LOOK TO THE ROCK

In Memoriam

John Wenham
(1913–1996)
with affection, gratitude and respect

LOOK TO THE ROCK

An Old Testament background
to our understanding of Christ

ALEC MOTYER

Inter-Varsity Press

INTER-VARSITY PRESS
38 De Montfort Street, Leicester LE1 7GP, England

First published 1996
Reprinted 1996

British Library Cataloguing in Publication Data
A catalogue record for this book is available from the British Library.

ISBN 0–85111–168–8

Set in Stempel Garamond

Typeset in Great Britain by Parker Typesetting Service, Leicester

Printed in Great Britain by Clays Ltd, St Ives plc

Inter-Varsity Press is the book-publishing division of the Universities and Colleges Christian Fellowship (formerly the Inter-Varsity Fellowship), a student movement linking Christian Unions in universities and colleges throughout the United Kingdom and the Republic of Ireland, and a member movement of the International Fellowship of Evangelical Students. For information about local and national activities write to UCCF, 38 De Montfort Street, Leicester LE1 7GP.

'Look to the rock from which you were cut
and to the quarry from which you were hewn'
(Isaiah 51:1)

'That rock was Christ'
(1 Corinthians 10:4)

Contents

Preface

For a long time now, I have wanted to try to put some Old Testament Theology on paper, and in the summer of 1994 I thought I had found an easy way to make a start. I remembered five lectures which I gave at the London Institute for Contemporary Christianity in 1982 at the kind invitation of Dr John Stott. The course was entitled 'The Old Testament and our Understanding of Christ' and, as I thought about it, I realized that it had brought together most of the things that I considered of central importance in Old Testament thinking.

I have, of course, discovered in the last ten months that it is easier to give a lecture than to write one up! An audience has to tolerate the airy sketching-in of a point with the wave of a lecturer's hand, the quick allusion to an avenue left unexplored or the rehearsal of a series of undeveloped points. The printed page is a resolute foe of all such easy fixes! And, of course, the lecture room does not allow the inclusion of notes.

The result is that the original lectures have grown in size, in coverage and in exploratory probings, while remaining as the overall shape of these studies, and their theme is the clue to the choice of topics. I have retained the original lecture titles, though now, in two cases, the material requires two chapters each. I have also retained the overlappings which characterize a lecture course – for basic truth always benefits from being expressed in the different contexts appropriate to it.

The lectures as given did not follow their theme through into the New Testament in any detail and I have on the whole accepted that limitation, but at my editor's suggestion I have added a short section at the end of chapters 2 to 8, entitled 'Avenues into the New Testament'. It was, however, the purpose of these lectures to point up the glory of our Lord Jesus Christ, and it is my prayer and longing that this will be achieved – more fully and plainly, if God so will – in this enlarged presentation. For the 'Rock'-metaphor which now figures in the title of these studies compels us to look in two directions: back to the great Old Testament quarry in which we originated, and on to Jesus, the Rock revealed in the Old Testament and manifested in the New.

My thanks are due – and gladly given – to Dr Stott, whose kind invitation first sparked this line of study; to David Kingdon, Theological Books Editor of Inter-Varsity Press for his friendship, encouragement and advice; and, most of all, to my wife Beryl, who is my unfailing joy and has (yet again) accepted heavy inroads into time we would otherwise have spent together.

Alec Motyer
Bishopsteignton
1995

Chief abbreviations

BDB   F. Brown, S. R. Driver and C. A. Briggs, *Hebrew and English Lexicon of the Old Testament* (OUP, 1929).

BST   The Bible Speaks Today.

CBG   Crossway Bible Guide.

EBC   *The Expositor's Bible Commentary*.

GKC   W. Gesenius, E. Kautzsch and A. E. Cowley, *Gesenius' Hebrew Grammar* (OUP, 1910).

IBD   J. D. Douglas *et al.* (eds.), *Illustrated Bible Dictionary*, 3 vols. (IVP, 1980).

ICC   International Critical Commentary.

IDB   G. A. Buttrick *et al.* (eds.), *The Interpreter's Dictionary of the Bible*, 4 vols. (Abingdon, 1962).

JB   Jerusalem Bible.

JBL   *Journal of Biblical Literature*.

KB   L. Köhler and W. Baumgartner, *Lexicon in Veteris Testamenti Libros* (Brill, 1958).

KJV   King James Version (Authorized Version).

LXX   Septuagint (Greek version of the OT).

MT   Massoretic Text (Hebrew Bible).

NBC   D. A. Carson *et al.* (eds.), *New Bible Commentary – 21st Century Edition* (IVP, 1994).

NCB   New Century Bible.

NEB   New English Bible.

NICOT   New International Commentary on the Old Testament.

NIDNTT C. Brown (ed.), *New International Dictionary of New*

Chief abbreviations

	Testament Theology, 3 vols. (Paternoster, 1975–78).
NIV	New International Version.
RSV	Revised Standard Version.
TDOT	G. J. Botterweck and H. Ringgren (eds.), *Theological Dictionary of the Old Testament*, 4 vols. (Eerdmans, 1974–80).
TOTC	Tyndale Old Testament Commentary.
TynB	*Tyndale Bulletin.*
VT	Vetus Testamentum.
WTJ	*Westminster Theological Journal.*

< >   Indicates the verse numbering system of the Hebrew Bible.

√   Indicates Hebrew verbal roots.

Introduction

A LOST CONFIDENCE

John Buchan is not quite in the same vogue today as he was forty years ago, and the same can be said for some of the characters which he portrayed with such acute perception.

Here, for example, is Mr Muirhead, on the subject of 'worthy Mr Macmichael':

> He was aye a pious and diligent minister ... I've heard that he preached for a year and sax months on Exodus 15 and 27, the twelve wells and the three score and ten palm trees of Elim, a sabbath to ilka well and ilka tree.[1]

In frankness, Mr Muirhead felt obliged to add, 'I've a notion that he was never very strong in the intellectuals.' Maybe not – but what confidence he had that the Old Testament was, even in its minutest detail, the Word of God, a book of divine revelation for the church, testifying about Christ to the people of Christ, with direct bearing on faith and life! If we have not only abandoned his exegetical methods but also lost his assurances, we have surely had the worst of the bargain.

KNOWLEDGE

Then there was Ephraim Caird, the church elder who, for all his devil worship in Witchwood, could greet his minister with 'The voice of the turtle is heard in the land' and, when the hour of repentance was long past, could register the pitiful claim that:

> I aye ettled to repent, for I was sure of the Mercy Seat ... It is written that Solomon went after the abominations of Moab and yet was numbered among the elect.[2]

If Ephraim failed tragically to work out his aspirations in practice, who are we to criticize? But do we not at the same time marvel at that mastery of the content of the Scriptures which allowed him to move with such fluency from the Song of Songs to Kings and Exodus?

And the same is true of Mr Proudfoot, preaching at the excommunication of David Sempill:

> The history of Israel was searched to show how Jehovah the merciful was yet merciless towards error. Agag was hewn in pieces, the priests and worshippers of Baal were slain to a man . . . Barak the son of Abinoam . . . with ten thousand of Naphtali and Zebulun . . . went down from Mount Tabor and fell upon Sisera . . . 'Let us smite the chariots and the host with the edge of the sword, for in this day hath the Lord delivered Sisera into our hand and let us pursue after the remnant even to Harosheth of the Gentiles!'

– a climax grievously destroyed by the interjection of Mark Riddell from the back of the church: 'Harosheth of your grannie!'[3] We no longer move with that dovetailing of knowledge and certainty where the Old Testament is concerned, but rather in the realm of half-truths – like Hugh Walpole when he revealed his own hand in describing Mrs Clopton, governess to the children of Timothy Bellairs: 'Her God was the real God of the Israelites, revengeful, on the watch for every blunder, cruel in punishments.'[4]

ILL-DEFINED AND MISLEADING CATEGORIES

The prophet Micah is a surer guide to the God of Israel when he cries out:

> Who is a God like you,
>> who pardons sin and forgives the transgression
>> of the remnant of his inheritance?
>
> You do not stay angry for ever
>> but delight to show mercy.
>
> (Micah 7:18)

We, however, belong to a generation which has lost its grip on the Old Testament and, over and over again, we mislead ourselves with caricatures of the truth. We polarize the Old and the New, seeing the former as the book of wrath, law and works, with the latter as the book of love, grace and faith. Undoubtedly, for all his weakness in 'the intellectuals' and his fanciful treatment of the wells and palm trees, 'worthy Mr Macmichael' knew better than that!

STRIPPING THE ENGINE DOWN

A century in which Old Testament study has been preoccupied with the 'nuts and bolts' of Old Testament literature has frankly not helped. This is not necessarily a comment on the integrity of the approach which concentrates on fragmenting Old Testament literature into what, it is urged, are its original components, but simply on its utility. It has made the Old Testament a mystery to the average person – indeed to the average theological student too! It has removed the book from the hands of the church and put it into the hands of the specialist. It has broken down one confidence without replacing it with another. The bits and pieces spread out on the bench have ceased to be a car.

OLD TESTAMENT THEOLOGY LOST

There has been, furthermore, an inevitable spin-off from the literary fragmentation of the Old Testament. If, for example, the Pentateuch can no longer be seen as a single work, substantially the product of one mind and time, but is, instead, a late amalgamation of very different 'sources' spread far from each other on a time-line spanning centuries, the possibility of a single Pentateuchal theology is remote indeed. If, in addition, the Pentateuch is long post-Mosaic and much of it post-exilic, it has become totally detached from the actual history of the Exodus and, exacerbating the situation, the more the historicity of the Exodus events is viewed with scepticism, the less the doctrinal statements of the Pentateuch possess the quality of objective revelation. God and the acts of God are no longer at their root, and all that can be said is that this or that 'truth' is what people happened to believe at certain points in the history of Israel. Theology has been replaced by Believing.

EICHRODT AND VON RAD

In this way the entire Old Testament became, in the words of W. C. Kaiser, the record of 'a collection of detached periods with little or no unity'.[5] Kaiser perceptively sees the work of W. Eichrodt (1933)[6] and Gerhard von Rad (1960)[7] as brackets around a period in which

15

an attempt was made to recover Old Testament Theology – but without fundamental success. Eichrodt was convinced that something more was possible than writing a history of the religious ideas of Israel, and he set out to restore Old Testament Theology to its proper place and function. He did this by asserting that Old Testament thought finds its unity in the doctrine of the covenant, and his two large volumes, packed with interest and instruction, attempted to show this.

Von Rad rightly pronounced this attempt a failure. Eichrodt had neither given sufficient reason for making 'covenant' the central and organizing idea of Old Testament thought, nor, indeed, had he succeeded in demonstrating that it was the covenant which gave coherence to each and every aspect of it. For himself, von Rad turned back to seeing 'the Bible [as] not so much the source of the faith of OT men as . . . the expression of their faith' and considered that:

> . . . each historical epoch had a theology unique to itself with internal tensions, diversity, and contradictions to the theology of other OT epochs . . . The OT possessed no central axis or continuity of a divine plan; rather, it contained a narration of the people's religious reading of their history, their attempt to make real and present older events and narratives.[8]

RECOVERING THE WHOLE:
A WELCOME NEW DAY

The last decades of the twentieth century have seen a welcome move towards a sense of the wholeness of the Old Testament and of its individual books.[9] A search for rounded artistry has replaced a passion for fragmentation. Whether with longer books or shorter pieces like individual psalms, new understandings of the literary skill of this ancient literature have revealed conscious development and sequence – a beginning, middle and end – where once all was treated as an unorganized anthology.[10]

This is long overdue and highly welcome. Kaiser's own work constitutes a notable contribution in this area. He holds, with Eichrodt, that the Old Testament needs constants, normative concepts, to hold it together; equally, he holds, with von Rad, that the proper approach to the Old Testament is to take each epoch in sequence, but in each area he is determined to establish a clear exegetical base. The Old Testament displays real progress in revelation resting on real history in which God was at work. The central ideas of one epoch prepare for, and are subsequently integrated into, the central ideas of the next epochs. He uses the analogy of a tree-trunk and its branches: the interconnected ideas of the different epochs are the trunk.

> More often than not growth was slow, delayed, or even dormant, only to burst forth after a long period in a new shoot off the main trunk. But such growth, as the writers of Scripture tell it, was always connected to the main trunk . . . a growth of the record of events, meanings, and teachings as time went on around a fixed core that contributed life to the whole emerging mass.[11]

Dr Tim Bradshaw, though his concern is not the Old Testament but the nature of the church, has expressed exactly this vision in relation to the totality of Holy Scripture:

> The Bible, for traditional theology, contains a vast range of materials from centuries of time. Some is obscure and difficult to grasp; some is fairly plain. But whatever the type of literature in question, the mind can address it and seek to understand it . . . The texts do say something which we can *understand*, therefore they are 'propositional' in the sense that they make statements or 'propositions' which the mind can understand . . . Scripture therefore has a clarity and a content . . . Written words are written words, and they tell us something . . . they have a content with which we may agree or disagree. The devastatingly simple fact is that the whole Bible tells a story which is basically intelligible . . . [Jesus] interpreted himself to his disciples after his resurrection, according to Luke's account of the journey to Emmaus, with reference to a 'corpus of revealed propositional truths', which he claimed concerned himself.[12]

Bradshaw has set the scene for what this book will now attempt – to explore the 'wholeness' of the Old Testament in its expression of its great, central,[13] messianic hope.

CHAPTER ONE

The master theme of the Bible

The division of the Bible into two books or Testaments is not really helpful towards a proper understanding. Once a unity is sundered it is not always a simple matter to restore the lost wholeness. But centuries of tradition, along with our own education from childhood, have drilled our minds into accepting a two-testament, instead of a holistic, model for the Bible.[1]

MODELS OF UNITY

There are any number of ways of exploring the unity of the Bible and seeking to bring the two-testament model into a more helpful perspective.[2]

1. THE BOOK WITH THE ANSWERS AT THE BACK

The Old Testament does not bring all its teaching and evidence into a secure integration. We reach the end of Malachi with, for example, glowing expectations of the Messiah but without knowing how they can possibly be fulfilled: how can the son of David be David's Lord? How can one with a plainly human ancestry be truly 'the Lord our righteousness'? Such questions could be multiplied over the whole area of Old Testament revelation. They are not exclusive to the messianic theme. But they do suggest that we should see the Bible as *the book with the answers at the back*.

Like all attempts to reduce the huge question of biblical unity to a single model, this can be caricatured. For we are all familiar with mathematical textbooks where the answers to problems set en route are given in the final pages, or with introductions to biblical Hebrew or New Testament Greek where a 'key' to the parent book is provided in a subsequent volume. Needless to say the New Testament is not a set of 'answers' or a 'key' in quite that way! Maybe, therefore, a detective novel would be a better illustration, where problems and clues multiply in the course of the book and are solved in the final denouement. This offers a greater approximation to unity in diversity.

2. A TWO-ACT PLAY

John Bright wrestled penetratingly with ways to understand the place of the Old Testament in the Christian pulpit.[3] He was determined to resist the concealed Marcionism of much of what is called the 'liberal' handling of the Old Testament for, as he understood it, 'no part of the Bible is without authority' and the Old Testament must be used 'as a part of normative Scripture' from which 'the Church must never part'. In illustration of this view of the unity which binds the two Testaments he offered the analogy of a two-act play, pointing out that (a) without either act the play is incomplete; (b) that each act has something individual to say; and (c) that neither act can stand without the other. The fact that he proposed only two acts is a by-product of the dominance of the 'two-testament' model, and it is not altogether satisfactory to make the interval curtain fall between Malachi and Matthew. None the less the concept is useful and profound. As Act One unfolds, tensions begin to appear, for example, in the sacrificial system. There are sins which it does not explicitly cover and for which, since the Lord is a forgiving God, repentance must avail (Ps. 51); there is the basic inadequacy, discerned by Isaiah, that in the ultimate only a Person can substitute for people (Is. 53). Thus Act One awaits the denouement in Act Two. Yet the testimony of Act One is irreplaceably valid, that by the will of God the substitution of the innocent for the guilty is the divine principle for dealing with sin. Act Two sweeps in on the flood-tide of Act One: here is the human perfection of a willing Substitute: without the realities of Act One even the terminology of Act Two would be incomprehensible. But yet Act Two has something distinctive to say: that when the ultimate substitution was made, it was God himself who came and stood in our place.

3. DOCUMENT AND SEAL

If we prolong for a moment the artistic metaphor, we can move from the dramatic unity of a play to the visual-compositional unity of a picture which

... is the same kind of problem as unfolding a long, sustained, interlocking argument. It is a proposition which, whether of few or numberless parts, is commanded by a single unity of conception.[4]

Could the Bible be better described?

THE AUTHORITATIVE JESUS

In the final analysis, our authority for anything we believe is the Lord Jesus Christ. Our highest dignity is to be made like the Son of God in all things – and this includes how he thought and what he thought. The most blighting form that Marcionism can take is to pick and choose at the very heart of divine revelation: the person, work, life, teaching, example and directives of Jesus. We can put the same truth another way: the divine act of raising Jesus from the dead was an unconditional validation of everything he was in his incarnate life on earth. In a memorable passage, E. J. Bicknell says that the resurrection 'was God's public attestation of the claims of the crucified . . . the Amen of the Father to the "It is finished" of the Son'.[5] But to what did the Father say 'Amen'? Certainly to the saving work: that by his death on the cross Jesus had indeed saved eternally all those whom the Father had sent him to save. But the Old Testament insists that only the perfect can act as a substitute for the imperfect (*e.g.* Ex. 12:5; Is. 53:9): so the divine scrutiny prior to the great 'Amen' must also cover the moral character and life of the Lamb of God. Also, Jesus spoke of his sign-acts in the course of his ministry as works that the Father had given him to do, and it was his claim that he had finished this work (Jn. 5:36; 17:4): did he perform all the Father's works and leave nothing undone or imperfectly done? And finally, was Jesus true to his vocation as the Word of the Father so that he declared all the truth the Father sent him to declare, left nothing half-said and taught nothing that had any admixture of untruth?

It is in this sense that the resurrection is an unconditional divine validation of the teaching as much as of the saving efficacy of Christ.

This great Lord Jesus came from outside and voluntarily and deliberately attached himself to the Old Testament, affirmed it to be the word of God and set himself, at cost, to fulfil it (*e.g.* Mt. 26:51–54).[6] This fact of facts cuts the ground from under any suspicion that the *doctrine* of biblical authority rests on a circular argument such as, 'I believe the Bible to be authoritative because the Bible says it is authoritative.' Not so! It was Jesus who came 'from outside' as the incarnate Son of God, Jesus who was raised from the dead as the Son of God with power, who chose to validate the Old Testament in retrospect and the New Testament in prospect, and who is himself the grand theme of the 'story-line' of both Testaments, the focal-point giving coherence to the total 'picture' in all its complexities.

There is an old jingle which is certainly simple and verges on the simplistic, but our forebears were fundamentally right when they taught that: the Old Testament is Jesus predicted; the Gospels are Jesus revealed; Acts is Jesus preached; the Epistles, Jesus explained; and the Revelation, Jesus expected. He is the climax as well as the substance and centre of the whole. In him all God's promises are yea and amen (2 Cor. 1:20).

Christ as fulfilment:
The themes of King and kingdom

We begin our studies on the Old Testament background to our understanding of Christ by considering the themes of 'king' and 'kingdom' starting, perhaps surprisingly, with the book of Judges.

WHY WAS THE BOOK OF JUDGES WRITTEN?

It is not intended to be frivolous to give the obvious if silly answer that Judges was written to fill a gap that would otherwise exist between Joshua and Samuel. Certainly, the continuation of the history of the people of God is one of the functions of the book. Those who used to see Judges as exemplifying the same 'documentary' structure as the Pentateuch and Joshua,[1] along with those who now advocate the notion of a 'deuteronomistic history',[2] are essentially subscribing to a 'gap' theory of the composition of Judges, for neither view can offer an explanation why it ever came to be seen as an individual book with an individual title: it simply fills in years that would otherwise be left blank in a sweeping historical review.

But another group of writers have, more recently, advanced a more perceptive understanding of Judges.[3] Barry Webb can speak for them all when he describes his work as 'an exploration of the meaning of the book of Judges considered as a whole, and as distinct from what precedes and follows it in the canon'.[4] He was responding to a call issued in 1967 by J. P. U. Lilley for 'a fresh appraisal of Judges as a literary work starting from the assumptions of authorship rather than redaction'.[5]

When Judges is approached along this avenue, its coherence as a work of literary art and also its central thrust – the purpose of the author in writing, what he would have said in an 'Author's Preface' had this convention existed – are alike plain. Without entering into minutiae, the historical content of Judges looks like this:

Great leaders	Great failures
(3:7 – 16:31)	(3:11, 30; 5:31; 8:28 – 9:57; 10 (*passim*); 12:7; 16:31)
Great problems	The great solution
(17:1 – 21:25)	(17:6; 18:1; 19:1; 21:25)

There were two sides to the history of the people of God. What captured the headlines (Jdg. 3:7 – 16:31) were the scintillating deeds of a great line of charismatic men and one woman. These were the Judges, the divinely raised up Saviour-Rulers, whose activity in deliverance was the outreaching of divine mercy to an undeserving and recalcitrant people. Nevertheless, the Lord's agents though they were, they were essentially episodic and ultimately failures. They came, they delivered, they went, they achieved no permanent blessing or security; they interrupted but did not change the deadly sequence of apostasy and captivity. The coda to the story of the first judge, Othniel, can be allowed to speak for them all: 'the land was at rest for forty years' (3:11, lit.). That is to say, limited relief was achieved but with no permanent solution.

AT GROUND LEVEL

Meanwhile, among ordinary people, out of the limelight of great deeds, things were very far different. One would need to be remarkably lacking in literary appreciation if one failed to feel the enveloping darkness and to catch the smell of corruption as soon as one enters the final section of the book. Religiously (17:1–13), politically (18:1–31), morally (19:1–30) and socially (20:1 – 21:25) Israel is in disarray – and for all the mighty deeds of derring-do at the top, this is what life was like at the bottom, a situation which the judges did not manage to touch or influence at all. Gideon, the most lovable of the judges, left a disastrous legacy of religious falsehood and social disruption; Samson, the great buffoon, created havoc wherever he turned and the book of Judges comes to a climax in a howl of despair. The noble Othniel, the impressive Deborah, the attractive Gideon, the blunt, honest and confused Jephthah – and the host of semi-unknowns – all alike left things as they found them. And if such people, God-given and God-endowed, failed, what was there to be done for ordinary folk in a collapsing society?

THE GREAT SOLUTION

Point by point, as the book traces the religious, political, moral and social collapse of Israel, it announces its remedy, and does so in a balanced form, evidence of the author's sense of the wholeness and perfection of the solution he offers:

17:6 In those days Israel had no king;
everyone did as he saw fit.

18:1 In those days Israel had no king.

19:1 In those days Israel had no king.

21:25 In those days Israel had no king;
everyone did as he saw fit.

THE MONARCHIC IDEAL

Thus Judges trumpets its monarchic ideal and prepares for the request for a king in 1 Samuel 8. It is as if it were saying to us: 'Why be surprised that things have come to such a pass – we have no king! It stands to reason that unless we have a king no aspect of national life is as it should be.'[6]

1 Samuel offers a complex but coherent account of how monarchy was actually instituted in Israel. Our understanding of the course of events has not been helped by the common insistence that the Bible offers two (or more) conflicting accounts of the appointment of the first king.[7] This is an insecure hypothesis. While it is clear that the narrative of the institution contains anti-monarchic (1 Sa. 8:1–22; 10:17–19; 12:1–25) as well as pro-monarchic (9:1 – 10:16; 10:20 – 11:15) feeling, no attempt to isolate 'documents' or 'sources' has succeeded, even to the point of Weiser's counsel of despair that we have a collection of hetero-geneous literary units drawn together without any attempt at harmonization – a suggestion that sounds suspiciously like the assumption of lunacy among ancient editors. The older comment-ators like H. P. Smith[8] who found the description of feudal/despotic kingship in 1 Samuel 8:11ff. as 'hardly conceivable . . . before the fall of Jerusalem', or even W. McKane's opinion[9] that the form of verses 8 to 13 reproduces features of Solomonic despotism and is dependent on experiences during his reign, collapse before the evidence cited by J. Mauchline.[10] He says that 'the account is an authentic description of the semi-feudal Canaanite society as it

existed prior to and during the time of Samuel'. It follows that Samuel could have described kingship in this way and 'the whole situation makes it highly probable that he did so'.

SAMUEL AND THEOCRACY

Furthermore, within the institution narrative, anti-monarchic feeling is wholly confined to the person of Samuel himself. Attempts to make the narrative a back-reflection of later feelings founder on the fact that our records know nothing of an anti-monarchic movement in Israel or Judah – not even after the downfall of the kingdoms and the plain evidence that monarchy had been a failure. Herein, of course, lies the almost savage irony with which the story is told – for the people are found putting their trust for ongoing security in a system of succession at the very same time as they are affirming that succession does not work! 'Look, you are old, and your sons do not walk in your ways' (1 Sa. 8:5, lit.). And not only so, but Samuel himself was the antidote to the failure of the principle of succession in the house of Eli for, in a dramatic phrase, the Hebrew states that 'the sons of Eli were sons of Belial' (2:12).

The hostility of Samuel to kingship was human and understandable. He was an outstanding representative of a system which, within limits, had served the people well, and the old man's unthinking pride when he mentions himself as the current deliverer in a long succession (12:11) is natural and forgivable. But when he brought the matter to the Lord (8:6) his perspective was reshaped (8:7): the real issue was not judgeship but theocracy. As far as the people were concerned, Samuel was acceptable. – If only Samuel could live for ever! But now that he was old an uncertain future opened before them, and by asking for a permanent monarchy they were tacitly admitting that an invisible divine King was not enough for them – 'they have rejected me, that I should not be king over them' (8:7, lit.).

Under God, it was, from that moment, Samuel's task to make sure that monarchy in Israel was itself founded as, and was known by all to be, a theocratic institution. It is to this end that the narrative is shaped. By divinely overruled circumstances (9:1–24), Saul was brought to Samuel and was authenticated as God's chosen king by a predictive word (9:15–17). He was privately anointed (9:25 – 10:1) and the word of divine choice was confirmed both internally (10:9a) and objectively (10:9b). The will of God was publicly confirmed by the sacred lot (10:17–24); Saul was acclaimed as king and, when he proved his kingship by his deeds (11:1–11), he was confirmed in office (11:12–15) and Samuel prepared to bow out.

SAMUEL'S SERMON

The old man's farewell sermon (1 Sa. 12:1–25) explains everything. According to 12:17 he was preaching at the celebration of the Feast of Weeks and this accounts for the shape of his sermon. The Feast celebrated the wheat harvest (Dt. 16:9–11), recalled the Exodus (Dt. 16:12a) and summoned the people to renewed obedience (Dt. 16:12b). In his preaching, Samuel brought his hearers back to the exodus-acts of God (12:6–8) but reminded them that they had responded to their redemption not by obedience but by forgetfulness (12:9). Their sin indeed brought chastisement, but the Lord never deserted his unworthy people: he exercised his kingship of mercy in raising up deliverers for them (12:10–11). Instead, however, of learning the lesson of their own past, namely that the Lord is to be trusted in every situation, the Ammonite threat (12:12) exposed their unbelief. They could not trust the divine King; they needed a human king (12:12–13).

This brought Samuel to the second part of his sermon and the second theme of the Feast of Weeks, obedience to the law of the Lord. The fact of an earthly monarchy has changed nothing. King and people alike are under obligation to obey (12:14) and under threat if they disobey (12:15) – truths which are repeated as the sermon ends (12:20–23, 24–25). The incident of the thunder storm, threatening their harvest and livelihood (12:16–19) is a visual and practical enforcement of this truth: they may now have a king but they are still under the rule of God, for good or ill.

THE THEOCRATIC KINGDOM

The narrative of the institution of the monarchy and Samuel's sermon can be summed up in four truths: first, the request for a king arose from a failure of faith. The strain of living without visible means of security was more than the people could any longer endure. Notwithstanding that the Lord had always proved reliable, they were not strong enough in trust to face seen dangers whilst looking to the unseen. They wanted an enduring institution, taking responsibility for the welfare of a small, vulnerable nation in a threatening world. Secondly, the Lord did not abandon his rule over his people. He is still their King and it is to him directly that they are responsible. Monarchy is the new form the theocracy is to take. Just as, formerly, the Lord expressed his theocratic rule by raising up judges to meet emergencies, now he will express his rule through a chosen king and a line of kings. Thirdly, since the theocracy remains, the call to faith and obedience remains. It is as true as ever it was that obedience leads to blessing, disobedience to cursing. This is the basic covenant-situation (Lv. 26; Dt. 28 – 29); it obtained all through the period of the judges; it remains the same in the monarchy. Fourthly, there is the astonishing mercy of God. It is true that the request for a king was evidence of their weakness, faithlessness, ingratitude and forgetfulness; it is also true that in asking for a king they were not rejecting Samuel but rejecting the Lord. But into this situation of bleak unspirituality the Lord came in mercy, accepting the people at their own self-valuation, agreeing to their request – and proceeding to make what they asked in unbelief into the primary and golden vehicle of his eternal purposes and blessings. His king would come and reign, a supreme gift of grace to an unworthy people.

THE SEARCH FOR THE KING:
1. EXPECTATIONS AND FAILURES

All through the reigns of Saul, David and Solomon, how marvellously the record conveys the impression of a fresh, young people rising enthusiastically to the opportunities of a new, hopeful start! There was great hope and great disappointment.

According to the ideal implicit in Judges 17 – 21, a king would be the solution to religious, political, moral and social evils. Each of the first three kings had resounding successes to his credit, but each in turn failed when judged by one or more of these criteria. Saul succeeded, for instance, religiously (1 Sa. 28:3) but failed politically: not only was there considerable discontent, unprovoked by David but none the less focused on him, but Saul could not, in the end, withstand the Philistine threat, and he died with his kingdom under the heel of the conqueror (1 Sa. 31). David, however, succeeded religiously and politically but failed morally (2 Sa. 11 – 12).

Solomon, the king who started with more advantage than any king before or after, failed – of all things! – religiously (1 Ki. 11:1–6). In a word, it is one thing to entertain the correct expectations of the book of Judges that a king will prove to be the solution; it is another thing to possess a monarchy with plain divine authentication; but it is quite a different matter to find one who is worthy and able to be king.

2. THE MOVING SPOTLIGHT

It is against this background that the books of Kings bring us such a strange way of recording the history of the kings of Israel and Judah. We might well ask if it would not have been easier to write the histories of the two kingdoms quite separately following the schism provoked by the inept Rehoboam (2 Ki. 12). It certainly would have been easier but it would not have achieved the historian's purpose, which was, to continue the search for the true king who would match the Judges-ideal. He does this by allowing his spotlight to swing backwards and forwards: south and north, north and south. In the south there was the covenantal, institutionalized monarchy of David, reigning on the Lord's throne (1 Ch. 29:23), with son following father in ordered succession, for five centuries. It was very different in the north. There men rose to kingship by their own abilities and ambitions, and dynasty succeeded dynasty as each in turn failed and another came to power. Monarchy was ordered in the south; in the north it was charismatic. The two stood in essential contrast but both ran into the sand. Natural human abilities were given full room for expression in the north. There were in total nineteen different kings of whom only a minority succeeded in passing the throne to their sons, and the kingdom ended in a climax of unrestrained individual ambition with six kings reigning briefly in quick succession until the kingdom ended ingloriously in Assyrian exile (2 Ki. 17).

The south lasted longer but fared little better. The kings who were in any way worthy could be counted on one hand. The kingdom was set on its course of failure by the nincompoop Rehoboam (1 Ki. 12) and brought to its heartbreaking end by the born loser, Zedekiah (2 Ki. 24 – 25). The swinging spotlight failed to find the true king either in a monarchy underwritten by divine covenant or in the natural abilities of very gifted men.

3. THE UNQUENCHABLE HOPE

It is unrealistic to postpone the rise of 'messianic hope' until the disappearance of the monarchies, in 721 and 586 BC respectively,[11] even though the principle on which that view rests is itself correct: namely, that disappointment is the seed-bed of hope. But disappointment was present from the start: Saul, David and Solomon all alike failed to achieve the Judges-ideal, and in the time of all three kings there is evidence of at least some who would have said: 'There must be something better than this!'

Samuel knew that Saul was not the Lord's ideal king, and he saw by Saul's first failure in obedience that he would not found a lasting dynasty (1 Sa. 13:13–14), and by his second failure that he could not personally continue as king (1 Sa. 15, especially verse 23).[12] David's reign was beset by two rebellions, which succeeded in commanding the support of 'the men of Israel' (2 Sa. 15:13; 20:2). Jeroboam the son of Nebat became Solomon's adversary through a strong undercurrent of hostility to the king expressed by Ahijah the Shilonite (1 Ki. 11:26–40). The very possibility of the question 'Is this what we were led to expect?' could have provoked either a rejection of monarchy (which it never did) or a forward-looking hope that the ideal would yet be realized. And if the tragedies of Saul, David and Solomon, *per impossibile*, were not a sufficient experience of disappointment to give birth to hope, surely the incompetence of Rehoboam must have done so. The need for a true king was now plain.

FOCAL POINTS IN EXPECTATION

The Old Testament does not make it clear by what steps this hope moved from a longing for a better ruler to the expectation of the perfect ruler. The beginnings of hope are firmly set in the days of the David by the foundational oracle of Nathan in 2 Samuel 7, yet it promises no more than an endless Davidic line, ever under the blessing of the Lord: 'Your house and your kingdom shall endure for ever before me; your throne shall be established for ever' (7:16).

It is not unreasonable to presume that there was a constant interaction between, on the one hand, the expectation of a continuing Davidic line and, on the other hand, the Judges-ideal that a true ruler would be the solution of personal and national needs. Two things can be affirmed with confidence. First, many of the royal psalms are best explained if we assume that they were composed deliberately in order to hold up before a new Davidide at his coronation a mirror of the true ruler. Since Psalm 101, for example, claims Davidic authorship, it is easy to see it as David's own statement of the ideals he will pursue as king,[13] and what could be a better norm to set before each new king to ascend David's throne? But, secondly, alongside this persistent notion of the ideal ruler there was a backward look of longing to the 'golden days' of David himself, for, without a doubt, in spite of all his frailties, he was, by the standards of those who followed him, beyond compare. It was no mere *pietas* or unrealistic glamorization of the past for the Kings-historian to ask of each successive king whether he was like or unlike his father David (*e.g.* 2 Ki. 14:3; 22:2). In the light of these two facts, it is a short step from saying 'If only David could come back!' to saying, 'But he will!'[14]

AN EXPECTATION LARGER THAN LIFE

Whatever be the truth of the growth and individualization of this great hope, it is certain that

> . . . with each new king, Israel hoped anew. He [Israel] hoped that this one would be God's perfect Messiah, the one who would bring in the golden age. Of each of its kings, Israel asked, 'Are you the one who is to come, or shall we look for another?' From the time of David onward, Israel expected a ruler who would save his people, a ruler who would restore to them all of the goodness of the creation.[15]

It is possibly slightly ambitious to trace quite so much back to the actual time of David, but in principle Paul and Elizabeth Achtemeier are surely correct in stating this. The passing years, however, made the promise grow until it not only outgrew the capacity of any foreseeable member of David's line to fulfil it but also the capacity of any mere human being. It never lost touch with reality but it became decidedly larger than life.

Summarizing the material offered in Psalms, the expected king would meet world-opposition (2:1–3; 110:1ff.) but, as victor (45:3–5; 89:22–23) and by the activity of the Lord (2:6, 8; 21:1–13; 110:1–2) he would establish world-rule (2:8–12; 45:17; 72:8–11; 89:25; 110:5–6), based on Zion (2:6) and marked by a primary concern for morality (45:4, 6–7; 72:2–3; 101:1–8). He would rule for ever (21:4; 45:6; 72:5), in peace (72:7), prosperity (72:16) and undeviating reverence for the Lord (72:5). Pre-eminent among men (45:2, 7), he would be the friend of the poor and the enemy of the oppressor (72:2–4, 12–14). Under his rule the righteous would flourish (72:7). He would possess an everlasting name (72:17) and be the object of unending thanks (72:15). He is the recipient of the Lord's everlasting blessing (45:2), the heir of David's covenant (89:28–37; 132:11–12) and of Melchizedek's priesthood (110:4). He belongs to the Lord (89:18), and is devoted to him (21:1, 7; 63:1–8, 11). He is his son (2:7; 89:27), seated at his right hand (110:1) and is himself divine (45:6).[16] No wonder the swinging spotlight of the books of Kings could find him neither in the ordered line of David to the south nor amongst the personally gifted leaders of the north!

THE PROMISED SEED, THE SECOND ADAM

Another focal point in messianic expectation was created by the way in which Nathan worded his oracle regarding the house that the Lord would build for David. A major link is forged between David and Abraham by Nathan's description of the coming 'line' of David as his 'seed',[17] a key word in the Abrahamic covenant.[18] The coincidence of one word might seem a slender tie between David and Abraham, but it must be noted additionally that this 'seed' is qualified by the description 'who will come from your own body', an expression taken directly from Genesis 15:4 (lit.).[19] A further link between David and Abraham is formed by the motif of 'making the name great'. This was the Lord's promise to David (2 Sa. 7:9), but it was first made to Abraham (Gn. 12:2) and is found only in these two places in the Old Testament.[20]

Psalm 89

The evidence is therefore more weighty than might appear at first sight for urging that Nathan saw the Davidic covenant as the inheritor of the Abrahamic, especially in terms of the promised 'seed' on whom the blessing would be suspended. However, it fell to Psalm 89 to develop, covenantly, what thus lay implicit in 2 Samuel 7. As we noted above (see also note 17 on pp. 192–193), Psalm 89 emphasizes the theme of the 'seed' of David but it does so within a telling structure.[21] The psalm opens and closes with references to the 'love' of the Lord (89:1, 49). In each case, the word is plural and this, of itself, is sufficient to arouse attention, for the plural only occurs thirteen times in the almost two hundred and fifty occurrences of the word in the Old Testament.[22] In the psalm, the plural in verse 1 is 'spelled out' in the two occurrences of the singular in verses 24 (literally, 'My faithfulness and my love will be with him') and in 28 ('I will maintain my love to him forever'). The former promises David world-dominion (see verse 25), and the latter an enduring throne (see verse 29). Both of these pledges are secured by the Lord's commitment of love and these are the 'loves' mentioned in verse 1 and prayed for in verse 49.

This is the world-dominion of blessing which was promised to Abraham's seed (Gn. 12:3; 22:17–18) and which, as Isaiah foresaw, would be fulfilled through the work of the Servant, a world-blessing based on a universally offered free salvation.[23]

Genesis 3:15

Nathan's reference to the 'seed' of David, however, reaches back far beyond Abraham to the 'seed' of the woman who will crush the serpent's head (Gn. 3:15). Von Rad argues that this verse cannot be considered as a protevangelium for two reasons: first, it 'does not agree with the sense of the passage' and, secondly, 'the word "seed" may not be construed personally but only quite generally with the meaning "posterity"'.[24] Taking von Rad's second point first, it is simply not true. The word has a rich ambience, but it is flying in the face of all reason to deny that it is best explained as referring to a single offspring in at least Genesis 4:25; 15:3; 38:8–9 and in 1 Samuel 1:11. G. J. Wenham goes far beyond von Rad and beyond the banal etiological interpretations favoured so widely[25] when he writes:

> Once admitted that the serpent symbolizes sin, death, and the power of evil, it becomes much more likely that the curse envisages a long struggle between good and evil, with mankind eventually triumphing.[26]

Wenham also notes that, while the interpretation of 3:15 as a messianic protevangelium has a very long history and can be justified in the light of other scriptures, 'it would perhaps be wrong to suggest that this was the narrator's own understanding'.

Wenham's view is, of course, judicious but ought, legitimately, to be brought into a slightly sharper focus. We can certainly go further than saying that 'the serpent symbolizes'. For within the narrative-complex of Genesis 1 – 3, snakes are part of the good creation of God (1:24). The serpent of 3:1ff., therefore, in a way that Genesis does not explain, is not part of that creation, for it is not an animal pure and simple; it reveals itself as far from what the Creator would call 'good' and, indeed, this serpent is not 'it' but 'he', so that the woman enters into conversation as with another person. This revelation of 'the serpent' and this attitude towards him is sustained throughout Genesis 3.

In respect of ongoing human history (3:15), the serpent is not a 'principle of evil' but a parent giving birth to a 'proliferation of adverse powers . . . other evil spirits, the disciples or spiritual sons of the devil'[27] and yet also himself continuing in full personal reality until the day of his final demise, the crushing of his head. We must be careful not to allow the use of serpent-imagery – crawling, and death by the crushing of the head – to make us think that the serpent as such is merely part of the imagery. The serpent is 'he', the usurper of the divine right to direct the creation, the corrupter of the word of God, the one who denies the truth of divine judgment on sin and rebellion, the deceiver of humankind, the author and instigator of a fallen creation – but destined, at last, to be crushed.

NEW ADAM, SECOND DAVID, RESTORED EDEN

Can we take Genesis 3:15 further than seeing, with Wenham, 'mankind finally triumphing'?[28] The whole of Scripture is not packed into every scripture, but we may allowably expect every scripture to prepare and make room for the whole. This is what happens in Genesis 3:15. There is an ambiguity waiting to be solved. We saw above that the word 'seed' leaves the door open for an individual fulfilment[29] and it would be insensitive indeed not to feel some movement in the verse towards a 'single combat' situation in which the heel is crushed on the one side and the head on the other. This is what Old and New Testaments alike progressively make of the protevangelium.

Taking the matter no further than the 'major' prophets, we find an impressive dove-dailing of teaching. Starting with 'a shoot . . . from the stump of Jesse', *i.e.* by implication, a new David, Isaiah

(11:1–9) advances step by step from the king's character (verses 2–3) to his rule (verses 3–5) and on to the new creation within which he reigns (verses 6–9).[30] Jeremiah and Ezekiel carry the vision forward. Jeremiah (23:5–6; 33:14–17) uses the 'family-tree' motif of the coming king as David's 'branch', but also he sees the promised line of David actually culminating in David, the righteous king. To Ezekiel, the coming David is the Shepherd Prince (34:23–25; 37:24–27), tending his flock in a peaceful creation and in peace with the resident God. We will return later to the enigma of a 'shoot of Jesse' who is also the 'root of Jesse' (Is. 11:1, 10) and of a Davidic 'branch' who is also 'the Lord our righteousness' (Je. 23:5–6), but this compound picture presented by Isaiah, Jeremiah and Ezekiel adds up to another David reigning in a restored Eden.

Isaiah contributes two other important insights. In accordance with the whole 'build-up' of the Isaianic literature, he interlocks his developing messianic vision by identifying the Servant of the Lord with the Davidic promises (55:3).[31] But on each side of this identification the key word 'seed' occurs. Both the Servant, in his covenant work of salvation (53:10), and the Anointed Conqueror, in his covenant work of salvation and vengeance (59:20–21),[32] are 'fathers of a family'.[33] This motif (and reality) not only identifies the Isaianic Messiah with Abraham but also with Adam, adding, therefore, to the compound picture[34] the dimension of the new or second Adam as the Davidic king in the new Eden.

THE KING-PRIEST MELCHIZEDEK

Without the Old Testament background it might well be thought that the book of Hebrews (*e.g.* Heb. 7:11–14) is indulging in special pleading when it introduces Melchizedek to solve the problem of the priesthood of the Christ who arose from the non-priestly tribe of Judah.

The Old Testament, of course, does not tell a complete story but offers enough facts to allow us to construct a convincing scenario. Melchizedek appears by name only twice: first when, as king of Salem, he emerges to bless the victorious Abram, to receive the offering of a tithe and to contribute the theology of 'God Most High' to Abram's understanding of Yahweh (Gn. 14:18–21);[35] his second appearance is in the Davidic Psalm 110. A middle-member between these two references is found in Joshua 10:1, where a certain Adoni-zedek appears as king of Jerusalem. It is plain that in form and meaning the two names, Melchi-zedek and Adoni-zedek are the same, and this gives rise to the reasonable assumption[36] that a line of priest-kings reigned in Salem/Jerusalem. The consequence of this would be that when David conquered the city he, in his own person, became Melchizedek, the King-Priest whose priesthood and theology had both been validated by Abraham. This might very well explain the otherwise enigmatic statement that 'David's sons were priests' (2 Sa. 8:18, lit.), *i.e.* functionaries in the priesthood of the royal house, but at all events it provides solid background for the visionary Psalm 110 and for the subsequent Melchizedek messianism of the book of Hebrews. In this as in so many other psalms, David, sensitively aware of his own failures, looks forward to the perfect Priest-King of whom he is but a pale shadow cast beforehand by coming events.

THE MESSIANIC ENIGMA

In so many areas the Old Testament prepares for the New by unanswered questions, and this is true not least regarding the kingly Messiah. We have already noted the basic enigma of a portrait of the king immeasurably larger than life whereby we are forced to ask who such a king could be and where he might come from. In some ways the Old Testament solves this problem, but in others it leaves us with questions, not answers.

A KING MORE THAN OF THIS WORLD

The shoot of Jesse is also his root (Is. 11:1, 10); David's successor, veritably born in his line, is also the Mighty God (Is. 9:6–7);[37] the king is God (Ps. 45:6) and yet worships God (Ps. 45:7); the Branch of David is 'the Lord our righteousness' (Je. 23:5–6); the virgin's son is 'God with us' (see Is. 7:14); the 'root out of dry ground' (Is. 53:2) is 'the arm of the Lord' (Is. 53:1).

Thus we sample the enigma of the person of the coming King, but the solution to the enigma awaits its realization in the Lord Jesus Christ. Until then, the Old Testament remains the expectant book.

A KINGDOM NOT OF THIS WORLD

The Old Testament uses its own times and characteristic norms and forms as building-blocks of the future reality which it foresees, much as Jesus used the ordinarinesses of his own time in his parables of the kingdom. Within the Old Testament, the Exodus events provided funds of imagery and motifs regarding the future acts of God for his people; so also Old Testament life and institutions became the bearers of a still-yet-future vision much larger than themselves.

There is, for example, the foreseen emergence of a world-wide 'Israel', *e.g.* in Isaiah 19:24–25; 45:25.[38] Isaiah elaborated this in his depiction of an 'Israel' within 'Israel' (8:9–20) and his expectation of world-wide accretion into this company (*e.g.* 56:8). The then people of God (Is. 54) and a freely invited world (Is. 55) join alike in the salvation and banquet of the Messiah (*cf.* Is. 25:6–10a). Alongside this vision of people there is a vision of 'place'. In chapters 13–20, 21–23 and 24–27, Isaiah progressively develops his understanding of the panorama of the coming Davidic kingdom, starting with what he saw around him (13–20), feeling forward into a more dimly discerned future (21–23) and finally envisaging the end-time (24–27) where the whole of earthly reality is encapsulated as two contrasting cities: the city where meaning has ceased to exist (24:10), and the city of peace, salvation and faith (26:1–4). When we couple this vision on a truly grand scale with the evidence that for the prophets Edom, for example, has ceased to be a nation and a place and has become a symbol of undying hostility to the Lord and his people, the spirit of the world, fighting to the last and at the last overthrown (Is. 34; 63:1–6; Ezk. 35), we realize that, by its national and territorial pictures, the Old Testament is preparing us for a kingdom that is not of this world (Jn. 18:36), a redeemed, believing people who already live 'in the heavenly realms' (*e.g.* Eph. 1:4, 20; 2:6) and who belong here and now to the heavenly Zion (Heb. 12:22). In the same way, the Old Testament both affirms the Messiah as the 'Prince of peace' (*e.g.* Is. 9:7) and sees him as slaughtering foes over the wide earth (Ps. 110:5–6) and possessing a sword-bearing people (Ps. 149:6). The motifs are understandable: if the Messiah is king then he will extend his kingdom by kingly means – the militarism that is endemic among monarchs. But the enigma remains of a prince bringing peace by war and a people resting in their beds with a two-edged sword in their hands! The enigma is only solved when we see the Gentiles falling before the conquering David (Am. 9:11–12) through the all-prevailing 'sword' of the gospel of Christ (Acts 15:13–18), for he is more than 'the end of the law' (Rom. 10:4); he is the consummation, too, of every expectation.

◇ AVENUES INTO THE NEW TESTAMENT

The New Testament solves the chief messianic enigma of the Old Testament in the single Person of the Lord Jesus Christ, who is both son of David and Son of God (Lk. 1:32–33), and who reigns in Zion, his unshakeable kingdom (Heb. 12:22–24, 28). He is also the second Adam (Rom. 5:12–21), who will reign in the restored Eden (Rev. 22:1–5), and the promised Melchizedek Priest-King (Heb. 6:20 – 7:28; *cf.* Heb. 4:14–16).

The kingdom is *present* (Rev. 1:9), because where Jesus is the kingdom is (Lk. 17:20–22); it is also *future* (Rev. 11:15), because its full reality awaits his second coming (Mt. 13:30, 39, 47–50; 25:1–13; 2 Tim. 4:1). *Entrance* to the kingdom is by new birth (Jn. 3:3, 5; 1 Cor. 15:50), blood-purchase (Rev. 5:10; *cf.* the kingdom as the fulfilment of the Passover, Lk 22:16, and of the Supper, Lk. 22:30), repentance (Mt. 4:17), and response to the gospel invitation (Lk. 14:15–24). *Life* in the kingdom is one of conflict (Mt. 13:24–43; Acts 14:22–23), calling for commitment (Mk. 9:43–48; Lk. 9:62), and marked by spirituality (Mt. 18:21–35; Rom. 14:17). The *work* of the kingdom is world-wide gospel preaching (Acts 1:3–8; *cf.* Mt. 8:11; Col. 4:11) for to enter the kingdom is to be saved (Mk. 10:23–26), the gospel is the good news of the kingdom (Mt. 24:14; Lk. 8:1), and the kingdom is characterized by the word of God (Mt. 5:19). The *truth* about the kingdom is the truth about Jesus and the gospel (Acts 8:12; 19:8–10; 20:21, 24–25, 27; 28:31). Eternal destinies are involved (Mt. 25:31–46; Mk. 9:45, 47; 10:23–31; Eph. 5:5–6).

Alongside 'church', 'flock', 'temple', 'bride', *etc.*, 'kingdom' expresses one aspect of the present enjoyment and future consummation of the saving work of Christ: namely, regarding him, his present and future reign with all authority in heaven and earth; regarding us, our present commitment of loyalty, obedience and service as due to the King, and our future bliss in his fully realized kingdom.

CHAPTER THREE

Christ as climax:
The themes of covenant, grace and law

If there is one line more than another in which it can be seen that Christ is the master theme of the Bible, it is the subject of this chapter: covenant, grace and law.[1]

THE GREAT VISUAL AID

Several lines of evidence converge to prove that Mount Sinai was not a chance caravanserai for the Exodus-people but was, rather, the primary goal of their journey. First, in Exodus 3:12, 'worshipping God on this mountain' is the sign given to Moses that the Lord was personally the agent in the Exodus enterprise. There is thus a tension between what Moses was sent to do and what actually happened. The journey to Canaan (Ex. 3:8) would not pass by way of Sinai, and Moses may well have wondered how the sign would be fulfilled. Secondly, there was the leadership of the pillar of cloud and fire (Ex. 13:20–22) so that there was never a question which road the people were meant to take. The Lord who brought them out led them along – and brought them to Sinai! And, thirdly, on arrival at the mount (Ex. 19:1–3) Moses immediately went up, without any summons or invitation to do so. He recognized that he had arrived at the place where he would 'report back' to the Lord who sent him: and, sure enough, the Lord was there to greet him as he ascended the mount.

THE PRIORITY OF GRACE

Looking at the whole complex of events – Egypt, Exodus, the wilderness and Sinai – and allowing the picture and pattern of them to become a huge visual aid before our eyes, we see that what the Lord *does* precedes what the Lord *demands*, as the work of redemption prepares for the promulgation of the law.

39

Since we have described the Egypt-to-Sinai history as a 'great visual aid', it may help to set it out just like that and then to dwell on what we see:

Egypt: ⟶ The wilderness: ⟶ Sinai:
    Liberation   Provision   Home-coming
    Redemption   Perseverance   Law-giving

HISTORY

First of all, the visual aid shows that it is history which rescues theology from the realm of make-believe.[2] To remove historical veracity and reality from the Exodus complex of events is to consign Exodus 'truth' to the realm of the religious ideas of ancient Israel with the story-component introduced as an illustration. We will explore this important matter further in the next chapter.

This is the place of history in the Old Testament. It is a rock-foundation laid beneath the edifice of revealed truth.[3] The way the story is told underlines key truths. It is a story of the Lord bothering with Israel when no-one else would, of divine perseverance when any other would give up, of God being good when neither deserving attracts nor merit persuades that such goodness should be extended. In a word, it is a story of grace being grace, pure and simple.

GRACE

The Sinai event itself is a further statement of the priority of grace. At two key points the initial word of the Lord to his people is the word of grace. The very first message that Moses mediates from the mount begins like this:

> You yourselves have seen what I did to Egypt, and how I carried you on eagles' wings and brought you to myself.
>
> (Exodus 19:4)

In terms of Exodus theology, as we shall see, this is the double message of liberation ('what I did to Egypt'), and of redemption ('brought you to myself').

But, secondly, when the Lord addresses his people from the mount (Ex. 20:1–17) he begins thus:

> I am the Lord your God, who brought you out of the land of Egypt,
> out of the house of bondage.
>
> (Ex. 20:2, lit.)

Once more it is stressed that what God has done takes priority in both time and statement over what he may demand. Grace – liberating, redeeming – comes before law.

LAW

Nevertheless, law is really and truly law. The terrors of Sinai were real and palpable (Ex. 20:18–21; Heb. 12:18–21). This was no contrived display of religious 'fireworks' designed merely to cow and awe. The cause of the whole manifestation of fire and cloud, earthquake, thunder and lightning was simply this that 'the LORD descended . . . in fire' (Ex. 19:18). This is what he is like. His holiness is not a passive attribute but an active force such as can only be symbolized by fire, a force of destruction of all that is unholy. At Sinai this holy God came to declare his holy law.

It is at this point that the sequence of events in the great historical visual aid bears its distinctive fruit: in the Old Testament, as in the whole Bible, the law of the holy God is not a ladder of merit whereby sinners seek to come to God, to win his favour and climb 'into his good books'; his holy law is, rather, his appointed and required pattern of life for those who, by redemption, have been brought to him already, who already belong to him and are already 'in his good books'. The law of God is the life-style of the redeemed.

THE HEART OF THE GRACE-LAW COMPLEX: THE COVENANT

The book of Exodus is in its entirety a covenant document, and it brings to its Old Testament climax and completion the covenant working of God.

In Exodus we begin face to face with a sheer mystery. We are never told why the sovereign purposes of God required that his people should go down to Egypt or why, having pledged them his presence in that alien land (Gn. 46:4), his care of them should take the strange form of persecution (Ex. 1:8–10), cruel sorrows (1:15–16) and threatened genocide (1:22). The early narratives of Exodus make us face the fact that 'days of darkness still come o'er me; sorrow's path I often tread'.[4] Yet the chapters are equally clear that there is a mystery of care parallel to the mystery of suffering, a secret power of preservation and increase which proves greater than the power of the enemy (Ex. 1:12). The chosen agents of infanticide prove to be moved by a spiritual fear that turns them from their grim task (1:17) and, marvel of marvels, out of that hostile, genocidal royal house, there emerges a tender-hearted princess, moved by an infant's tears (2:6). Exodus 1 – 2 are fully a match for the book of Esther in its understated theology of the hidden providences of the God of Israel.

Nothing overt, however, happens on earth until a significant fact is recorded regarding heaven. In answer to prayer (2:23), 'God heard their groaning and he remembered his covenant with Abraham' (2:24). Thus the Exodus-events proclaim themselves continuous with earlier acts of God and, specifically, with his covenanting work.

THE COVENANT:
1. NOAH, GRACE AND OBEDIENCE

The word 'covenant'

'Covenant' occurs for the first time in the Bible in Genesis 6:18. As a word, its meaning is the subject of much discussion. Is it related to the verb 'to eat' and does it therefore have in mind the sealing of an agreed relationship in a meal (Gn. 31:44–46, 54; Ex. 24:3–11)? Or does it mean 'bond', the binding of two hitherto separate entities into one? Or possibly 'a between/a mediation', the thing which stands between two parties so as to unite them?[5] Whatever the truth may be regarding the etymology of the word 'covenant', these three suggested meanings converge at one point: the coming into existence of a stated and continuing relationship between two parties who were previously apart from each other.

The 'finding grace' formula

The Bible does exemplify covenants between equals where there is a mutuality of promise and of obligation (*e.g.* Abraham and Abimelech, Gn. 21:21–32), but in the case of the divine covenant this mutuality disappears: the relationship between the sovereign, transcendent God and those on whom he wills to bestow his promises is totally asymmetrical. It comes about without discussion or negotiation; it is an imposition of grace.

This is very plain in the case of Noah, where the facts are set out in such a way as to exclude human initiative, contribution or desert: if anything is to be done, it must originate in and be carried through by God. The sequence in Genesis 6:5–7 tells it all, 'man . . . man . . . man'.[6] Without exception, the whole human race is involved in wickedness (6:5), outwardly ('on the earth') and inwardly ('the thoughts of his heart'); equally without exception the whole race has excited divine grief and pain (6:6); and, once more without exception, the race is under judgment of death (6:7). All have sinned; all are alienated from God; all must die. 'But Noah found favour in the eyes of the LORD' (6:8). A new factor operated in this situation of total loss; there was a man named Noah and he 'found favour'.

The formula 'x found favour in the eyes of y'[7] is found about forty times in the Old Testament. Naturally it evidences some mobility of emphasis in relation to different contexts. Sometimes it is a purely formal politeness not really intended to be taken seriously; at other times it is used in a way not wholly in accord with its basic force but, when the impression of all the passages is gathered, it becomes clear that in its strict intention it deals with a situation where 'x' can register no claim on 'y' but where 'y', contrary to merit or deserving, against all odds, acts with 'grace'.[8] In a word, it is a formula which safeguards the pure understanding of 'grace' as the outreaching of free, unmerited favour.

The 'generations' formula

Taking Genesis 6:8, then, in its preceding context, we meet Noah for the first time as a typical man among men. Like the rest, because he too is part of humankind, he is wicked outwardly and inwardly, a grief to God and under divine sentence. But in distinction from the rest of humankind a grace of God, as unexplained as it is unmerited, has come to him. He has not 'found' this grace by merit or effort; rather it has found him.

But what of the following context, where we read in 6:9 that Noah was in fact very different from the rest of mankind: in character 'righteous', in public conduct 'blameless among the people of his time', and spiritually 'walking' in fellowship with

God? U. Cassuto is typical of many when he comments that 'only *Noah*, who was, as the Torah stresses immediately afterwards (v. 9), a wholly righteous man . . . *found* FAVOUR . . .'[9]

This view would, of course, contradict the meaning of the formula 'x found favour in the eyes of y'; it would also infer an Old Testament doctrine of the grace of God contradictory of the New Testament: that grace comes as the reward of merit. While this immediately throws doubt on the interpretation that sees verse 9 of Genesis 6 as explanatory of verse 8, the killing blow to such a view is the 'generations formula' with which verse 9 opens.

The introductory heading which NIV represents as 'This is the account of Noah' (6:9) occurs throughout the book of Genesis,[10] where it uniformly marks a new beginning. This fact in itself constitutes a difficulty in seeing verse 9 as prior to and explanatory of verse 8. Why should an explanation be prefaced by a formula which proclaims a new start? But there is more to be said than this somewhat theoretical observation. 'Account' is a poor representation of the meaning of the word *tôlᵉdōt*. This word derives from the verb 'to beget, bear, bring forth' and is, in particular, a product of the hiphil mode of the verb, namely, 'to give birth to, cause to bring forth'. By its formation[11] the noun expresses 'the verbal idea in action', hence, in this case, 'a product', an 'ensuing event', an 'ongoing and emerging story'. In this way the word compels us to see verse 9 not as the explanation but as the consequence of verse 8 – it is what verse 8 'brought forth' – and, seen in the light of this, the story of Noah preserves the exclusive reality of grace as grace, while at the same time demonstrating that when grace comes (verse 8) it produces the changed and distinctive life of the new man (verse 9).

Covenant implementation

It is to all this that God looks back when he says to Noah that, when the destroying flood comes, 'I will implement[12] my covenant with you' (Gn. 6:17–18, lit.). Even though this is the first time the word 'covenant' has been used, the reality of it is plainly already present, awaiting implementation. On the divine side, therefore, the grace which has freely come to Noah is saving grace, grace which protects and preserves him and his family in and from the judgment of God on a sinful world.

On the human side, Noah's enjoys the benefits that this saving grace bestows in the context of responsive obedience. The narrative almost labours to underline that Noah is the obedient man, acting only at the divine word (Gn. 6:22; 7:5, 9, 16; 8:15–18). If the building of the ark itself was the most striking act of obedience (Gn. 6:22), perhaps Noah's patience in leaving the ark, not on the basis of the evidence of his eyes (7:13–14) but only when the divine word was given (7:15), is the most revelatory of his submissiveness.

THE COVENANT:
2. ABRAHAM, REGENERATION AND OBEDIENCE

The covenanting theme re-surfaces in Genesis with the Lord's new beginning in Abraham.

Covenant signs

The distinct emphases of the Abrahamic covenant can be appreciated by comparing the covenant sign given to Noah and that given to Abraham, the 'bow in the clouds' (Gn. 9:11–17), with circumcision (17:9–14): the one massive and public, the other tiny and private; the one pledging universal benefits, the other full of intimate, inward and domestic promises; the one full of God's concern for the human race, the other indicative of his transforming power in the individual.

Both signs, of course, have this in common: they are visible expressions of the promises of God, intended to excite and provide a foundation for faith. In the case of the 'bow in the cloud',[13] it expresses and guarantees the promise that never again will the earth be destroyed by a flood. Significantly, God does not say to Noah 'This is what the sign of the bow means to you', but 'This is what it means to me': 'I will see it and remember the everlasting covenant' (Gn. 9:16). The Bible risks the anthropomorphism of representing God as being in need of a reminder in order to make this point of major importance, that the revelation of what the sign means to God makes it the bearer of eternal truth to Noah the covenant man. He can be certain of its changeless meaning and rest in faith on what it says to him. In this way the basic meaning of a covenant sign is established: *covenant signs express covenant promises to covenant people.*

This principle applies without alteration to the sign of circumcision.[14] In Genesis 17, the covenant is first of all defined as a series of promises:

Personal: 'your name will be Abraham'. Abram became Abraham, the new man, regenerated, with the ability to be the father of many nations (17:5).

Domestic: 'I will make you very fruitful', with a family of 'nations' and 'kings' (17:6).

Spiritual: 'Your God and the God of your seed after you' (17:7, lit.). A divine commitment, expressed in the circumcision of the eight-day-old child (17:7).

Territorial: 'The whole land of Canaan' (17:8).

Following on from this magnificent, multi-faceted promise, circumcision is commanded and is called 'the sign of the covenant' (17:11). The identity of the sequence of promise (Gn. 9:11; 17:3–8) and sign (9:12; 17:9–14), along with the identical expression 'the sign of the covenant', used alike of bow and circumcision (9:12, 17; 17:11), indicates an identity of significance: just as the bow in the cloud sealed and spoke covenant promises to the covenant man Noah, so circumcision sealed and spoke covenant promises to the covenant man Abraham. The movement in each case is from God to man. Just as Noah, trembling in case a storm-cloud betokened the onset of another flood, would look on the sign of peace appearing at the very heart of wrath and rest believingly in the promise God had made, so Abraham, waiting through long years for the promised son, could take note over and over again that he was bearing in his very flesh the token of the divine promise and so continue trusting in faith and patience.

The two signs, however, differ in a very important way. Noah received the sign of the bow by divine action: 'I have set my bow in the clouds' (Gn. 9:13, lit.). But Abraham was required to impose the sign upon himself and his family (17:23). Careful understanding is needed at this point: circumcision symbolized the gift of God's promises but required the responsive obedience of the covenant man; it expressed promises and exacted obedience. As a symbol circumcision speaks of God and grace and the downward movement of the promises of God to the covenant man and his family; as an act it involved the response of obedience.[15] Obedience was, as we saw, intrinsic to the Noahic covenant, but the essential dovetailing of the very covenant sign itself with the responsive act of obedience integrates obedience into the very heart of God's covenanting purpose, and it takes us one significant step nearer to its Old Testament consummation in Moses, the Exodus, the Passover and Mount Sinai.

THE COVENANT:
3. MOSES, THE BLOOD AND THE LAW

We can trace the development of the covenant from Noah through Abraham to Moses by the following diagram:

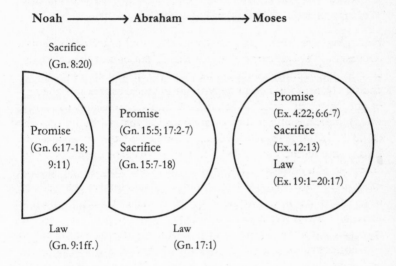

Noah ⟶ Abraham ⟶ Moses

Sacrifice
(Gn. 8:20)

Promise
(Gn. 6:17-18;
9:11)

Promise
(Gn. 15:5; 17:2-7)
Sacrifice
(Gn. 15:7-18)

Promise
(Ex. 4:22; 6:6-7)
Sacrifice
(Ex. 12:13)
Law
(Ex. 19:1–20:17)

Law
(Gn. 9:1ff.)

Law
(Gn. 17:1)

The whole diagram figures a gradual development from a crescent to a full moon. (1) The constant factor within the covenant 'circle' is God's promise, because that is what the covenant is: the promise of God. (2) In the case of Noah, the covenant idea is expressed in its central simplicity: in his free grace God comes and makes a promise. Yet within the covenant narrative (Gn. 6:8 – 9:17) there lie two related concepts: Noah offers a sacrifice in which the Lord found delight, and Noah's obedience was formalized in a minimal law. Yet neither law nor sacrifice are as yet integrated into the covenant idea. (3) In the case of Abraham, however, sacrifice comes right into the covenanting concept, for we read that the covenant was inaugurated[16] 'on that day' (Gn. 15:18), *i.e.* the day of the sacrifice which the Lord appointed (15:9, 'Bring me', lit. 'Take for me'),[17] but, as far as

47

Genesis 15 is concerned, the meaning of that sacrifice remains unexplained. Law too, through its indissoluble link with the covenant sign of circumcision, is brought within the covenant circle but it remains totally unelaborated, consisting of no more than a single, undeveloped though comprehensive spiritual principle: 'Walk before me and be blameless' (17:1). (4) With Moses, the whole sequence comes to full flower: sacrifice is basic and its meaning is clarified; law is promulgated in detail and its place and function are explained. The Old Testament has nothing further to add to covenant theology, nor indeed, in principle, has the New Testament.

Passover

From its inception, the Exodus narrative distinguishes between the acts of God in which there is no deliverance, and the climactic act which does deliver (Ex. 4:21–23).[18] This raises two important questions. First, why the plagues? If nothing will be achieved for Israel until the dire contest of the firstborn, why the nine plagues? But, secondly, if the tenth plague accomplishes deliverance (Ex. 11:1), why the Passover?

In answering the first question, the nine plagues are Egypt's probation. They demonstrate and prove the forbearance of God who delays wrath and offers every chance to repent and obey, and the justice of God who, when every probationary exercise has failed, finally inflicts the wrath which has been proved to be deserved. The nine plagues arise from and reveal the character of God. With regard to the second question, the relation between the tenth plague and the Passover has, by contrast, to do with the objectives at which the work of God is directed. According to the prospectus set out in Exodus 6:6, the Lord purposes both deliverance ('I will free [deliver] you . . .') and redemption ('and I will redeem you'). Deliverance is not redemption, salvation is distinct from liberation. A change of address is not a change of heart nor is the dissolution of an old bondage to Pharaoh the initiation of a new relationship with the Lord. There are two sides to the Exodus work: 'out of Egypt' and 'to myself'.

Living with a holy God

The inclusio around the Exodus narratives is formed by the fire in the bush (3:1–5) and the fire on the mountain (19:18). In each passage, this fire is linked with the reality of a holy God and the threat which that holiness constitutes to the trespasser. Theologically, the problem which the book of Exodus sets out to solve is how sinners can be brought into the presence of such holiness and live. The fact that, onwards from Sinai, the people did actually live with the burning fire at the heart of their community (Lv. 6:8–13) indicates that the problem was solved. The solution began – and in every real sense was completed – at the Passover.

Passover night redefined Israel's problem. Hitherto they had lived under threat of a genocidal king, but now a new factor came into the situation: 'I will pass through the land of Egypt . . . I will bring judgment' (Ex. 12:12, lit.). Another King is on his way, even more to be feared and more inescapable than Pharaoh. In relation to this King there is no negotiation. The ensuing death of the firstborn of Egypt, a judgment no less dire for being restricted to a token divine act, showed how real the threat was. But while there was no negotiation there was a provision: 'When I see the blood, I will pass over you' (12:13) and '. . . he will not permit the destroyer to enter your houses . . .' (12:23). The God of judgment decreed that which would protect from his judgment – even if all we may at present say is that, somehow, he was so satisfied at the sight of the blood that he no longer has any claim to make against that house. Likewise, the people who have taken shelter in the blood-marked houses discover that they are safe from the fearful judgment exacted on all others. Putting the case experimentally, the blood effected a change in God.

Satisfied acceptance

In so far as words can summarize the Godward aspect of Passover, it is that the holy God is satisfied to accept those who have acted on his prescription of the blood of the Passover lamb. He came to their houses in judgment; he passed over in peace. This basic Passover concept is continued in the levitical sacrificial system by the recurring assurance that the sacrifices are made in order 'that (the offerer) may be accepted before the Lord' (Lv. 1:3, lit.).[19] The drama of this can be caught by reading straight through from the end of Exodus into the beginning of Leviticus. No sooner was the tabernacle inaugurated (Ex. 40:33) than it was found to be a system of exclusion: not even Moses could enter, because of the presence (cloud) and glory of the Lord (40:35). But out of this forbidden Tent

(Lv. 1:1) a voice came speaking about 'coming near'. In Leviticus 1:2, the verb 'brings' and the noun 'offering' both alike express the idea of 'being near'/'bringing near'. Those who are excluded in their own right can 'come near' by the right which the blood of sacrifice confers and, coming near in this way, find 'satisfied acceptance' by the holy God.

Substitution and equivalence

Returning to Exodus 12, does the Passover narrative offer any explanation why the shed and applied blood of the lamb has this double effect of satisfying God and keeping the people secure? The story makes two things clear: first, that on Passover night there was a death in every house in Egypt without exception. In Egyptian houses, where there was no sheltering blood, there was the grim, sad death of the firstborn (Ex. 12:29–30), but in the houses of Israel lay the dead body of the lamb providing the Passover meal (12:8–11) for those who took shelter beneath its blood. This does not emerge from the narrative as a 'homiletical' truth: that is to say, a so-called 'devotional' thought marginal to, even possibly only tenuously related to, the content. Rather, it is an exegetical necessity, for it belongs to the way the story is told and is inseparable from the details the narrator chose to include. Otherwise, why, for example, did he dwell on the obvious and tautological truth of the dead body in every Egyptian house? Where the lamb died, the firstborn son did not die; where there was no lamb, the firstborn lay dead.

This lamb has been meticulously selected in each case so that it was as nearly as could be assessed equivalent to the *number* and *needs* of those who were to eat it (Ex. 12:3–4).[20] In this way the terms of the story make the point of equivalence. There has been a counting of heads and an assessing of appetites leading up to the choice of a suitable lamb so that the name and the need of every man, woman and child in Israel had been 'counted into' the lamb. Those who are mathematically minded might be inclined to say that had any household in Israel refused to obey the Passover regulations and failed to operate its provisions, it would have been 'only' the firstborn of the house who would have paid the penalty[21] and that therefore the notion of equivalence between the lamb and the total company of Israel is flawed. This logical conclusion, however, would contradict the terms in which the Exodus-sequence is set up. The Lord sent Moses into Egypt with the words ringing in his ears 'Israel is my son, my firstborn' (Ex. 4:22, lit.), and it is this corporate reality which is contrasted with the singularity of the firstborn of Pharaoh (4:23). On Passover night it was this corporate 'son' who was covered by the lamb so carefully chosen. The death of the lamb meant the safety and security of a whole people, the redeemed people of the Lord.

Atonement

In the levitical sacrifices, the concept of substitution was, as we shall see, particularly linked to the requirement that the offerer lay his hand on the head of the sacrificial beast, and this constant act in each category of sacrifice[22] was vividly explained by its use on the Day of Atonement.

First, however, it will be a help to note that the ideas of equivalence and substitution are prolonged in Old Testament thinking and practice by its atonement-vocabulary. The verb 'to make atonement'[23] is rooted in the idea of 'covering', and when it became part of the technical vocabulary of the levitical sacrifices it did not lose this basic meaning but developed into a price-paying concept. We today have not lost this either. We speak of a sum of money as sufficient to 'cover' a debt – not at all meaning that it hides the debt out of sight or sweeps it under the carpet, but rather that, because it is the exact 'covering', it actually cancels the debt by an equivalent payment. This is precisely what the Old Testament means by 'atonement'. Thus the noun *kōper* means 'ransom price'[24] and, says Leon Morris:

> . . . upon every occasion on which it is used it can be shown that there is the thought of a payment to be made. In its biblical usage it refers to the sum paid to redeem a forfeited life . . . [it] necessarily involves thought of a ransom price, a substitute, this being demanded by every occurrence of the term.[25]

Morris calls particular attention to Exodus 30:11–16, where the noun *kōper* and the verb *kippēr* are found together.

> The thought of payment . . . is clear [and] it is twice said 'to make atonement for your souls' (verses 15, 16). The verb . . . has here the sense of atonement, and of atonement by the payment of a . . . ransom.[26]

Morris's main conclusions are so exact that it is helpful to quote them:

> When *kippēr* is used in the Old Testament to denote the making of an atonement by means other than the use of the cultus, it usually bears the meaning 'to avert punishment, especially the divine anger, by the payment of a *kōpher*, a ransom', which may be of money or which may be of life . . . a substitutionary process . . . [Further, within the cultus,] the verb *kippēr* carries with it the implication of a turning away of the divine wrath by an appropriate offering.[27]

Morris rightly holds that this non-cultic use is the key to understanding *kōpēr/kippēr*[28] within the cultus. In this regard the key verse is Leviticus 17:11, which can be set out, reasonably literally, as follows:

> The soul/life (*nepēš*) of the flesh is in the blood.
> And I, for my part, have given it (the blood) to you
> on the altar to make atonement (*kippēr*) for your souls/lives (*nepēš*).
> For the blood is what makes atonement (*kippēr*)
> at the expense of/in the place of/as the equivalent of the soul/life
>   (*nepēš*).

The meaning of blood in the sacrifices must be consistent with its function. The verb 'to make atonement' is thus a key word in understanding Leviticus 17:11, and it is decisive when it relates the shedding of the blood and its cultic use to a basic 'hiding' and 'price-paying' function. The idea of 'hiding' could derive from the Passover situation itself when the people 'hid away' in the blood-marked houses, but the terms of the Passover story would not be satisfied if we failed to press beyond the pictorial elements of 'hiding' to the spiritual realism of being covered by an equivalent and satisfactory payment designed to 'propitiate' or satisfy the hostile intent of the God of judgment. Thus S. R. Driver commented on Leviticus 1:4:

> Though the burnt-, peace-, and meal-offerings were not offered *expressly*, like the sin- and guilt-offerings, for the forgiveness of sins, they nevertheless (in so far as *kipper* is predicated of them) were regarded as 'covering' or neutralizing the offerer's unworthiness to appear before God, and so . . . as effecting (atonement) in the sense ordinarily attached to the word, viz., propitiation.[29]

In Leviticus 17:11, the other key word is 'soul/life' (Heb. *nepeš*), which – and the above rendering shows – appears three times. This gives rise to alternatives of translation. If the third occurrence (line 5) refers back to the first (line 1), then it means that atonement is achieved 'at the expense of'[30] the life of the beast which has been killed. While its flesh and blood were united it was a living entity,[31] but the spilling of the blood on the altar necessitated the death of the beast, and this was the price paid for the sinner before God. Alternatively, the third use of *nepeš* may refer back to the second (line 3), in which case the reference is to the way in which the atonement price is equivalent to the sinner's need: it pays the *kōper* in the place of the *nepeš* which would otherwise die for its own sin.[32] The difference between these two possibilities is chiefly one of emphasis: the former stresses how the blood *makes* atonement (*i.e.* by an equivalent price), the latter how this *applies* to the individual's need (*i.e.* by paying a price exactly equivalent to the offence).

Substitution

We have seen how the idea of substitution is intrinsic to the way the Passover story is told. The remarkably strong emphasis on the element of 'equivalence' in the choice of the lamb (Ex. 12:3–4) coupled with the reality of a death in every house (12:30), and the balance between the firstborn of Pharaoh and Israel as the corporate firstborn of the Lord (4:22), are, without question, best summed up by saying that the Passover lamb was a substitute.

The concept of substitution is now more readily recognized by Old Testament theologians, even if in some cases there seems to be a residual unwillingness to do so. But in connection with the rite of the laying-on of the hand,[33] required in all the sacrifices, it can hardly be denied. Thus, for example, M. Noth writes:

> The 'laying' of the hand on the animal brought to the holy place for sacrifice is hard to explain. It may have its origin in special sacrificial rites, as in Lev. 16:21, in the sense of the transference of the offerer's own person to the animal, thus making the latter his substitute . . .[34]

Frankly, however, the rite is only 'hard to explain' if one wishes to resist its obvious meaning. Furthermore, the evidence does not really support the idea that its presence in the 'ordinary' sacrifices was in any sense derivative from its use on more 'special' occasions, but rather that the idea of substitution was fundamental to the sacrificial system as such – and indeed that it had always been so, for in Genesis 22:13 Abraham on Mount Moriah needs no divine instruction as to what to do with the ram caught in the thicket. As one doing a practised and accustomed thing, he took it and 'sacrificed it as a burnt offering instead of his son',[35] recognizing this as what the Lord had provided. Noth, however, is correct in calling attention to Leviticus 16:20–22 as the occasion on which the rite is given maximum exposure and full explanation.

On the Day of Atonement, the act of laying on hands was associated with the recital of 'all the iniquities of the children of Israel, and all their transgressions, even all their sins' (Lv. 16:21, RV),[36] and the 'force' of the act was that all this adverse moral weight was (literally) 'put . . . on the goat's head' making the beast one which 'shall bear on itself all their iniquities'. In this way the ritual of the Day of Atonement counterpoised secrecy and publicity. On the one hand, where none could enter and observe, and where the cloud of incense prevented even the High Priest from open vision, the blood of sacrifice was sprinkled on the 'atonement cover' (Lv. 16:11–17). William Tyndale devised the curious, beautiful and emotive rendering 'mercy seat' for the word *kapporet*, which NIV renders more exactly as 'atonement cover'. True indeed, it is where the Lord sits enthroned (Ex. 25:22); it is the place of mercy, for the ark's lid was the object of special specification whereby it was the exact covering over the tables of the Law which the ark contained (Ex. 25:17). On the Day of Atonement exact covering and blood-covering met together. But, since no-one was there to see and the rite was shrouded away from the assembly of Israel, the Lord provided also a visible demonstration of this secret transaction: a live goat, identified and loaded with the sins of the people, bearing sin, carrying away all their iniquity, never to be seen again (Lv. 16:20–22). The laying-on of hands effected the identification of the sinner with the guiltless, and the transference of sin and guilt from the one to the other.

The Servant of the Lord

The full Old Testament development of the principle of substitution came through the towering genius of Isaiah who saw that, in ultimate reality, only a Person can substitute for persons.[37]

Theodorus Vriezen, who voices unconvincing doubts about a general concept of substitution in the sacrifices, is yet frank enough to affirm that 'biblical theology cannot do without the idea of substitution but it is only in the personal sacrifice that it can be found in its fulness . . .'[38] This is exactly the point Isaiah reached in his portrayal of the Servant of the Lord who, literally, 'was pierced as a result of our rebellions, crushed as a result of our iniquities', upon whom was imposed 'the chastisement of our peace', 'at the price of' whose 'wounds there is healing for us' and upon whom 'the Lord caused to meet the iniquity of us all' (Is. 53:5–6).[39] The substitutionary death of the Servant is made even more explicit in the precise 'sin-bearing' terminology that Isaiah uses when he says that 'their iniquities he himself shouldered' (53:11) and 'he himself bore the sin of many' (53:10).

In the general Old Testament concept of the substitute, as realized in the animal sacrifices, there are three main strands: perfection (Ex. 12:5), that is to say, free from any stain of our sin; identification, the laying-on of hands which made the beast and the sinner one; and acceptance by the Holy God – the recurring stress first made in Leviticus 1:4 that what was achieved in the death of the beast met the requirements of the Lord. These three are explicitly linked with the Servant of the Lord: the verses instanced above express his identification with us in our sin, yet it is clear that he is himself free of sin. Isaiah 53:9 uses the idiom of comprehensiveness by contrast. In outward behaviour ('violence') and in inner mind and heart ('deceit') he was free of fault. The outward and the inward is the whole man – and with a typical adroitness Isaiah specifies a purity of speech that sets the Servant off from his own acknowledged sin and that which he sees as the hallmark sin of his people (Is. 6:5). Likewise, this Servant, in his work of blood-sacrifice and sin-bearing, is acceptable to the holy God for 'it was the Lord (himself) who made to meet upon him the iniquity of us all' (53:6, lit.), and who, when all was accomplished, 'gave him the many as his portion' and 'the strong as his spoil' (53:12, lit.).[40]

Identification

One final Exodus-Passover note requires brief comment – though in principle it has been mentioned in passing. The verb 'to redeem' which occurs in Exodus 6:6 proves to be a growing-point in Old

Testament soteriology.[41] In sixteen out of the forty places where the Lord is spoken of as Redeemer, the reference is to the Exodus. The passages fall into two groups: those which speak of the Exodus as an act of redemption,[42] and those which use the Exodus as a model of redemptive work.[43] The Lord announces himself as the typical and perfect redeemer, and in true redemption terms depicts himself as the husband undertaking for his wife (Is. 54:5), the father for his children (Is. 63:16) and the king for his subjects (Is. 4:6). Psalm 69:18 appeals to the Lord as 'next of kin', where the verb 'come near' is to be compared with its related noun 'nearest relative' who is the redeemer in Leviticus 25:25. The book of Ruth,[44] with its moving history of the identification of the wealthy Boaz as next of kin to the impoverished Ruth, is a central tract on redemptive kinship, and the Old Testament confidently takes up the figure of the Lord as the archetypal 'next of kin'. It does so without falling into the heathen notion of a quasi-physical relationship whereby the tribe or people are thought to have derived directly (sexually) from their god. The Exodus safeguards the truth: the relationship is one of grace, fashioned at a particular time in history and through historical action. The Lord came to Egypt to claim and constitute a people as his son (Ex. 4:22; Dt. 14:1–2); Jeremiah (2:1ff.; 31:31–34) and Hosea (2.1ff.) see the Exodus as establishing a marriage; Numbers 23:21 speaks of the Lord as Israel's king in the wilderness days, a royal relationship explicitly related to the Exodus in 1 Samuel 10:18–19. The 'price-paying' aspect of the Lord's redemptive work is found in Isaiah 43:3 which is best seen as a reference back to the Exodus[45] when the Lord brought Israel out at the expense of Egypt and the Egyptians. The thrust of the passage is that there is no price that the Lord would not be willing to pay as the Redeemer of his people. But at the heart of the whole redemptive exercise is his condescending identification of himself with his needy ones, just as, at the Exodus, he proclaimed himself as the God who himself came down to deliver (3:7–8).

COVENANT ENACTMENT:
GRACE, LAW AND MORE GRACE

At Mount Sinai, Moses embodied the whole meaning of the Exodus in a dramatic ceremony (Ex. 24:4–8). The altar with twelve surrounding pillars stands for the fulfilment of the Exodus purpose of God: he is now in the midst of his people and they, in literal, rock-solid, reality are gathered to him. Following the offering of the appropriate sacrifices of burnt- and fellowship-offerings, half of the blood is first sprinkled on the altar. For, as at Passover, the first 'movement' of the blood is Godward in atonement, the paying of the price that 'covers' the debt of sin. But, secondly, there is the reading of the covenant law and the people's response. That is to say, as the Lord's redeemed, the people hear, receive and commit themselves to the way of life pleasing to him. Finally, the remainder of the blood is sprinkled over the people: *i.e.* as sinners committed to obedience, they live under the shelter and continual cleansing of the blood which has atoned for them, before God.

The sequence of 'Grace → Law → Grace' is thus established. Grace redeemed; the law is proclaimed to the redeemed as the way they are to live; grace shadows and shelters them as they set their feet on the road of obedient pilgrimage. Grace and law are bound together in a great and blessed unity of divine saving mercy.

COVENANT EXPECTATIONS: ISAIAH, JEREMIAH AND EZEKIEL

Moses laid the foundation for the whole of the Old Testament. The redeemed are a people resting on grace for a life of obedience. The prophets inherited this situation but with centuries of experience making them long for a further work of God which might supply what was lacking or inadequate in what already existed.

Isaiah

As we have already outlined, Isaiah saw the need for a true Substitute who would perfect all that the Mosaic system of sacrifices had shadowed and, just as the Mosaic sacrifices secured the covenant status of the Lord's redeemed people (Ex. 24:4–8), so too Isaiah saw that the atoning work of the Servant of the Lord would effectuate the perfection of the covenant. It is the function of Isaiah 54 – 55 to spell out the benefits secured by the death of the Lord's servant, first (chapter 54) as they are enjoyed by the Lord's people, and then (chapter 55) as they await those whom John will later decribe as 'the scattered children of God' (Jn. 11:52). Thus in Isaiah 54:3 the 'seed' begotten by the saving work of the Servant (53:11) is now the otherwise inexplicable 'seed' of the derelict Zion, and, at the other end of the chapter, the 'righteousness' provided by the Servant (53:11) is the divinely given 'righteousness' (not, NIV, 'vindication') of (all) 'the servants of the LORD' (54:17). Chapter 55 reaches out to the widest audience of all who will respond (55:1-2) and, appropriately to Old Testament thinking, links this world-gathering (cf. 25:6-10a) with David (55:3) and the 'faithful loves' promised to him. The background to this relatively uncommon plural[46] is in Psalm 89, where it provides an inclusio of the psalm (89:1, 49 <2, 50>) and is explained by the same word in the singular (89:24, 33 <25, 34>). The Lord's 'loves' for David are respectively the love which pledges David's world-dominion and the love which pledges an enduring throne. In this way the Servant's work issues in the fulfilment of the covenant ideal: all the benefits of salvation are secured for the church in perpetuity by 'my covenant of peace' (54:10, cf. 53:5); and the world-wide gathered community enjoys the blessings of the universal and unending rule of the perfect king by an 'everlasting covenant made in your [plural] favour' (55:3, lit.).[47]

Jeremiah

The prophet Jeremiah, too, saw the culmination of the purposes of God in a covenant, and he was, indeed, the first person recorded to have used the expression 'a new covenant' (Je. 31:31–34). With all his sensitive awareness of human weakness, Jeremiah longed for a more radical work of grace in the heart such as Moses also had foreseen to be necessary (Dt. 5:29; 30:6). Jeremiah specifies four new covenant truths: first, he exposes the particular weakness of the former covenant (Je. 31:32), then the remedy that the Lord proposes (31:33), thirdly the result which follows upon that remedy (31:34a–d), and finally the groundwork upon which the new covenant rests (31:34e–f). In 31:32, the translation 'husband' could (see NIV mg.) be rather 'master/lord' and some favour this.[48] In context, however, 'husband' seems preferable, because it introduces at the start the concept of intimate relationship which, as we shall see, is intrinsic to the envisaged new covenant. As the divine Husband of his people, the Lord was totally faithful to his husbandly, covenantal obligations, but his wifely people were unfaithful: 'they broke my covenant', finding the obligations it imposed on them more than they could or were ready to meet. Significantly, this passage is about a 'new covenant' not a 'new law'. When his people could not rise to the height of his standards, the Lord does not lower his standards to match their abilities; he transforms his people. This is the meaning of 'my law within them', written on their heart (31:33, lit.). The Lord purposes and promises a work of regeneration bringing inner transformation, creating a human constitution that will be the exact 'match' of the Lord's law, and which will 'naturally' flow out in obedience.

Personally and experimentally this will result in a new and perfect 'marriage' between the Lord's people and the Lord. They will each 'know' him (Je. 31:34). To 'know the Lord' is quite different from knowing about the Lord. Samuel, for all his ministering to the Lord (1 Sa. 2:18) and growing up before the Lord (2:21) and in his favour (2:26), 'did not yet know the LORD' (3:7). 'Knowing' involves person-to-person union and intimacy, as indeed we read that 'The man knew his wife, Eve' (Gn. 4:1, lit.). This form of words arises not because the Old Testament coyly disguises sexual intercourse under a euphemism, but because it would instruct us in what marital intercourse is and is intended to be: the deepest person-to-person involvement and intimacy. The broken marriage of the former covenant is not a good idea that failed but an essential covenantal reality which the Lord will realize in the new covenant. When Jeremiah now counterpoises the ideas of 'teaching' and 'knowing', his intention is to contrast the thing that only humans can do with the thing that only the Lord can do. We can communicate truth, but we cannot create conviction or renew the mind of those we teach. Only God can do that: the new covenant is a transforming, regenerating work of grace effectuating a new nature and a new relationship.

The basis on which all this rests is a divine dealing with sin. The two words that Jeremiah uses in 31:34 point respectively to sin as the inner corruption of human nature (NIV 'wickedness'), and to sin as a fact in human life (NIV 'sins').[49] This combination of the inner and the outer, nature and conduct, is the Hebrew idiom of 'comprehensiveness expressed by contrast'. It is a total dealing with sin as it infects and marks us. On the other side, there is the divine work of forgiveness and forgetfulness. In relation to God, forgiveness is something he does, dealing with the offence that sin causes, breaking down the barrier it erects between us and him; forgetfulness is internal to his nature, the dismissal from his mind, eternally, of every recollection that we were once sinners and that we committed this, that, or the other sin. How the Lord proposes to do this work of forgiveness Jeremiah does not say. Maybe he felt that Isaiah had already said all that was to be said on the point.

Ezekiel

His love of intricate complexities led Ezekiel to see the future in all the baffling detail of his visionary temple (Ezk. 40–48). It was natural for him as a priest to furnish the future out of the stock in trade in his mental storehouse. But, happily for our briefer concerns here, Ezekiel also made a succinct statement of what he foresaw. News of the fall of old Jerusalem (33:21) marked a turning-point in Ezekiel's ministry and he turned his face forward to the future: there would be a perfect king, David himself returned (chapter 34) bringing (as only David ever did) victory over Edom (chapter 35), seen not as the political entity of that name but as the eschatological reality of world-opposition and animosity.[50] Ezekiel 36 dwells on the new people, indwelt by the divine Spirit, who will live in the Lord's land, and 37:1–14 figures this in Ezekiel's hair-raising vision of the valley of bones. There will thus yet be one cleansed and obedient people under one true king (37:15–17), and the whole arrangement will culminate in the Lord's everlasting covenant of peace. The outward seal of covenantal reality will be the Lord's indwelling presence:

> I will put my sanctuary among them for ever. And my tent-dwelling will be over them; and I will be their God and they will be my people. And the nations will know that I myself, Yahweh, am sanctifying (setting apart) Israel (for myself) when my sanctuary is in their midst for ever' (37:26–28, lit.).

For Ezekiel (as indeed for all the prophets), the future is the realization of the ideals of the past. Of old the Tabernacle was pitched as God's Tent at the very heart of the camp of Israel (Nu. 2).[51] It symbolized the Lord's identification with his tent-dwelling people and was the focus of his communion with them (Ex. 29:42–45) and theirs with him (Lv. 1:1–2).[52] At that time, he put his tent among them but it was not open to them (Ex. 40:34–35); the time will come, says Ezekiel, when his tent will be 'over them' (*cf.* Is. 4:5–

6): they will be his family, at home with the Lord.

In all this, even the greatest of the prophets were not innovators. They built on the Mosaic foundation – and the edifice they erected was Christ Jesus our Lord in his final work of redemption, transformation and indwelling. The fulfilment of Ezekiel's visionary temple is found in Ephesians 2.

AVENUES INTO THE NEW TESTAMENT ◇

The New Testament sees the coming of Jesus (Lk. 1:72; Acts 3:25) and the saving work of Jesus (Lk. 22:20; 1 Cor. 11:25; Heb. 8:8–10; 10:15–18) in covenantal terms, and the same is true of the ongoing work of the church (2 Cor. 3:6). The key word regarding the new covenant in the Lord Jesus Christ is 'better': better in *assured hope* (Heb. 7:22–25), in that he is endlessly alive to administer its benefits; better in its *promises* (Heb. 8:6), for sins will be remembered no more; resting on a better *sacrifice* (Heb. 9:13–14, 23–28), the once-for-all death of Jesus (Heb. 9:28; 10:12). Thus, in the New as in the Old Testament, the covenant 'scheme' is:

Oath → Sacrifice → Holiness

The divine oath of commitment originates the whole sequence (Gal. 3:15–17; Heb. 6:13–20); the blood of Jesus as the covenant mediator establishes and implements the divine promises (Heb. 9:15–22; 12:24); and the result is a holy people, set apart for God, enjoying his blessings and committed to obedience (Heb. 10:10–14, 29).

Another way of putting the same point is to say that the New Testament affirms the Old Testament sequence

Grace ⟶ Law

See Titus 2:11–14; 3:4–8. John, therefore, can affirm that all the grace and truth of the Mosaic law 'came real' in Jesus (Jn. 1:17). In Jesus, the blood-sacrifices with all their blessedness for forgiveness and atonement were made, consummated and ended (Heb. 10:11–12, 18); and the law as a life-giving code – that is to say, a code which empowers what it commands (Lv. 18:5) – is also actualized. He is the 'end' of the law (Rom. 10:4; 13:8–10), the one in whom law is brought to its full meaning and application (Mt. 5:17–48) and to its full efficacy in and for the obedient life (Acts 5:32).

CHAPTER FOUR

Christ as revelation (1):
The theme of the image of God

Two very different people provide a starting-point for our third study in the Old Testament background to our understanding of Christ.

THE SO-HUMAN GOD

First there is Miss Rodway. She lived in Bristol in the early 1950s and was a lady with undoubted psychic powers. In fact, after she became a Christian and renounced her life and work as a spiritist medium, she used to say that she had to make a constant, conscious effort not to 'see' the dimension of the often strange spiritual entities in which she had once lived. But after her conversion she became a delightful and richly helpful Christian, as much in demand as a speaker about Christ and the Scriptures as formerly she had been as a medium. She spoke once to a group of what would now be called 'teenagers' (they had not yet been 'invented'), and the thrust of her remarks was that they should and could live close to God in Christ, that his ear was open to their every cry, his longing was to supply their every need and that, as Miss Rodway put it, God's kindness and understanding were such that 'Dear young people, you must never be afraid to come to him: he's so human'.

Our other source is very different – the dinosaur weightiness of J. Pedersen in his marvellously suggestive study, *Israel, its Life and Culture*:[1]

> In all the law codes . . . it is a common feature . . . that the assertion of Yahweh and the rejection of images is the same thing . . . The conception of Yahweh that came to prevail was entirely determined by his human character.[2]

They make an ill-assorted pair, the ex-spiritist medium and the professor from Copenhagen, but they put their fingers alike on a deeply important Old Testament and biblical truth: to be sure, the Lord's transcendence exceeds our vocabulary of exaltedness; indeed his distinctness, difference and 'otherness' is not to be denied; but at the same time the highest, greatest and best biblical thinking about God is anthropomorphic, that is, couched in terms of human attributes, feelings, actions and reactions. This is just as true (if more unobtrusive) in the majesty of Genesis 1, where we meet the speaking God, as in the homelier ways of Genesis 2, where he sits like a potter to 'fashion' man or comes visiting in the Garden like the squire from the big house calling on one of his tenants. Pedersen rightly insists that:

> The raising of Yahweh above the world did not mean that he was made into an abstraction . . . His soul is built like a human soul . . . he looks after his children like a father . . . chastises his enemies like a mighty king . . . is affectionate to the affectionate.[3]

ANALOGICAL THINKING

God's ways, of course, are not our's, nor our thoughts his (Is. 55:8) and therefore we must use analogies cautiously. Isaiah is our careful mentor in 40:11–12. In 40:11, the Shepherd God is described in the most moving terms as he tends the flock, keeps the lambs together, carries them in his arms and matches the journey to the capabilities of the nursing ewes. But, following immediately, the revelation of God explodes into transcendence as, in 40:12, we meet One whose mere cupped hand is sufficient to hold all earth's waters, whose ruler and compasses plotted the heavens, whose scales weigh out mountains and hills. U. E. Simon, with typical perceptiveness, comments on this dramatic change of emphasis:

> If God be a shepherd, is he also like a cowherd, a swineherd, a cattle-dealer, an auctioneer, a butcher, a director of meat-purveyors? . . . We deal, in fact, with absurdities to show how analogies may go hopelessly astray . . . The analogy of the shepherd might have opened the floodgates to fantasies . . . Paganism succeeds precisely because men employ the analogies with which they are most familiar [and], apparently sensing the danger of being misunderstood, the prophet returns to cross swords with

the antagonist at a somewhat deeper level: 40:25 'To whom, then, says the Holy One, will ye compare me . . . ?'[4]

In this way, the analogy of the Shepherd-God, helpful and beautiful within its limits, must be contextualized within the doctrine of a God who is incomparable. Yet, as Simon also notes, the bridge between the simple analogy of the Shepherd (40:11) and the interrogatives (40:18, 25) which assert the breakdown of all analogies is (simply) another essay in analogical thinking: the master Craftsman (40:12), the self-sufficient Wisdom (40:13–14), the all-Sovereign (40:22–24) – Carpenter, Counsellor and King!

FORM OR NO-FORM?

Miss Rodway and Professor Pedersen, whose ignorance of each other could not have been more profound, in their distinctively individual ways put a finger right on one of the pulse-points of the Old Testament.

Old Testament religion was distinct from its religious environment in its repudiation of images.

> The goddess Hathor was represented as a cow; Thoth could be manifested as a baboon or as an ibis . . . other deities were represented in a cross between animal and human form . . . Several Egyptian deities were represented as birds, one of the most important being Horus, who was represented as a falcon.[5]

It was not to be so in Israel. In Israel religion was inseparable from theology and theology inseparable from revelation. The second commandment follows the first by necessity, just as the first arises by equal necessity out of the divine self-proclamation which forms a preamble to the Decalogue: *i.e.* because he is Yahweh, the Redeemer-God (Ex. 20:2), nothing less than total devotion to him alone is in order (20:3). But since 'total devotion' is a concept that can mean anything or nothing, the question arises 'How shall I be a totally devoted person so as to keep the first commandment?' The second commandment (Ex. 20:4–6) supplemented by Deuteronomy 4 provides the answer. It touches worship, belief and behaviour. The first thrust of the commandment is not to wean Israel away from pagan gods – this has been secured by the first commandment – but to safeguard the divine acceptability of worship.

It is at this point that Deuteronomy 4 and Numbers 12 bear their testimony. According to the latter passage (Nu. 12:8), Moses enjoyed a privileged distinctiveness in that the Lord spoke with him 'face to face' (lit., 'mouth to mouth') and he saw 'the form of God'; according to the former passage (Dt. 4:10–14), Israel's experience at Horeb was one of receiving teaching and hearing commandments but they 'saw no form'.[6] When, therefore, Israel is forbidden the use of visible representations of the Lord in worship, it is not because they are impossible but because they are impermissible. Visible representations inevitably lead to corruption (Dt. 4:16).[7]

SPIRITUAL OR MATERIAL: TENSION

The religions of Canaan would speedily have impressed this fact on Israel. No doubt Baal-worshippers considered their god to be a non-material or 'spiritual' and invisible force, but the depiction of the Baal-nature in terms of bull-images gave rise to a brutish and orgiastic religion of the most debased kind. The 'spiritual' was absorbed in the material and Baal became the bulls that (in theory) only symbolized part of 'his' nature.[8] It was to be precisely the reverse in Israel. In so far as the Lord is to be 'visualized' in worship, it is in terms of the truth he has revealed about himself in word and deed.

Deuteronomy affirms this in general terms (4:10, 12); the second commandment specifies the 'visualizing' of the Lord in terms of the truths of jealousy and judgment, unfailing and tender love. But both passages insist that worship must lead to obedience to what the Lord has commanded. In Israel's religion, therefore, truth determines ceremonial and rite; and, in its life, truth determines conduct: the primary 'manifestation' of the Lord is his revealed word.

MAN IN THE IMAGE OF GOD

When we think, therefore, about the Old Testament understanding of the revelation of God, there are two foci of discussion. There is, on the one side, the 'form' of God which Moses enjoyed to a special degree and (as we shall see) others experienced in lesser but significant ways; on the other side, there is the word of God, his spoken disclosure of himself. The element in which these two find their unity is humankind, for it is to humans that the revelatory word is addressed and it is in them that the revelatory 'form' is specifically present.

The Genesis poem of Creation (1:1 – 2:3) surrounds the appearance of man on the earthly scene with great solemnity. Foremost among the preparatory marks of man's speciality is the careful use of the verb 'to create' (Heb. *bārā'*). It is the first main verb in Genesis 1:1 and the last main verb in Genesis 2:3, thus forming an *inclusio* around the whole poem, *i.e.* looking forward to what is about to happen and then back over the finished work. Within the poem, it marks first the incoming of animate life in the shape of the 'great sea-monsters' (1:21) and, secondly, the arrival of man in the image of God. At this point (1:27) the verb occurs three times. It is tempting to match the 'created . . . created . . . created' of the nature of man with the 'Holy, Holy, Holy' of the nature of God (Is. 6:3) – and the very uniqueness and speciality of the latter[9] suggests an equal significance in the former. Just as the Lord is the 'super-superlatively holy One', so man is the super-superlative creature, the creature par-excellence, the one whose essential nature is unique creatureliness. Only by recognizing themselves as the unique Creature and by discovering how to live as such can human beings be true to themselves and enter upon a truly human life.

These observations about the uniqueness of man are reinforced by the fact that the verb 'to create' is, in the Old Testament, God's exclusive verb. Outside the Old Testament, related languages used cognate verbs to cover the whole field of creativity, human as well as divine,[10] but not so the Old Testament. When the verb 'to create' has a subject, it is always God; when it is used with a presumed subject, it is always God. It is not used in any other way. 'To create' is his exclusive act. As to its meaning, while in Genesis 1 it must include the notion of *creation ex nihilo*,[11] it is used throughout the Old Testament of acts or events which either by their speciality or novelty or both point to God as their originator. Thus man as the creature par excellence is by this very fact also the most special and greatest work of God.

The speciality, uniqueness and dignity of man, heralded by the threefold cluster of the verb 'to create' is defined by saying that man was created 'in the image and likeness of God' (Gn. 1:26). Once more the solemnity with which this is announced is evident. 'Let there be light' is essentially a bare imperative but 'Let us make man' is deliberative. For the one and only time in the whole creative process we are invited into the mind and counsels of God: there is a pause in the onward flow of the poem. The Creator is thinking and has reached a conclusion; in the whole of a wonderful, mysterious, revelatory creation there is to be this deepest wonder, this especial mystery, one who is wholly and essentially a creature but also the bearer of the divine image.

Neither the poem of Creation (Gn. 1:1 – 2:3) nor the emergent narrative of the beginnings of history (2:4ff.) defines the idea of 'the image of God', and the search for a definition has spawned a library all its own.[12] In Genesis, however, two things are reasonably clear: first, that 'the image of God' is descriptive of human nature in its entirety and is not to be linked with or limited to any particular part or aspect. The distinctiveness is as much in one part as another; it is the common denominator of the whole. This, at any rate, is the plainest implication of the words in Genesis 1:26–27 where 'man' and 'image' are mutually correlative.

Secondly, in Genesis 1 and 2 certain human distinctives are isolated, which mark man off from the beasts, associate man with God and to that extent, even if not defining or 'locating' the image of God, at least focus on the ways in which this great, fundamental definition and uniqueness of human nature displayed itself.

1. THE IMAGE: PHYSICAL

We start with the words 'image' and 'likeness' themselves (Genesis 1:26–27).[13] In their Old Testament use, both words – which must be treated as synonyms – have a primary reference to what is outward and visible. We can feel the 'scandal' of the idea the words convey by translating 'Let us make man in our form and shape' as 'Let us make a "lookalike"'.

Seeing God

But how can this be entertained even for a moment? In the Old Testament as in the New, the God of Israel is essentially invisible. There can be no argument about it and, for this reason, some have sought to play down the insistent outwardness of the two words.[14] But to do so runs counter to another line of evidence which must be considered.[15] The Old Testament records people as claiming to have 'seen God'.[16] Very often an element of mortal fear follows on the 'seeing'. In the case of Isaiah, this was very precisely explained by H. H. Rowley as 'not the consciousness of his humanity in the presence of divine power but the consciousness of his sin in the presence of moral purity',[17] and there is no reason why Isaiah cannot here speak for all those who trembled for their lives before God, even if, equally, their reactions were more instinctual and less articulated than those of the prophet. But more related to our theme is the remarkable fact that whether it is the Lord or the Angel of the Lord who is seen, wherever any further description is offered, it is in human terms. According to Judges 13:3 'the angel of the LORD' appeared but, in 13:6, Manoah's wife reports that 'a man of God' came to her. In response to Manoah's prayer (verse 8) 'the angel of God' (verse 9) returned, and Manoah's wife ran excitedly to her husband with the words, 'He's here! The man who appeared to me . . .' (verse 10). Manoah 'came to the man' and asked (lit.), 'Are you the man who spoke to the woman?' (verse 11). And so things remain. Manoah is under the impression that he is talking to a 'man' until 'the angel of the LORD ascended in the flame' (verse 20) and Manoah, now realizing the truth of the matter, cries out, 'We are doomed to die. We have seen God' (verse 22). In this way, 'God', 'the angel of the Lord', 'a man of God' and a 'man' are all the same person.

In so far as our thought-processes can bridge between these two aspects of the divine nature – God's essential, spiritual invisibility and his occasional visible presentation of himself to individuals – we would have to say that there is a visible 'form' which is specially and exactly appropriate to the invisible glory of God. In this 'form' man was created. The physical is as much 'the image of God' as are those aspects of human nature which (with our 'Greek' background) we might more readily think of as our 'higher nature'.

2. THE IMAGE: MATRIMONIAL

The sequence of thought in Genesis 1:26–27 associates the image of God in man with the creation of male and female. Thus, in 1:26 the initial determination to 'make man in our image' is at once modulated into a plural: 'and let them rule'. Verse 27 defines this plural as 'male and female', the two components of the single entity (*hā'ādām*) embraced by the threefold 'created' which signals a unique work of God. J. J. Von Allmen can say that:

> Marriage is not an accidental but an essential element of creation, to the extent that man is . . . complete, capable of reflecting and displaying his Maker, only if he is 'male and female' . . . it was not until the human couple was formed that God was content with his work.[18]

Unity in diversity

The implication, however, of the verses is that the image of God is not found in sexual diversity as such but in marriage, the two who become one and so become 'fruitful and increase' (Gn. 1:28). Genesis 5:2 expresses the same thought when it says (literally) that 'male and female he created them . . . and he called their name Man'. They are Mr and Mrs Adam – not because, according to modern custom, she had taken his name, nor because he had taken hers, but because, in their oneness, they are the essential components of that unique entity in creation, 'man in the image of God'.

The narrative of the making of woman in Genesis 2:18–25 puts this in its own striking way. The Creator brings the female into being by making the male incomplete. In order to 'build' (Gn. 2:22, lit.) the woman, the Lord God 'took a something from his sides'. Henceforth the male will only become complete by receiving back that which was taken from him. Likewise the female is 'built' in separation from her true origin or context so that she will only 'come home', return to where and what she should be, by union with the male. Rightly, therefore, the narrative declares them to be 'îš and 'iššâ (2:23), the male and female components of a single reality.

This is not, of course, to say that the unmarried do not possess the image of God or are deficient in their enjoyment of humanness in its revealed definition. In the early chapters of Genesis, the matrimonial is only one of six ways in which the distinctiveness of humankind in creation is marked out. But this must be said: there is a distinct truth about the image of God in man expressed and safeguarded by the union of man and woman in marriage. It is the revealed secret (Paul's 'mystery', Eph. 5:31–32) of biblical marriage that when the two become 'one flesh', one personal entity, their diversity in unity and unity in diversity[19] are themselves a revelation of the divine nature.

3. THE IMAGE: GOVERNMENTAL

H. Ringgren well expresses the essence of this governmental aspect of the image of God:

> The rulers of the ancient Near East set up images and statues of themselves in places where they exercised or claimed to exercise authority. The images represented the ruler himself as symbols of his presence and his authority . . . Thus man's similarity to God consists in his dominion . . . exercised as God's representative.[20]

The early chapters of Genesis treat this idea very seriously, first, because their revelation of God is of the totally sovereign One. In Genesis 1:1 – 2:3 there is his calm mastery of the whole event of Creation. He 'speaks and it is done' (*cf.* Ps. 33:6, 9; 104; 148:5). This sovereignty of transcendence is matched, in Genesis 2:4–25, by a sovereignty of benevolence. There is the same unquestioned right to order life on earth as was evident in bringing the earth to existence and its living creatures to being.[21] The advent of humankind on the scene has not limited or altered the right of the Creator to impose his shape, order and will upon the world and the life of man. The man is not asked if he would like to be a gardener, nor is he consulted as to what would constitute a proper partner for him. The bounty of the Garden and the terms of life within it are alike a sovereign imposition.

In Genesis 3 man, prompted by the serpent, makes the great attempt to throw off the rule of God and break free from what is represented as an unnatural restriction on growth and development. But divine sovereignty is unaltered, exercising itself in judgment and mercy within a new situation: it is still the Lord's right and power to speak the authoritative word which carries its own effect with it, to decree the new framework of life on earth and both to impose and to restrain the results of sin.

The verbs in Genesis 1:28 indicate the reality of the dominion vested in man. NIV 'subdue' translates √*kābaš*, whose meaning of dominating and subordinating is reflected in the cognate noun *kebeš*, a 'footstool'. 'Rule' translates √*rādâh*, used in Joel 4:13 of 'treading' a wine-press, and in Isaiah 41:2 of the victorious progress of an invincible foe. The verbs do not, of course, direct humankind to walk on the rest of creation or to dominate with savagery as a conqueror would, but they must be allowed their weight as verbs of truly sovereign and authoritative government.

Joint-rule

It is important, in addition, to note that the imperatives in Genesis 1:28 are plural. Just as fruitfulness and increase are the joint and co-equal activities of male and female, so also are subduing and ruling. It is 'man in the image of God', the divinely created partnership and oneness of male and female, that is king[22] in creation.[23]

4. THE IMAGE: SPIRITUAL

The word 'spiritual' is used here to denote a relationship between the Creator and humankind such as is not enjoyed by any other entity in creation. This is very evident in Genesis 2:4–25, where humankind is plainly superintended by a special providence of the Lord God, but the ground for it is laid in Genesis 1:28. Two brief passages side by side reveal the point in question:

> Genesis 1:21–22: 'God created the great creatures of the sea . . . God blessed them and said, "Be fruitful and increase . . ."'

> Genesis 1:27–28: 'God created man in his own image . . . God blessed them and said to them, "Be fruitful and increase . . ."'

So much is identical between human and beast. The fact of creation, the blessing and the command are all the same, but there is this key difference: the command is imposed on the beasts as a fiat: it is communicated to the human pair as an address. Person to persons, 'thus', says Wenham, 'drawing attention to the personal relationship between God and man'.[24]

Genesis 2:25

Alongside this it is worth mentioning in passing that Genesis 2:25 may be understood as affirming that the human pair, alone in all creation, consciously shared the Creator's perfect and pure satisfaction in the created order. The idea of 'shame' in the Old Testament (here √*bôš*) is nothing like our sense of 'embarrassment' or of 'shyness'. Its two main shades of meaning are moral or spiritual shame (*e.g.* 2 Ki. 2:17; Ezr. 8:22; 9:6) and (much more frequently) disappointment, failure of expectation, reaping shame, public exposure to dishonour (Jb. 6:20; Pss. 22:5<6>; 71:24; Is. 19:9; 24:23). In this context, therefore, not to sense either moral opprobrium or any sense of disappointment or of failure of expectations to be fulfilled[25] is the negative counterpart of God looking at creation and finding it 'very good' (Gn. 1:31).

5. THE IMAGE: MORAL

Genesis 2:4–25, as we noted above, should not be thought of as a 'second account of Creation'. Rather, as the 'emergent story' (2:4, literally) it sets up, in a formalized manner, the basic essential principles of human life on earth. The structure of the narrative is all-important.

Genesis 2:4–25 falls into two sections. In verses 4–17, humankind is set within the context of the physical world, and in verses 18–25, in the context of the animal and personal world. In this way, Genesis 2:4–25 mirrors Genesis 1:1 – 2:3, where the creation of the physical environment (1:1–13, the first three days) is followed by the creation of the world of animals and people (1:14–31, the second three days). Within these 'frameworks', man is set to live and be. According to Genesis 2, in each sphere, man lives under the sovereign benevolence of the Lord God who, in the first 'frame' provides the Garden and, in the second, provides the 'matching/equivalent help' of a wife to remedy that which was 'not good' for the man. The structure of the verses is completed by the way in which each section concludes with the law under which man is to live within that department of his life: the law of the Garden (2:16–17), and the law of marriage (2:24).

Thus, for man, the merely instinctual life of the beasts is ruled out. Human life is not to be lived – as beasts do – in terms of needs and opportunities as if they were self-justifying principles. The man lives in a yes-no relationship with life – to choose one way and reject another, to live life with regard to foreseen ends. Furthermore, he is not left to ferret out these ends on the basis of intuition, logic or trial and error but has them declared for him by the word of God. There is, after all, no human logic in the link between a 'tree of knowledge of good and evil' and a consequence of death (Gn. 2:17). Nothing could quite so starkly reveal the ideal of government of life in terms of the foreseen good[26] and the basic definition of the good as that which God has revealed to be so. For the man the apparent immediate advantage (the acquisition of knowledge) must be subordinated to the 'real' good of doing the declared will of God.

The Bible never deviates from this basic position (which we shall explore further a little later). Humankind is designed for obedience to what God reveals. Neither does the Bible deviate from what is here implied about the place of obedience in the divine scheme. Just as later, in Exodus, law (Ex. 20) follows on grace (Ex. 12), so here law (Gn. 2:16–17, 24) follows on benevolence (2:8–15, 18, 21–23); and just as in the later covenantal order, obedience secured for the covenant people the blessings promised within the covenant, so, in the Garden, obedience was the key to the continued enjoyment of the bounties the Garden lavished on the fortunate first couple. Law was not an unnatural imposition or arbitrary restriction, but rather spelled out in its commandments the very life for which humankind was designed and, because it stated the revealed will of God, it was also the guarantee of the continued enjoyment of the Garden with all its prosperity and fulfilment.

6. THE IMAGE: RATIONAL

Genesis 2:19 recapitulates Genesis 1:24–25[27] and, consistently with the title (2:4) which speaks of this as the 'emergent story', takes things on to their next stage. By the will of the Lord God, evident in his action of bringing the beasts in parade before the man, man is set apart from and over the animal creation. He displays this distinctiveness by engaging in the rational, even philosophical, task of categorizing, matching like with like, setting group apart from group by means of significant names. Just as, in 2:5, the imposition of order on the vegetable creation awaited the advent of man's organizing hand, so, in the department of living things, he is the discerning and purposeful thinker.

THE IMAGE OF GOD AND THE LAW OF THE LORD

The foregoing review indicates that wherever we touch human nature, outwardly or inwardly, physically, spiritually, morally or mentally, we touch the image of God. Now finding fulfilment in life depends on knowing how to live in the light of a correct self-definition. Just as a car achieves optimum performance when it is used according to the 'law' of its construction, so with humankind. If we were nothing but bits of mechanism, possibly it would not matter if we put anti-freeze into the baby as well as into the car. So, with us also, optimum performance depends on knowing how to define 'human nature'.

Biblical revelation tells us how to define our true nature – we were created 'in the image of God'[28] – and also how to trigger that nature into activity so that we can enjoy a truly human life and a true personal fulfilment.

LAW = *TÔRÂH* = 'TEACHING'

The word 'law'[29] itself is not our best friend as we seek to understand the meaning and function of 'law' in the Old Testament (and in the Bible). It resonates with unattractive associations, from a small boy's memory of taking his new football to the local park only to be faced with a notice saying 'The Playing of Ball Games in this Park is Forbidden' to the use of 'the Law' as a synonym for the Police.

The Bible, of course, does not dissociate 'law' from the idea of an authoritarian imposition. Deuteronomy 6:2, for example, urges the people to 'fear the LORD your God . . . by keeping all his decrees'. But if this is the 'stick' of the law, the 'carrot' quickly follows in the promise that obedience brings security of tenure, life and enjoyment (6:3).

What is important is to grasp the foundation of all this, that *torah* means 'teaching'. In Proverbs 4, the exhortation of a loving father to beloved sons, is typical:

> Hear, sons, a father's instruction;
> pay attention so as to acquire a discerning knowledge;
> For I give you a sound grasp;
> do not abandon my teaching.
>
> (Pr. 4:1–2, lit.)

Line one speaks of a father's commitment to educate ('instruction') his sons; line two promises that beyond knowledge lies discernment (lit., 'so as to know discernment'), an understanding of the heart of things; line three expresses the father's confidence that he can lead his sons to abiding convictions ('a sound grasp'); and line four sums it all up as the father's *tôrâh*, 'teaching'. The whole procedure is within the family; it is prompted by the father's loving concern for his sons; no matter whether his teaching is promissory (Pr. 4:5–13) or restrictive (Pr. 4:14–17), its beating heart is the father's love. Life consists of choices, and he wants his sons to know the issues so as to choose soundly (Pr. 4:18–19).

LAW AND LIBERTY: THE PRECEPTUAL IMAGE OF GOD

We noted above how, in the Garden of Eden, law was both the guardian and the guarantor of liberty. As long as they obeyed the single precept of the law of the Garden (Gn. 2:16–17), the man and the woman were free to roam its acres, eat its fruits, revel in the joys of their marriage and walk with the Lord God. Far from cramping or marring their lives, the law of the Garden secured their joys and fulfilments. This was and remained the divine intention in the gift of the law. The key words come in Exodus 20:2 where, as a preamble to the law, the Lord announces himself as (literally) 'the Lord your God who brought you out of the land of Egypt, out of the house of slaves'. That is to say, 'your bondage is a thing of the past. The giving of the law is not a new bondage but a charter for the free, a token that slavery and bondage are over.'

The question must therefore be faced: how can the giving of *law* be a sign of *liberty*? And the answer lies in a chapter as full of significance as it is easy to overlook!

Leviticus 19

In Leviticus 19, the whole of life is brought together. There are precepts touching family relationships, religious objects and ceremonies, how to harvest your crops and love your brother, probity in working life, the honour due to the Name of the Lord, neighbourliness, gossiping, the proper care of the disabled and respect for the elderly, stock-breeding, vengeance, dress, sexual morality, arboriculture, the avoidance of bloody meat, spiritism, how to mourn, the protection of daughters, Sabbath-keeping, ethnic minorities. But it all seems so higgledy-piggledy: there is no apparent order of presentation; it is as if all the variety and muddle of life itself were intentionally reflected in this sweeping together of commandments. Possibly this was intentionally so: life is a varied, unpredictable thing, a hotch-potch of everything. But for the people of God there is one common factor amid all the flux and multiplicity of experience: there is the law of the Lord to obey. This is what gives coherence and shape to life.

Now, however, we must come closer to the heart of the matter.

Why is the Lord, the law-giver, so intent that his law should run throughout the whole life of his people in small matters as well as great, in their hearts and thoughts as well as in relationships and actions? Because he desires that they should be like him. The 'text' which this whole chapter expounds is announced in Leviticus 19:2: 'Be holy because I, the LORD your God, am holy.' Thus the intention of the law is to make the people like their God, and this, too, is the thread of unity running through the splendid diversity of the whole chapter. Fifteen times[30] the laws enunciated are driven home by the words 'I am the LORD/I am the LORD your God'. Thanks to the translational scruple of representing the divine Name, Yahweh, by the English convention 'LORD', this repeated sanction attached to the laws sounds like an assertion of authority: you must do this because, as your Lord, I command it. This is a misunderstanding. What is asserted fifteen times over is not the authority vested in the deity but the revealed nature of Israel's God, the 'I am what I am' of Exodus 3:14–15. Consequently, we can paraphrase the situation in Leviticus 19 like this: 'You are to obey all these laws, applying the law of the Lord to every detail of life in all its multiplicity, because I am what I am. It is for this reason that I legislate how you are to treat your parents, the disabled, the elderly, the alien, the poor . . . because I AM WHAT I AM'.[31] In a word, the law is the preceptual replica of the divine nature; by obeying the law the Lord's people become like him.

THE TWO IMAGES OF GOD

An illustration may be offered from the seventh commandment of the Decalogue: 'You shall not commit adultery' (Ex. 20:14). At first sight, it might be objected, this is a law which manifestly does not reflect the divine nature, for the Old Testament is clear that there is neither sexuality nor sexual diversity in the Godhead. This is true, but the 'maxim' enshrined in the seventh commandment is not sexuality but fidelity. Adultery is specifically the breaking of the matrimonial vow; the marriage covenant is one of the ways in which the Lord's earthly people can show themselves like their heavenly Covenant-Maker: when he pledges his word he 'will most certainly keep and perform'[32] what he has promised: and so should we.

In the life of obedience, therefore, two things come together: man in the image of God, and the law in the image of God. In declaring his law, the Lord declares what he is; in obeying the law we are being fundamentally true to what we are. Because the law reflects his image, it is the true law of our true nature. In obedience we are living according to our revealed definition, we are 'being ourselves'. The law of the Lord is the 'Maker's Handbook' for the effectuation of a truly human existence and personal human fulfilment.

In its biblical setting, this crucial understanding of life focuses down on to the life of our Lord Jesus Christ and our imitation of him. In his words that 'Anyone who has seen me has seen the Father' (Jn. 14:9) the Lord Jesus combines his claim to be the Perfect Man, Man in the image of God, and to be the divine Son, the Son in the image of his Father. He is the incarnate Word, in whom those with eyes to see saw 'the glory as of the Father's one and only Son' (Jn. 1:14, lit.). Furthermore, without trespassing into the solemn mysteries of the incarnation, his perfection of humanity was related to his perfect obedience. He always did what pleased the Father (Jn. 8:28–29); he insisted on the costly career of inflexible obedience to the Father's word (Mt. 26:52–54) when quicker and easier remedies were open to him by right as the Father's Son; Son though he was, he 'learned obedience' in suffering (Heb. 5:8), and along the pathway of obedience he grew from innocence to holiness. The Lord Jesus is the perfect example as well as the perfect proof that when 'man in the image of God' and 'the law in the image of God' coincide in the life of obedience, then perfect, true Humanity comes to its full realization.

◇ AVENUES INTO THE NEW TESTAMENT

The New Testament goes beyond the Old in not only rejecting images in worship but also rejecting the concept of the holy place. The groundwork is laid by Isaiah 8:13–14; Ezekiel 11:16; *etc.*; the superstructure is John 4:21–24; Ephesians 2:17–22. From one point of view, the locus of the Lord's presence is his people, individually (1 Cor. 6:19) and collectively (1 Cor. 3:16); from another, the new Temple is the Lamb of God (Rev. 21:22).

The anthropomorphic stresses of the Old Testament climax in the supreme anthropomorphism, the incarnation. Hint and illustration are replaced by the reality of the image of God in Christ (Col. 1:15–20) so that he is the manifested glory of God (Jn. 1:14; 2 Cor. 4:4–6);

to trust, see and hear him is to trust (Jn. 12:44), see (Jn. 12:45; 14:6) and hear (Jn. 12:50) the Father.

As well as being the Son and Image of God, Jesus is the Son of man (Jn. 5:22, 27), perfect human-ness. His assertion of complete present authority over heaven and earth (Mt. 28:18) is the realization of the intended rule of humankind over Eden and the world (Gn. 1:28). But, unlike Adam who snatched at glory for self, Jesus, both in heaven (Phil. 2:6–7) and on earth (Phil. 2:8) chose self-humbling and self-sacrifice, for the sake of obedience to the Father and the salvation of sinners (Phil. 2:8). Consequently, where Adam was banished, Jesus was received (Acts 2:33), crowned (Heb. 2:9), and highly exalted (Phil. 2:9–11).

The likeness of Jesus is the pattern for all those who are his, new-created by God (Eph. 4:24). This is sanctification, accomplished in its fullness by the cross (Heb. 10:10), experienced by us as an on-going work (Heb. 10:14), and consummated in the resurrection body (1 Cor. 15:42–45, 47–49) so that we shall be like him when we see him (1 Jn. 3:2).

CHAPTER FIVE

Christ as revelation (2):
The theme of the word of God

THE GOD WHO ACTS

William Temple may not have been the first to assert the principle that the revelation of God comes to us fundamentally through his acts, but it would be hard to find a more persuasively succinct statement of the position than that which he gave. He wrote, 'There is no such thing as revealed truth. There are truths of revelation.'[1] In this way, Temple refused to countenance what is called propositional revelation,[2] *i.e.* that God revealed himself by words directly spoken to chosen agents, couched in language and linguistic forms appropriate to them. And, of course, there is truth in what he says. At its widest level, who could deny that 'the apparently uniform process of the world is in its measure a revelation of God for those whose minds are alert to its significance'?[3] But is the same principle able to sustain the weight of special revelation? Temple believes so:

> The principle of revelation is the same – the coincidence of event and appreciation . . . He guides the process; He guides the minds of men; the interaction of the process and the minds which are alike guided by Him is the essence of revelation . . . [for] though revelation is chiefly given in objective fact, yet it becomes effectively revelatory only when that fact is apprehended by a mind qualified to appreciate it.[4]

THE INADEQUACY OF 'ACTS'

It would be discourteous to the memory of a very great man as well as absurd in the light of his huge abilities to fail to respect the care with which Temple stated his position and the truth which it enshrines. He is clear that a mere act carries no necessary meaning along with it: there has to be the association of a prepared mind before the act yields up its truth and becomes revelation. Thus – to go straight to the very highest – the sight of three crosses outside Jerusalem neither compels our attention to the central cross nor of itself imparts the truths of Christ and of redemption.

It is probable, however, that Temple would not have disagreed with the exposition by J. H. Hayes and E. F. C. Prussner of the 'God who acts' position.[5] 'Revelation in history', they urge, steers a welcome middle course between, on the one hand, 'conservative thought . . . that God was revealed in propositions' and that the Bible was the repository of these inspired words, and, on the other hand, the view of 'liberal interpreters' who saw 'revelation as the product of humanity's gradual progress in spiritual understanding'. Revelation in history safeguards the objectivity of revelation as coming from outside but safeguards too the place of 'humans who could understand and interpret the intervention of God. The Bible per se was thus primarily a record of this revelation . . . a book of history'. The Scriptures must, therefore, be taken with the utmost seriousness, yet there is room for 'historical criticism' and one is not committed 'to any form of the inerrancy-of-Scripture doctrine. Thus the position was clearly intended to occupy a middle ground between Fundamentalism and Liberalism'.

The theory is not, however, free of difficulty. Gerhard von Rad notes how 'historical investigation searches for a critically assured minimum – the kerygmatic picture tends towards a theological maximum'.[6] These two views of Israel's history are 'so divergent': the former is subject to historical-critical investigation 'but the phenomenon of the faith itself . . . is beyond its power to explain'. In other words, some tiny historical core has been used, not as a deposit from which riches can be mined but as a launching-pad from which rockets of faith fly off into free orbit. How else may we understand von Rad's contention that 'a great part of even the historical traditions of Israel has to be regarded as poetry, that is, as the product of explicit artistic intentions'?[7] This must mean that (to continue the 'launching-pad' metaphor) the rockets come back from time to time to add moon-rock to the platform from which they first shot into space. They have a direct relation to what was believed by Israel but 'only an indirect relation with historical reality', for the story-tellers are 'so zealous for Jahweh and his saving work that they overstep the limits of exact historiography and depict the event in a magnificence far transcending what it was in reality'.[8]

MIND OVER MATTER

J. A. Soggin wrestles with much the same problem in his commentary on Joshua. Regarding the 'deuteronomic history', he says:

> We cannot but be astonished by the wide range of an attempt at a historical, philosophical and theological synthesis which is without parallel either in classical antiquity or in the ancient Near East . . . On the other hand, we are perplexed by the inevitable distortions in a historical task of this scope [as] the writer gives new dimensions to the conquest of Palestine. [For] in a presentation like this the entry into Palestine is more than a historical and secular event; it is a theological fact.[9]

It is 'a thesis rather than established facts', a sermon more than a history-book.

Once again, therefore, it is the mind of the interpreter, not the raw historical fact, that is the locus of revelation. Is it this which results in an evident 'sitting loose' to what the Bible teaches? For example, in many commentaries on the historical books of the Old Testament, much attention is concentrated on 'the deuteronomic school' and 'the deuteronomic view of history',[10] but yet the commentator stops short of saying that this 'view' is a veritable divine revelation of how the world is and how it 'works' and how, under the rule of a sovereign and holy God, it is an unvarying system of justice and mercy, retribution and reward. To accept the 'deuteronomic view of history' as revelation, however, would outrun the limits of Temple's renowned definition and require a doctrine of 'revealed truth'. Von Rad, indeed, holed Temple beneath the water-line when he said that in the Old Testament 'there are no *bruta facta* at all; we have history only in the form of interpretation, only in reflection'.[11] As W. C. Kaiser puts it: 'Faith would need to go beyond any minimal assurances that historical criticism could yield'[12] or, as James Barr says, what we would find in the Old Testament is 'a history-related way of thinking'.[13]

COMING CLOSER TO THE BIBLE

Barr also observes that any rigid or even moderately rigid equation of revelation and history is too narrow a basis on which to rest many of the most significant 'blocks' of the Old Testament. Thus, for example, there is the wisdom literature in which:

   ... while it is known that God may and does act in human affairs, there is no impression that any particular series of historical acts are the sole or even the central foundation for all knowledge of him ... Something analogous can be said of many materials which have a cultic setting, mainly in the Psalms ... these texts suggest that God indeed acts in history, but that there is no reason to talk as if this acting were the sole foundation of relations with God.[14]

J. I. Packer tackles Temple head on. He rightly sees the exclusive wedding of revelation and historical act as vulnerable on five grounds.[15] It overthrows the biblical idea of knowing God in a person-to-person relationship, for all it can achieve is a knowledge of God in his acts. Putting it in a typical 'Packerish' manner, no amount of reading Wisden (the cricketer's 'bible') brings us to know the famous cricketer Wally Hammond as a friend! But, also, it destroys biblical faith as trusting what God has said and promised – as Abram in Genesis 15:4–6. Thirdly, the people of the Old Testament cannot be believed when they say they heard the voice of God, and we must be candid enough to recognize their experiences as 'actual hallucinations'.[16] The fifth of Packer's objections is that this charge of spiritual hallucination would apply equally to the claims of the Lord Jesus – 'and what, in that case, are we to make of His solemn assertions, "my teaching is not mine, but his that sent me"?'

Packer's fourth point, however, goes straight to the heart of the Bible's own claim regarding revelation and history and how they are to be related:

   In the case of all events of importance in the history of salvation ... God did not leave their significance to be perceived during or after their occurrence, but prefaced them, often at very long range, by verbal predictions of what he was going in due course to do.

Barr concurs:

   The function of the Old Testament tradition is not mainly to point back to a series of events from which the tradition has originated, but also to form the framework within which an event can be meaningful ... [This] can be said of the relation of one element to another within the Old Testament; for example, the relation between Moses' dialogue with God and God's acts of deliverance ...[17]

Exactly so!

WISE BEFORE THE EVENT

Take again the cross of the Lord Jesus Christ as a case in point. To dwell on the concrete historical *bruta facta* tells nothing. We might possibly learn that the One who died there was the Son of God, but even that fact as such provokes only wonder and puzzlement; we could note that the form of death was such as to involve copious blood-shedding, but again no amount of mere pondering will bring us to any significant truth. Some insightful person might even say, 'What a declaration of the love of God this is!' but this should only properly provoke the question 'Why?' – for what is there about dying as such to link it with love? On the face of it, it could be as much an act of folly as of affection. No, before it will yield up its secrets the bare act, the historical core, needs an ideological context, and this is provided in advance by Old Testament revelation and by the teaching of the Lord Jesus himself.

The point is of sufficient importance for us to remain with it a moment longer. This is the way R. W. Dale made the point in his great book, *The Atonement*:

> Unless the death of Christ has some direct end to answer in the redemption of the race, I confess myself unable to attach any meaning to the statement that the Death of Christ was a revelation of His love . . . If my brother made his way into a burning house to save my child . . . and were himself to perish . . . his heroic fate would be a wonderful proof of his affection for me and mine; but if there were no child in the house and if I were told that he entered it and perished with no other object than to show his love for me, the explanation would be absolutely unintelligible. The statement that Christ died for no other purpose than to reveal His love to mankind, is to me equally unintelligible.[18]

In a word, not even God's love can be known as love until it achieves some good for those whom he loves. The cross of Christ cannot be asserted as a demonstration of divine love until it is surrounded by biblical revelations of sin and redemption, wrath and propitiation, guilt and justification, and so on. It is the preceding context which makes the fact of the cross meaningful. It was in the same interest that the God of the fathers first addressed Moses before ever he performed any of his Exodus-redemptive acts.

Amos

A glance at Amos will help us to enter the Mosaic situation knowledgeably. Amos challenged the complacency and self-assurance of his day head on. 'The whole family I brought up out of the land of Egypt' (3:1, lit.) has been living in the conceptual frame expressed by the popular song 'Mary's Boy Child', still heard at Christmastime: 'Man shall live for evermore because of Christmas Day', except that for 'man' they were saying 'we' and for 'Christmas Day' they were saying 'the Exodus'. Amos saw that this reliance on the mere marking of a past date on the calendar was producing a spirit of pride, false security, religious frivolity and moral careless-ness among the people, and that the very privilege they were claiming must be their downfall (3:2). Only by asserting all the authority of his office as a prophet of the Lord can he hope to bring this unpalatable truth home to them.[19] Hence he says:

> Indeed the Sovereign Yahweh does nothing at all
> unless he has opened his mind to his servants the prophets.
> A lion has roared –
> who would not be afraid?
> The Sovereign Yahweh has spoken:
> who would not prophesy?
>
> (Am. 3:7–8, lit.)

It is good to balance the persuasive succinctness of Temple's view with one even more succinct and persuasive! Behind prophecy there lies the speaking God; the prophet is one whom the speaking God has made wise before the event. The key idea above, 'opened his mind', involves a word (*sôd*) which is rich in meaning. In Psalm 5:14<15> it combines the broad idea of a trusting 'fellowship' with that openness of sharing that is fitting in such a case; in Proverbs 11:13 it is a 'confidence' shared (as it happens, with the wrong person); in Psalm 111:1, parallel to 'assembly', NIV translates it rightly as 'council'. When Jeremiah, therefore, draws a distinction between the false and the true prophet by asking 'which of them has stood in the council of the Lord to see or to hear his word?' (Je. 23:18, *cf.* 23:22), he is bringing rich ideas together: that there is a heavenly 'council' within which the Lord makes his decisions (*cf.* 1 Ki. 22:19); the decisions he reaches are his 'counsel', the confidences he shares; to be within that council, to hear that counsel, is to be in intimate fellowship with the Lord himself. 'Opened his mind' seeks to go some way to bringing these three strands of meaning together. But, be that as it may, this opening of the divine mind, says Amos, is prior to any and all divine action. This was the conviction of the prophets,[20] and they derived it from the founder of their order, the normative prophet himself, Moses (Dt. 34:10).

THE WAY OF THE LORD WITH MOSES

The temptation to re-write the Bible, whether on the smaller scale of textual emendation or on the larger scale of re-allocating whole passages, has proved to be an occupational hazard among Old Testament specialists.[21] The extent, however, to which the Old Testament evidence must be either ignored or adjusted if it is to fit the theory of 'the God who acts' reaches a magnitude which surely must call such a procedure in question.

The evidence of the book of Exodus is unequivocal. Divine speech preceded divine action, and, at that, divine speech on no meagre scale, but offering a full and rounded revelation of the God of the Exodus. The passages in question are Exodus 3:1–22; 4:21–23; 5:22 – 6:8. The following summary of the divine speech to Moses is not elaborated so as to offer a Mosaic theology of the Exodus, but simply observed so that we may sense the breadth of the divine speech, that is, of the propositional revelation involved:

1. The Lord's self-announcement as the God of Moses' family and of the patriarchs (Ex. 3:6);
2. The holy God (3:6), the first explicit linking of God and holiness in the Bible;
3. The delivering God, the gift of the land (3:8);
4. The divine Name, the eternal revelation of God (3:13–19);
5. The Lord as the father of Israel (4:22);
6. The course of coming events (3:18–22; 4:21–22). The distinction between the wonders that will effect no deliverance and the act which forms their climax (and by implication effects deliverance);
7. The Lord the redeemer (6:6), a work of God distinct from deliverance;
8. The normative form of the covenant promise (6:7).

Much more could be said about each of these eight items and, doubtless, much more could be mined from these chapters, but nevertheless here is the length and breadth of the Mosaic revelation of God: how it links back to earlier revelation; the foundational fact of divine holiness, basic to the understanding of the place of both law and sacrifice in the coming Mosaic economy; the distinct divine acts of liberation from Egypt and redemption unto God; the new intimacy between the Lord and Israel in the revelation of the meaning of Yahweh; the course of coming history. All this, Exodus insists, was spoken by God before any act of God occurred. It is indeed a perplexity and vexation to Moses that his first efforts with Pharaoh were backed by no action on the Lord's part (5:22) and this, in turn, is followed by the emphatic divine 'Now' (6:1) of the dawning of the time for the Lord to work.

ALTERNATIVES

It is plain, therefore, that either we must re-write the book of Exodus or else accept that propositional revelation preceded the acts of God and provided the context in which they were seen to be the acts of God and in which their meaning was understood. Exodus, as we have received it, provides a sequence which the rest of the Bible accepts and develops: (a) the revelation of truth by divine speech; (b) the acts of God, fulfilling and thus confirming what he had earlier said, and themselves only understandable because of that foregoing word; and (c) further elaboration of the meaning of the acts of God by the reiteration and expansion of the primary spoken truth. In this way, the post-Exodus Mosaic deposit and the books of the prophets elaborate and re-apply foundational Exodus truth. In the ultimate this is the pattern of the whole Bible: the Old Testament and the words of the Lord Jesus lead up to the Calvary act of redemption; the redemptive act of Christ fulfils and confirms all foregoing revelation and cannot be understood without it; the words of the apostolic New Testament Scriptures elaborate the meaning of the act of redemption in the light of the primary revelation of truth.

The first and fundamental reality is not the God who acts but the God who speaks, the God of the Word of God.

THE GREAT PROPHETIC CONVICTION

The idea of the communication of the word of God through the lips of humans runs through the Old Testament. 'The Lord said to

Moses' is the loom on which the Exodus and post-Exodus literature is woven and, indeed, in the case of Deuteronomy, the claim is explicit both that what the Lord said Moses said, and that what Moses said the Lord said: the divine and human words perfectly and exactly coincide.

We can dip almost anywhere into the prophets and find the same insistence. Amos, at the outset of written prophecy, is a case in point: 'The words of Amos . . . Thus Yahweh has said . . .' (Am. 1:1, 3, lit.); Haggai, at the other end of the prophet period is another: '[They] paid heed to the voice of Yahweh their God and to the words of Haggai the prophet . . .' (Hg. 1:12, lit.). Jeremiah, with that sensitive personal emphasis so typical of him, felt the touch of the Lord's hand on his mouth and with it the explanation: 'Yahweh said to me: "Behold, I have put my words in your mouth"' (Je. 1:9, lit.). Ezekiel was commanded, 'You are to speak my words to them' (Ezk. 2:7, lit.) . . . 'Son of man, away with you to the house of Israel and speak with my words to them' (3:4, lit.). The plural 'words' must not be overlooked: the prophet did not understand that he was commissioned to communicate the general 'drift' of the mind of God – however accurately – but that he was to speak the truth of God in the very words of God as they had been donated to him.

A credible mystery?

The Old Testament expression rendered conventionally as 'the word of God came to . . .'[22] involves, in Hebrew, not a verb of motion, but the verb 'to be': 'the word of God was to', that is to say 'became a living reality to'. It stresses the end-product, the fact, but is silent about the mechanisms of revelation. Yet the occasional 'secular' use of the same formula indicates that modes of communication are included and presumed. Thus, for example, 'Yahweh appeared again in Shiloh, for Yahweh revealed himself to Samuel in Shiloh by the word of Yahweh, and the word of Samuel "was" to all Israel' (1 Sa. 3:21 – 4:1, lit.), or 'And his words "were" with Joab . . . and with Abiathar' (1 Ki. 1:7, lit.). In each case, the implication is of an effective word brought home by whatever means of communication was appropriate. But in respect of the revelatory purposes of God and the human agents who enjoyed 'verbal inspiration', the verb 'to be', while implying the use of appropriate means of communication, divulges nothing about them.

Ezekiel

Suitably to his almost over-active imagination, Ezekiel had a very vivid experience in which he claimed to have received the word and the words he was to minister (Ezk. 2:8 – 3:3). Once more it must be stressed that this visionary experience told him, and tells us, nothing of how the Lord actually works in inspiration, but it makes important affirmations about the essential realities involved.

Firstly, there is a stress on objectivity: (a) the scroll is *given*: a hand was stretched out (2:9), the command was 'eat what you find' (3:1, lit.), namely 'the scroll I give you' (3:3); (b) the scroll was *complete*, written on both sides (2:10), leaving no room for additions, that is to say the word of God came as a complete entity neither inviting nor allowing human contribution; and (c) in its contents it was *clear* in meaning and implication – 'lament and mourning and woe' (2:10). But in the donation of the scroll the Lord dealt with Ezekiel in his real manhood, for he is required to make a personal response ('open your mouth and eat', 2:8) as an intelligent, moral and responsive being: (a) Ezekiel 2:10 describes the unrolling of the scroll, for Ezekiel is not a carrier pigeon but is required to be the first to read and understand the message. Plainly the Lord opened the scroll, held it, turned it at the appropriate point and waited until Ezekiel had read and grasped its contents. This is the *mental* aspect of the prophet's office, his intellectual integrity in fulfilling his vocation. (b) Before the scroll is even seen, the prophet is required to pre-commit himself to obedience (2:8). This is to be his foremost distinctiveness among the people to whom he is sent: they are rebellious but he must 'hear what I am speaking', that is, hear, heed and obey. This is the *moral* aspect of the prophetic office. (c) On eating the proffered scroll, he found that he was *emotionally* moved and engaged with the word of God: 'it was in my mouth like honey for sweetness' (3:3, lit.). This two-sided transaction – the whole word absorbed by the whole man – is succinctly stated in the previous verse: 'I opened my mouth and he made me eat' (3:2, lit.). Divine action and human response came together in a perfect marriage.

Nothing, of course, is explained in all this, but equally could anything make us see more clearly Ezekiel's self-understanding of the prophetic office? Barr has appraised the importance of this exercise with typical clarity:

This does not mean that we have to *believe* that the prophetic messages originated just as the prophets themselves, or their contemporaries, thought they did. It does mean that any evaluation of the prophetic message has to be an evaluation of the prophets who understood themselves in the way in which they did understand themselves. Otherwise our picture of the prophets is unhistorical and accommodates them to what it suits us to believe about them.[23]

But their self-understanding is surely plain enough: as typified by Ezekiel, the prophets understood themselves to be called to be channels of the word of God, and the divine exercises of revelation (imparting the truth) and inspiration (enabling to receive and transmit the truth) were such that the prophets spoke the actual words in which the Lord desired his message to be conveyed. The sequence in Ezekiel is significant and important: (a) the command (2:7), 'speak my words'; (b) the divine imparting of the message (2:8 – 3:3) and (c) the reiterated command (3:4) as if to say, 'Now you really can "speak with my words".'[24]

Jeremiah

But do we have to distance ourselves from the way in which the prophets understood themselves? We need to take care at two points in particular.

First, it is plain that Ezekiel's experience rules out any explanation that overdrives impersonal or depersonalizing 'models' like that of the typewriter or the tape-recorder. Far from depersonalizing him, the Lord seemed to go out of his way to affirm Ezekiel's personality: as we noted above, he not only gave him the very sort of experience that matched his restless and vivid temperament but also so planned the experience that, because of it, Ezekiel was all the more established as an intellectual, conative and emotional being. The most superficial recollection of the rest of the prophets (whether they recorded for us any account of their call and their understanding of prophetic inspiration or not) confirms this: they are all, if anything, larger than life; their personal distinctives are to such an extent evident in their ministry that there is no way in which the majestic, 'Miltonic' Hebrew of Isaiah could be taken for the pedestrian style of Jeremiah or the fidgetiness of Ezekiel; nor could the native thought-forms of Hosea be confused with those of Amos, nor could the lively impression Malachi makes of being an open-air preacher ever be mistaken for the austere and bookish Zephaniah. Any and every model which we might try to use is capable of being over-stretched, but it is totally unfair to reason that, because verbal inspiration suggests an unacceptable, depersonalizing typewriter model, we can therefore sit loose to the claim to verbal inspiration. We must not make our incompetence in finding a suitable model the yardstick of truth.[25]

Secondly, inspiration is a mystery. The Bible affirms it but does not describe or explain it. We need, therefore, to be aware beforehand that no model we conceive and no explanation either of divine activity or of human psychology is going to 'cover' the fact as the prophets affirmed it. The 'crunch-point' must be faced whether we are prepared here as elsewhere to make the same precommitment to Scripture that was in principle required of Ezekiel; what the Bible is found to affirm I hold myself bound to believe.

Jeremiah, however, can take us a significant step further into the mystery. Conformably to his sensitive, self-questioning nature, Jeremiah was tormented by the need for certainty, the need to be sure that he was indeed the true prophet of the Lord when so many others were making the identical claim and preaching opposite messages. He wrestled with this problem throughout his ministry but centrally in chapter 23 of his book.[26] It is not germane to the present purpose to pursue Jeremiah's controversy with the false prophets in all its details. F. D. Kidner sums up Jeremiah's charges against them well by saying that:

> The most damning comment on the self-appointed prophets . . . besides the mounting absurdity of having no mission, no message and no access to God (21–22), is the fact that they have nothing to say about sin and repentance (22b).[27]

They had become, as J. Guest puts it in his commentary, 'part of the problem' . . . 'instead of being part of the solution'.[28] All this is true of Jeremiah's analysis of the false prophet, but the thing which would appear to be central to his understanding of the essential difference between the true and the false was the matter which Kidner calls 'access to God': to 'see' and 'hear' the Lord's word, it is essential to 'stand in the council/counsel of the Lord' (23:18) but this the false prophets had never done (23:22).

'Council/counsel' is, in Hebrew, *sôd*.[29] J. A. Thompson recalls that Jeremiah used the word in 15:17 of 'the company of the merrymakers' and remarks that here in 23:18 it is 'the circle of those who are privy to the deep purposes of Yahweh and are in his confidence'.[30] In a word, they have been brought into the Lord's intimacy, to stand in his presence, to share his thoughts, to be made aware of his plans and intentions and, in Jeremiah's case, then to be the emissary of that heavenly intimacy to the church.[31] More than anything else, the prophet is a person brought near to God.

Applying to the prophets and their unique inspiration what we learned about the image of God in the previous chapter, we can put the matter this way: the closer a person comes to God, the more real, true and human such a person becomes. The Man Christ Jesus, always perfectly one with the Father, is necessarily the Perfect Man. In the case of the prophets, the unique oneness with God which they enjoyed by his will for the reception and communication of his word meant that they were now more truly and fully themselves than they had ever been before. Consequent upon this, by being themselves they were also the organs of his will, by saying what was theirs to say they were also saying what was his to impart. The coinciding of the human and the divine word was not by some external working (as the 'typewriter' and all such models suggest) but by an internal, personal and spiritual reality of intimacy with God.

Stained-glass windows

If illustrations help at all, then possibly the nearest we can come to the blending and maturing of the prophetic person within the intimacy of God is the experience of a true marriage, wherein the 'two become one flesh' and where it is not alien to a husband to know his wife's mind, nor unnatural for her to know his, but where each partner is truly himself/herself by being at one with the other. This is the divinely intended 'good' for the man, the divinely planned return to home and wholeness for the woman; it is the flowering of each personality by identification and identity with the other. Certainly it was so with the prophets and their Lord.

All other illustrations are external, but there are ways in which the stained-glass window proves helpful. Like every illustration, it can be driven to a misuse. Thus the 'pure' light of the sun strikes the colorations of the glass and emerges 'tarnished' on the other side. So the pure word of God emerges tainted from the sinfulness and capacity for error of the human channel. Left to itself, the illustration is, of course, subject to this interpretation, but if we follow it along these lines we are moving rapidly away from biblical evidence. Let us start again.

Every stained-glass window is built to the artist's design, and the tinting of the sunlight that passes through is in fact what makes the sunlight tell the story that the artist intended – whether that story is a biblical or other scene or an abstract, symbolic design. The tints are not taints. True it is, of course, that sinners are subject to mistake and error and there is therefore almost a sense of rightness in thinking of the tints as taints, but even sinners do not have to be wrong all the time. Error is not a necessary element in the definition of humankind, and it is no interference with person or personality for the Sovereign Lord to guard his chosen ones from error for the purposes of an inerrant revelation of himself. Indeed it was for this very purpose that they were born.

Again it is Jeremiah who records that the Lord let him into this secret: 'Before I fashioned you in the uterus I knew you; and before you emerged from the womb I sanctified you; a prophet to the nations I appointed you' (Je. 1:5, lit.). Jeremiah had a tripartite history with God. He was a 'twinkle in the Lord's eye' before he was a twinkle in his parents' eye! Prior to his earthly conception, he was a known plan and person in the mind of God. During the months of gestation, the Lord set him apart for himself, to belong to God and to the divine order and sphere of reality.[32] And now that he has grown to manhood, he must see himself, not according to his own self-estimate (Je. 1:6), but according to the divine appointment to be a prophet to the nations. So there he is, with all his hesitations and insecurities, his awareness of immaturity and inability, God's stained-glass window with every tiniest fragment of glass in exactly the appointed place, every tint exactly right, every aspect of the design pre-planned, God's man, at God's time, for God's people, with God's word.[33]

WORDS, WORDS

The Old Testament understands 'the word' as a dynamic force let loose into the world. This is true of the words of people, particularly important, influential people. How much more therefore of the word of God!

The wide ambience of *dābār*, 'word', is indicative of this. The book of Nehemiah, for example, is headed 'the words of Nehemiah' (1:1) for which the Revised Version margin, with some cogency, offers 'history', for the 'word' is that which is formulated in the mind, expressed in speech and effectuated in action. The Hebrew title for Chronicles is 'the words of the days' – the things planned, uttered and accomplished, the 'journal' of the Davidic kings. Over and over the books of Kings (*e.g.* 1 Ki. 11:41) round off a reign with 'now the rest of the acts of . . .', where 'acts' is *deḇārîm*, the plans, words and actions. It is in this light that Ecclesiastes (12:11) says that the words of the wise are 'goads' and those of the masters of assemblies are 'nails': they are effective both to prompt and to secure. Sometimes 'word' approaches what we might think of as 'authority' or 'force of personality' (*e.g.* 'The king's word has power', Ecc. 8:4, lit.); 'the king's word prevailed against Joab', 1 Ch. 21:4, lit.), for the word of the king is full of the position and person of the king. Joab, tough customer though he was, felt the force of the king's personality and the weight of his authority. Thus J. Pedersen can say that:

> The close connexion between the soul and all that originates in it is the presupposition of the strong power of the *word*. This *power* does not consist in the word being something material, acting by its very existence in the same way as a projectile. On the contrary, the power of the word consists entirely in its mental essence. The word is the form of vesture of the contents of the soul, its bodily expression. Behind the word stands the whole soul that created it . . . He who utters a word to another lays that which he has created in his own soul into that of the other and here then must it act with the whole of the reality it contains. He who speaks good words to another creates something good in his soul, and he who speaks evil words creates unhappiness in his soul.[34]

But, of course, if the originating soul is empty of content, the word too is empty as was that of the wimpish Hezekiah when he was weakly and vain-gloriously drawn into rebellion. Rightly the Rabshakeh called it a 'word of the lips' (2 Ki. 18:20, lit.; *cf.* Pr. 14:23), a word with no 'soul' or power of accomplishment behind it, a mere movement of the mouth.

BLESSING AND CURSING

There are two modes in which we see the 'spiritual' power of the word operating with particular clarity, the blessing and the curse.[35] When Isaac blessed Jacob, mistakenly as it happened, there lay behind the blessing all that at that moment made up the soul of the head of the chosen people solemnly transmitting the divine promise resident in the family. Isaac was 'the blessed of Yahweh' (Gn. 26:29, lit.) and all this spiritual potency was gathered into the word. The subsequent tears of Esau are of no avail. The blessing has gone forth and cannot be recalled or redirected; it has lodged in the soul of Jacob and there it will fructify: 'I have blessed him – and blessed too shall he be!' (Gn. 27:33, lit.). The same is true of the word of malediction which Balaam was able to utter. Indeed, the strange and fascinating Balaam pericope is at heart a contest of words, for Balaam is explicitly presented as a challenge to the Abrahamic promise: 'I know', said Balak, 'that he whom you bless is blessed and he whom you curse is cursed' (Nu. 22:6, lit.; *cf.* Gn. 12:3). Such is the force of the word and such the strange power with which Balaam was able to invest the word he spoke. But the word of man cannot prevail against the word of God: the divine soul invests the divine word with divine power for, said Balaam, acknowledging the Lord's mastery:

> The transcendent God is not a man that he should tell a lie; nor a mere human that he should change his mind. Is he the one to say and not do? To speak and not make it happen?
>
> (Nu. 23:19, lit.)

THE WORD OF GOD

By definition, then, the word of the Lord is dynamic. Isaiah 31:1–3 is particularly telling. In verse 1, the contrast is between earthly and heavenly power, Egypt and its armaments and the Holy One of Israel; in verse 3, the contrast is between that which is (mere) flesh and the Lord who is Spirit, who has but to stretch out his hand and all the vaunted forces of earth stumble and fall; in verse 2, the arising of this great God is the uttering of his word. Pedersen is, of course, right to insist that the word is no mere projectile, but the idea of an arrow shot towards its mark is not an unacceptable metaphor in biblical thought: the Lord's promises do not 'fall' (Jos. 21:45; 23:18) like useless arrows (Ezk. 39:3); his word 'falls' where he directs it (Is. 9:8<7>). Equally true to biblical imagery, the word is the divine messenger or plenipotentiary in Isaiah 55:8–11, the expression ('out of my mouth') and accomplisher of the Lord's purpose. By his word the Lord performed the work of creation (Ps 33:6, 9); by it he controls the workings of the created order (Ps. 147:15, 18; 148:8). But in the same way he moulds events in history to his will. The soul of the great King is expressed in his word, and even when humans would resist they are compelled to bow down: 'this word [thing] is from me' (1 Ki. 12:24, lit.). In Isaiah 28:13 and 19, the 'word' is made flesh in the invading barbarians who become the unmistakable 'message' of the Lord. Indeed, more, in Isaiah 45:23 the whole sweep of history moving inexorably to its consummation in the kingdom of God is governed, controlled, lead on by 'a word'[36] which has 'gone out from my mouth in righteousness' (lit.).

Zechariah looked back across the vistas of the captivity to the pre-exilic prophets. The forefathers are dead and so are the prophets who then spoke, but the word is alive and triumphant:

> Your fathers – where are they? And the prophets – they do not live for ever, do they? To the contrary, my words and my statutes which I commanded my servants the prophets – did they not catch up on your fathers and they turned round and said, 'Just like the Lord of hosts planned to do to us, as our habits and actions deserved, so he has done to us.'
>
> (Zc. 1:5–6, lit.)

Truly the Lord's word runs swiftly (Ps. 147:15). But the word is also the Lord's agent to heal and rescue (Ps. 107:19–20). It is an unerring and irrevocable agent. In Ezekiel 12:23 the fulfilment of the Lord's purposes is called 'the word of the vision' (lit.); expression and final reality are the same thing, like the actions of fire and hammer (Je. 23:29).

There is no essential conceptual difference in thinking of the word of man and the word of God. In each case, the word encapsulates the power of the soul of the speaker and the word of the Lord is annexed to the Spirit of the Lord (Ps. 33:6)[37] who is explicitly 'the Spirit of his mouth'. In Genesis 1:2, the Spirit[38] is the 'middle member' between the Creator God and the created though as-yet-unformed material substrate of the world, and is the implied activator of the word, hovering in waiting for God to speak. It is interesting to note that in Genesis 2:7 it is Yahweh Elohim himself who is the agent of the divine word in 'forming man'. Thus from the very outset there is a nexus between God, the Spirit of God and the word of God. In 1 Samuel 3:19 the Lord watched over his word spoken by Samuel; in Jeremiah 1:9–12 he pledges to Jeremiah that 'Wakeful am I over my word to do it' (lit.). In this way, the 'word of God' is an extension of the divine activity, the active presence of God in the world. The word spoken by the prophet is as if spoken by the Lord himself: it has all the potency of the divine 'soul' within it. To put the matter another way, the word of the Lord pledges the active presence of the Lord.

THE WORD AND THE LORD

There is thus a certain 'divineness' if not divinity about the word of the Lord. Samuel put it like this in speaking to Saul: 'Because you have spurned the word of Yahweh, Yahweh has spurned you from being king' (1 Sa. 15:26, lit.). The word rejected is the Lord rejected, and provokes a violent divine reaction.

G. A. F. Knight sums the situation up well:

> Just as the human word was a 'living thing', so was the word of God. It was part of God, the living God . . . and being part of God, it contained the whole potency of God's Will and Person in it when it was uttered and became 'separate' from God. The word both was 'with God' and 'was God', as John 1:1 puts it. And so we discover that the Word of God . . . seems to be an . . . *alter ego* of God.[39]

THE PROPHETS AND THE WORD

The prophets were raised to positions of extraordinary privilege and dignity as the personal agents of the very words of the Lord. The Lord himself used Moses and Aaron as figures of the true. Moses urged his hesitant speech as a reason why he should not go to Egypt, and the Lord graciously condescended to this acknowledged deficiency by providing Aaron as the spokesman, but this is the way he put it: 'He, for his part, will be a mouth for you and, as for you, you will be God to him' (Ex. 4:16, lit.).[40] In other words, it is the part of God to provide the words; it is the part of the prophet to speak them.

Yet the prophets were never masters of the word but always its, and the Lord's, servants. The Lord was their master in that they could not, so to speak, turn on the word at will like a tap. No technique was put at their disposal whereby they could command a word: they could only wait till the word was given.[41] When the word was given, it became their master. Micaiah the son of Imlah, when urged to do himself a favour by conforming his word to popular whim, replied, 'What the Lord says to me, that is what I will speak' (1 Ki. 22:14, lit.) – a commitment not of arrogance but of subservience. The word is the master of the mouthpiece. Jeremiah, out of distaste for his prophetic work and message, tried silence only to find that 'it is in my heart like a fire burning, shut away in my bones, and I am tired of holding it in, indeed I am not able' (Je. 20:9, lit.).[42]

By word of mouth

The prophets adopted two main means of communication of the God-given word. On every occasion their communication was by word of mouth. Even when they used other media there was still always the plain, explanatory word. As G. A. Smith said of the 'live coal' from the altar (Is. 6:7):

> It is not a dumb sacrament, with magical efficacy. But the prophet's mind is persuaded and his conscience set at peace by the intelligible words of the minister of the sacrament.[43]

So it always was in prophetic ministry. The hearer was left in no doubt;[44] the mind and conscience were addressed by the perspicuous word.

Patient thought and holiness

We have already noted that the mechanisms of inspiration are not revealed to us, and this is an area into which we should only venture with caution. A passage like Jeremiah 42:4–7 indicates that patience and prayer at least sometimes provided the context in which the word 'came'; 2 Kings 3:15[45] reveals a prophetic awareness of the need to cultivate receptivity of mind; like a watchman on the walls looking for an in-coming messenger, Habakkuk stood 'on duty' to 'look out to see' what the Lord would say (Hab. 2:1). We must not, of course, overdrive the verbs of seeing, as if Habakkuk was intent on or necessarily expecting a visionary experience. If he was, he was disappointed, for what 'came' was the Lord's word – 'Yahweh answered and said'. In Hebrew, as in English, verbs of 'seeing' can apply equally to the mind as to the eyes. By contrast passages like 2 Kings 20:4 (and see Is. 38:4) are best understood as a 'flash' of inspiration, the Lord's use of a sanctified faculty of intuition.

Spirituality

What, however, may broadly be called their 'walk with God', their spirituality, was certainly an important factor in prophetic experience. In Jeremiah 15:19, for example, while it is by no means obvious what (lit.) to 'take/bring out the precious from the vile' means,[46] it is plain that Jeremiah is called to 'repent' (lit. 'return/turn back again') and that this will result in a divine response whereby the Lord will 'restore' (lit. 'bring back again') him 'that you may serve me' (lit. 'that you may stand in my very presence').[47] To stand in the presence of the Lord is the equivalent of being admitted to his council/counsel. It is the hallmark of the genuine prophet. But here it is conditional upon a sensitive, penitently self-aware relationship with the Lord as well as upon the divine activity of ushering the lowly prophet in.

One side of the experience that Jeremiah records is fundamental to Isaiah. He needed to be overwhelmed by the holiness of the Lord (Is. 6:3–5) and to be made the recipient of his sovereign provision of atonement (6:7) before he could stand near enough to the Lord to hear what he was saying and respond (6:8).[48] By contrast, it is the other side of Jeremiah's experience that comes to the fore in Ezekiel. Like Isaiah, he was overwhelmed, but by the divine exalted majesty (Ezk. 1:4–28). This 'falling face down' is not, however, the relationship with the prophet which the Lord intends. The Spirit of the Lord (2:2) entered Ezekiel and set him on his feet, and it was then that the Lord spoke to him. In Ezekiel 3:22–23, the Lord puts on Ezekiel the responsibility of entering the place of revelation and, once more, it is the Spirit who comes upon him and enables him to stand before the Lord to hear his word (3:24). In all three 'major' prophets, therefore, there is this double feature of lowly self-awareness on the one hand, and, on the other, a divine activity of grace and enabling whereby the lowly one is brought close to hear the Lord's word.

THE PROPHET'S MIND

J. Lindblom has some very judicious remarks to make about the interior or psychic aspects of the experience of being a prophet. He notes that:[49]

> Unlike their predecessors, the great prophets did not experience ecstasy of a wild . . . type. Their revelatory states were of a more moral and personal character, with the tranquillity of sublime inspiration . . . the content of the revelation was more important than the psychic phenomenon itself . . . The revelatory state of mind was always regarded as brought about by dynamic influence [and] the revelatory experiences were mostly emotional and imaginative, not intellectual . . .

Jeremiah's apparently dream experience in Jeremiah 31:15–22, says Lindblom, is

> . . . a very valuable glimpse into the revelatory experiences of the prophets, the more valuable since such glimpses are rare in the prophetic literature. [Also] indications of intentional preparation are rare in classical prophecy . . . The theocentric character of the prophetic religion on its highest level becomes apparent. Yahweh acts when the right moment has come; and prophetic revelation is an action of Yahweh.

This is all very true, and much as we would like to do so we do not have the data to give any sort of account in depth of the engagement of the prophet's mind in the revelatory/inspirational process. There does not seem to be anything in the Old Testament quite like Luke's reference to a period of research leading up to and into his own inspired account of the life of the Lord Jesus Christ (Lk. 1:3).[50] There are, however, two evidences of the importance of the prophet's mind: the first is the invitation extended to prophets from time to time to appraise some significant object, as if the Lord were saying to them, 'What do you think?' Jeremiah found the word of the Lord as he looked at an almond branch (Je. 1:11–12);[51] and, with the same dependence on the punning effect of the Hebrew words involved, Amos was invited to ponder a basket of summer fruit (Am. 8:1–2);[52] in Jeremiah again, messages were derived from pondering the boiling cauldron and the potter's wheel (Je. 1:13; 18:1–2); was Isaiah down in the Negeb watching storms gathering and breaking when the 'harsh vision' was granted to him (Is. 21:1ff.)? This is, of course, meagre evidence of revelation 'coming' in the context of minds at work, but there is much more abundant evidence of the place of the mind in conveying and conserving the word of God.

THE PROPHETS' WORDS AND THE PROPHETS' BOOKS

The question whether the books of the prophets as we have them are the editorial work of the prophet in question or are the result of some, often prolonged, process of editorial work is too large to be pursued here[53] and does not in any case affect the point at issue: for whether a passage can be demonstrated to be the work of the named prophet or of later 'hands', the same processes of ordering the material are evident.

R. B. Y. Scott, for example, sees the oracles as we have them as the developed statement of a basic Yahweh-word given to the prophet.[54] 'Embryonic oracles' are seen in such places as Isaiah 8:10; 30:8-9; Jeremiah 1:1-11; Amos 8:1-3. The beautiful assonance of Isaiah 5:7 or 7:9 may be the way the truth first formulated itself in the prophet's mind. He then worked this core idea up into the oracle he preached. In this way the oracles as we possess them are an 'elaboration, clarification, and reflection. They are reflections of the word of God which was received . . . but they do not represent it with photographic accuracy'.

Interesting as this approach is, there is a major hurdle in its way. Every single unit of material in the prophetic corpus is a literary and not a homiletical entity. This is not always realized when the books of the prophets are broadly categorized as 'what they preached'. Whether we take Isaiah's application of the message of the vineyard allegory (5:8ff.) or Amos' diagnosis of foreign and domestic ills (1:3 – 2:16) or Jeremiah's temple oration (7:1ff.) or Malachi's challenge to the priests (1:6 – 2:9) – the list is endless – none of it is homiletically possible; no-one could preach like that and be listened to intelligibly. The material is too closely reasoned, too succinctly stated, too quickly come and gone to constitute a sermon. Much of the art of preaching is elaboration and repetition, for hearers must be given the chance to let their minds dwell on what is being said. To a minister who constantly allowed his nervous intensity to betray him into hurried and gabbled speech in the pulpit a member of his congregation remarked: 'You must learn to speak more slowly. I am a slow listener.' Were Isaiah's people –

or the audience of any of the prophets – different? All listeners need to be given time to hear.

PREACHERS AND WRITERS

This suggests a process precisely the reverse of that which Scott sketched out. However the prophets presented their spoken material to the people of their day, either before or after preaching, they concentrated the essence of it into carefully crafted and often highly poetical literary units. This conserved and concentrated essence (which by the mercy of God is our possession and treasure) is the inspired divine word. It is in this developed, crafted form that the 'voice of Yahweh' and the 'words of Haggai' (Hg. 1:12) coincide. Most if not all of these oracular units are of a length that would make contemporary publication a possibility: maybe Isaiah 8:1 and 30:8 offer us a 'wall-newspaper' model for the immediate public presentation of an oracle, just as Isaiah 8:16 and Jeremiah 36 are models for the way in which the prophets secured the conservation of their inspired ministry.[55]

This, pre-eminently, was the point at which the mind of the prophet came into play. The word of God had to be articulated. Nowhere is it so plain that the mysterious processes of revelation and inspiration, which secured the end-product as the very word of God, preserved intact the individual mental characteristics, powers, styles and preferences which each prophet possessed and used to the full.

The enacted word

Without abandoning the spoken word, the prophets frequently 'supported' what they said by what they did. This is usually called 'an acted oracle'. Isaiah made himself into an 'acted oracle' when he went 'stripped and barefoot for three years, as a sign and portent' (Is. 20:3); likewise Jeremiah, when he wore a yoke on his own neck (Je. 27:2; 28:10); or Ezekiel when he packed his belongings for exile (Ezk. 12:3). In all these cases, the word of the Lord became to a limited degree and for a set time 'incarnate' in the prophet. Much more incarnational was the action of Isaiah in naming his sons 'Shear-jashub' and 'Maher-shalal-hash-baz' (Is. 7:3; 8:3). In consequence the boys were, in their own personas and for their whole lives, identified with the word of God, in promise and judgment, and, in measure, Isaiah staked his veracity as a prophet on the lives of his boys. They were a permanent public declaration of his certainty that he had spoken the Lord's word and that that word would stand. Even if not more notably, certainly more painfully, Hosea embodied the word of God in himself as he submitted to the oracular reality of his marriage to Gomer, her desertion and their subsequent costly and disciplined reunion. In obeying the original command to marry a 'wife of whoredom' and even more with the second command to 'Go, love yet again . . . even as the Lord loves the children of Israel' (Ho. 1:2; 3:1, lit.), Hosea was making himself the word of God, and the embodiment spoke as loudly as the verbalization.[56]

The prophets also employed the device of the acted oracle in less personal but equally real terms when, for example, Jeremiah took and smashed the earthenware vessel (Je. 19), or when Ezekiel depicted the siege of Jerusalem on a tablet and accepted for himself the agonies and deprivations of a time of siege (Ezk. 4), or when Zechariah broke his two staffs, 'Favour' and 'Union' (Ze. 11:7–14).

VISUAL AIDS AND EMBODIED WORDS

Plainly these actions of the prophets acted as visual aids, supporting their spoken words. In Isaiah we can almost hear people whispering the question, 'Why-ever is he walking around like that?' In Jeremiah 19, it speaks volumes for the authority exercised by Jeremiah and the respect in which he was held that leaders in church and state were willing to go with him to the Postherd Gate, but what drama awaited them there! At the key moment of his address, Jeremiah hurled the earthenware pot he was carrying so that it shattered into fragments and was lost among the detritus of the potteries that gave the gate its name, and with the act came the word 'Even so will I break this people'. It surely was indeed a visual aid supreme!

But it was more. Important evidence of the conceptual backgrounds to the 'acted oracle' is provided in 2 Kings 13:14–25. Elisha on his deathbed was visited by the king of Israel. The king apparently saw the occasion as one on which he could patronize the old man with flattery, but the relationship was in fact quite the reverse. Elisha is still the man armed with the authority of the word of God and the initiative rests with him. He proceeded to set up an 'acted oracle' related to the Aramean threat to the kingdom of Israel.

The prophet did not explain to the king what was afoot but assumed, apparently correctly, that the king would understand. Together then (13:16), the two men held a bow and shot an arrow through the opened east window. This act was accompanied by an explanatory and oracular word: 'The arrow of the Lord's victory . . . you will strike the Arameans . . .' (13:17, lit.). A second acted oracle followed: the king was ordered to take the remaining arrows and to strike the ground with them. He struck thrice (13:18), to the prophet's dismay, for the number of blows struck represented the number of victories to be achieved over Aram (13:19), or, in other words, the extent to which the potent word of the Lord embodied and released in the sign would be realized.

The acted oracle was, therefore, much more than a visual aid. Visual aids help understanding, but acted oracles double the potency, for the word of the Lord released in speech is released all over again in act and runs on a twin-track to fulfilment.

Lindblom is quite mistaken when he says, that acted oracles

> . . . were akin to the magical actions which are familiar in more primitive cultures throughout the world; and the use of such actions by the prophets is no doubt an inheritance from lower stages of cultural development.[57]

In the Elisha incident, efficaciousness is related, not (magically) to the mere performance of the act, but (morally and spiritually) to the extent to which the king's faith can embrace and express the truth embodied in the act. We are at once out of the realm of magic and into the realm of understanding, faith and response.

AN ESSENTIAL MOVEMENT

Even more deeply, of course, the acted oracle expresses a movement essential to all biblical religion: the movement from God to his people. It was the very heart of the falsehood of Canaanite religion – and indeed is the hallmark of every false religion or false understanding of true religion – that rites, ceremonies, acts and observances are human attempts to press the god into action. Baalism was a deification and to an extent a personification of economic or market forces, and the motivation of Baal-religion was to make the economy work: *i.e.* in an agricultural economy like that of Canaan, to secure the essential processes of fertility for land, animals and humankind. Coming into this situation, Israel was offered and commanded a different security. For Israel's religion also was, in its own terms, a 'fertility' religion, offering agricultural and human blessings on the ground (not of pressuring Yahweh to Israel's will but) of Israel's submitting to Yahweh's will as expressed in his word.[58] In Israel the sacrifices too were (not a human technique to manipulate God but) a divine gift for the salvation of sinners (Lv. 17:11).[59] In this sense Israel here was intended to be an acted oracle: as she embodied his word by obedience, so the potency of the word that God first spoke through Moses was released with doubled and contemporary efficacy for her blessing. This is not magic, nor can sinners impose their logic upon the will of God by telling him how he must act: he alone decides, in perfect wisdom, justice, love and power, how to implement his word.

Lindblom, indeed, does come round to allowing such a view as this, noting

> . . . significant differences between the symbolic action of an Old Testament prophet and the primitive magical action. The power of the magical actions was dependent on the inner power connected with them and their performance in accordance with definite magical laws; the power of prophetic actions, like the power of the prophetic word was derived from Yahweh's will.[60]

THE SIGNS AND THE SON

The Old Testament understanding of the word of the Lord, spoken and enacted, forms a background to the covenant signs[61] in both Testaments and to the advent of the Son who is himself the word of the Father 'now in flesh appearing'.

Biblically understood, baptism and the Lord's Supper are 'acted oracles', embodying and releasing the efficacious word and promise of God which they express. It is for this reason that the New Testament so constantly uses positive and affirmative language about the signs: they *are* the word of God which cannot return void (*e.g.* Rom. 6:3–4; Gal. 3:27).[62] But since the word cannot return void, it is the instrument of blessing to those who meet it with faith and of death to those who abuse it – and the sign which expresses it (1 Cor. 11:29–30).

In the same way, in respect of the Supper, the central words of the

Lord Jesus that 'This is my body' must be understood in 'acted oracle' terms, not only because his literal body was at that moment present in its separate reality but because the required sense, 'This "means" my body', is so abundantly established in New Testament usage.[63] As our study of the acted oracle shows, this in no way diminishes the objectivity, power or importance of the Lord's Supper, but poses its power in truly biblical rather than magical terms and brings our understanding of it into line with the caveat of the Lord Jesus himself when he said that 'it is the Spirit that quickens; the flesh profits nothing: the words that I have spoken to you are spirit and are life' (Jn. 6:63, lit.).

Now all the power of the creative, irresistible, efficacious word comes to its full realization when a perfect life embodies the whole Word. The Old Testament doctrine of the word of the Lord is the intended background to the coming of the Word made flesh.

AVENUES INTO THE NEW TESTAMENT ◇

In Acts 2 it is the preached word that gathers and constitutes the church. The crowds are not left to contemplate the sign and interpret it as best they can; rather, they hear the truth and correct their (mis)understandings in the light of the apostolic preaching. In 2 Timothy where Paul writes the postscript to the apostolic age, he sends Timothy into the uncharted waters of the post-apostolic future solely as the possessor of revealed truth (1:13–14; 2:15; 3:14–17; 4:2), the Word of God inspired as to its content (2 Tim. 3:16) and as to its authors (2 Pet. 1:21). Jesus, himself the Word (Jn. 1:1–18), is the ultimate 'stained-glass window' in person (2 Cor. 4:6), word and deed (Jn. 14:10–11). In John 6 he provided his own perspective: the 'bare sign' (6:1–14) is elaborated in language of concrete symbolism (6:26–59), but finally the whole exercise is safeguarded from misunderstanding by a plain insistence on the word of truth (6:62–63). The people rightly saw Jesus as 'the Prophet' (6:14; Heb 1:1–3).

Like the prophets, Jesus left 'acted oracles' or 'enacted words'. In the Old Testament the repeated Passovers enacted the meaning of the first, once-for-all Passover. In accordance with the essentially repetitive nature of Old Testament ordinances (Heb. 10:1–4), the once-for-all sacrifice in Egypt was re-enacted by annual sacrifices, but the truly once-for-all sacrifice of Calvary (Heb. 10:12) is followed by enacted words of remembrance, with baptism acting out the initial blessings of Calvary in cleansing and new life, and the Lord's Supper the ongoing blessings in cleansing and pilgrimage provision. According to the Lord Jesus, the broken bread 'is my body', *i.e.* 'displays what my body means for you' – a meaning of the verb 'to be' found frequently in the New Testament (see note 63). Yet, as the affirmative language used (*e.g.* Rom. 6:4; Col. 2:12; *etc.*) shows, all the effective power of the word remains in the sign, putting the participant into a veritable crisis of faith to trust the promises which the sign encapsulates.

Christ our life (1):
The theme of sin

It is hard to believe that anyone has ever read the story of the first sin and its consequences without thinking that the Lord God was vastly over-reacting! On the one hand, such a tiny sin, so thoughtlessly committed; on the other hand, such comprehensive wrath, such a sweeping and all-enveloping divine curse on humankind, its circumstances, its environment and its seducer! But was it so?

HUMANKIND UNDER LAW TO GOD

In order to contextualize this discussion, it is essential to recall that humankind was created to live under law to God.

We noted in chapter 3 the importance of the 'generations formula', the word *tōlᵉdôt*, in the study of Noah.[1] It is equally important on its first appearance, Genesis 2:4. The translation 'This is the account' in NIV is accurate enough, but it fails to illuminate the central emphasis of the Hebrew word: 'the emergent account'. Once we see this, Genesis 1:1 – 2:3 and Genesis 2:4–25 fall into their correct mutual relationship and many of the problems alleged to exist between them disappear.

First of all, Genesis 1 and 2 are no longer misunderstood as two separate and contradictory accounts of Creation. C. Westermann speaks in many ways for the majority of commentators and Old Testament specialists.[2] First, he divides the opening chapters of Genesis into 1:1 – 2:4a and 2:4b–25. The reason for this is that Genesis 1:1 – 2:3 and the 'generations formula' in 2:4a are alike allocated to the P strand of the Pentateuch. Therefore they must belong together. In every other case the 'generations formula' begins a new section, but here:

> . . . the clause that concludes the priestly account of Creation . . . is in reality its title, added to the end to recall the towering clause (1:1) of the beginning.[3]

This, however, is highly unlikely. Is the theory dictating the conclusion? The place of a title is at the start, not at the conclusion and, as a matter of fact 2:3, with its concluding 'which God created so as to make' (lit.), provides all the features of *inclusio* that Genesis 1:1 could possibly require. Secondly, Westermann treats both sections as accounts of creation, calling the first the 'Creation of the World' and the second the 'Creation of Humanity'. He has much that is fine to say about the first account, but he seems to overlook the fact that the 'second account' in effect by-passes the theme of 'creation' in order to focus on the relation of Adam to his environment.

MAN IN HIS ENVIRONMENT

This, of course, is what the 'generations formula' properly considered would lead the reader to expect. Its essence, as we saw above, is to say what 'emerged' next, what the previous record 'gave birth to'. In this way Genesis 2:4ff. is the emergent consequence of Genesis 1:1 – 2:3. Westermann rightly and impressively says that the 'first account' 'does not speak of creation didactically, but in a way that confronts the hearer with its unfathomability'.[4] This austere though beautiful account, however, moves forward into precisely what 2:4a would lead us to expect: a homely, man-centred, down-to-earth statement about the beginnings of daily, earthly life and human history. At the level of telling the story of how all things, including humankind, came into being and how human life on earth started out, the two chapters belong together:

Genesis 1:	Genesis 2:
The physical world created (1:1–13)	Man in relation to his physical environment: the Garden (2:4–17)
The world made ready for living things and populated (1:14–31)	Man in relation to the world of living things (2:18–25)

The purpose of Genesis 2:4–25 is not to give any sort of diaristic account of 'what Adam did next' but to establish the platform and scene on which he will begin to live his daily life. It concentrates therefore on the matter of relationships: first, his appointment to care for the physical environment, and then his lordly relationship with the beasts and his relationship of equality and delight with his wife.

THE LAW OF GOD

But in each area of relationship, Adam is under law to God. The man may well be, by divine appointment, king in his world, but the Lord God is still King over all. Consequently, the man only has the run of the Garden with all its bounty as long as he keeps the law of the Garden respecting the tree of the knowledge of good and evil (2:16–17); likewise he only has the full fruition of the Lord's marriage-gift of the woman while the law of marriage is obeyed and the couple cleave together as one flesh. Genesis 2:4–25 is constructed so as to reveal and enforce this:

Genesis 2:4–17:	Genesis 2:18–25:
Situation and need (2:4–6):	Situation and need (2:18–20):
a world needing care.	a man needing a partner.
Provision (2:7–15):	Provision (2:21–23):
the man to till and work.	the woman, the 'help-meet'.[5]
The law of God (2:16–17).	The law of God (2:24–25).

Humankind finds its true reality in living under law to God. But in the Garden, the whole law was concentrated into one single prohibition. There was nothing else God required. Within the bounty and beauty of the Garden there was a life of unrestricted liberty save for this one matter. To violate this prohibition was, therefore, not a small thing at all; it was to contradict the total will of God. To break this law is to break all the law there was!

THE IMPLICATIONS OF SINNING

We turn now from what was done – the breaking of the whole law of God – to what was involved in the doing of it: the advent of temptation, the avenue of its approach, the nature, implications and consequences of the human response.

It is, of course, of the nature of biblical narrative simply to tell a story without pausing to explain or even to offer moral comment in praise or blame. The narrative in Genesis 3 contains two important features which it relates but does not explain. First, the story assumes that humankind can, freely and with open eye (*e.g.* 1 Tim. 2:14) flout the authority of the Sovereign God. James Orr says:

> Sin, in the biblical view, consists in the revolt of the creature will from its rightful allegiance to the sovereign will of God, and the setting up of a false independence, the substitution of a life-for-self for a life-for-God. How such an act should ever originate may . . . be a problem we cannot solve, but it is evidently included in the possibilities of human freedom.[6]

But how is it so included? Is selfishness somehow a possibility intrinsic to selfhood?[7] Or, narrowing the focus slightly, does selfhood necessarily impose such a limited view of reality that wrong decisions are inevitable because the part is confused for the whole?[8] C. S. Lewis put it all down to 'free-will' because:

> If a thing is free to be good it's also free to be bad. And free will has made evil possible. Why, then, did God give them free will? Because free will, though it makes evil possible, is also the only thing that makes possible any love or goodness or joy worth having.[9]

There is, however, a certain uselessness lurking at the heart of all such speculations. The Bible simply cuts in behind them by dwelling on the pragmatic reality of human rebellion. And, indeed, in the same way, the Genesis narrative is equally silent about the origin of evil itself, only insisting that the temptation to sin came to the first couple from the outside.

THE TALKING SERPENT

'It came from outside', says Genesis 3:1, through the medium of a serpent which addressed itself to Eve. What are we to make of this?[10] Are we to allow the presence of metaphor in Genesis 3 to indicate that it is all metaphor? In 3:15, the 'crushing of the serpent's head' alludes metaphorically to the final termination of the usurpation of 'that ancient serpent . . . the devil, or Satan' (Rev. 12:9). Is the serpent itself therefore a metaphor, and if so, for what? The question proves to be surprisingly hard to answer. Westermann speaks for many when he writes:

Up to a certain point we can explain why human beings break God's command . . . There is a force that compels them; it comes from within and approaches from without. What is prohibited is especially enticing: 'pleasant to look at and good to eat . . .' . . . The serpent is nothing more than the narrative symbol of this power of temptation . . . The serpent does not represent either a mythical being or the devil. It does not exist as a speaking, tempting force outside this scene. The narrator wishes to make it clear to his hearers . . . that he is not entertaining them with a story from the distant past . . . he is speaking of his hearers themselves, of the mysterious power of enticement and temptation inherent in human existence, familiar to every human being.[11]

Yes indeed, Westerman well describes *our* condition. *We* are all too familiar with the inner urging and the outer enticement, the magnetism of the forbidden, but Westermann's assumption that the Genesis narrator is 'speaking of his hearers' flies calmly in the face of what Genesis 2 and 3 themselves claim to be doing. The narration only addresses later generations – including ourselves – by telling us where we have come from, what we have lost, and how humanity has fallen from where and what it once was. For, like the rest of the creation, the Adam and Eve of Genesis 2 and 3 are 'good' and 'very good' in the divine estimation. It is mystery enough how such beings should contain within themselves the capacity to respond to temptation without multiplying mystery by making them also capable of generating temptation. But in any case, such a speculation is rendered unnecessary by the terms of the story: they were addressed from outside not from inside. The inner voice of temptation is not yet a reality.[12]

So then, did a serpent really talk to them? The direct answer is that someone/something must have done. The impossibility of an inner voice requires the action of an external voice. Were Satan to manifest himself in his own person – if it is possible for him to do so – he has given the game away before it has started; he must hide himself behind some innocuous reality, and a voice out of the beauty and goodness of creation perhaps offers the best hope of success.

It is, however, a secure course to look back from the vantage-point of the rest of the Bible and to concur with Revelation 12:9 that we meet here the ancient serpent, the devil. The characterization matches. In the broad picture, here is one who opposes the work of

God (Rev. 12:7; *cf.* Zc 3:1; 1 Thes. 2:18; Jude 9), who is a murderer (Jn. 8:44), a deceiver (2 Cor. 11:14; Eph. 6:11) and a liar (Jn. 8:44); and, more particularly, one who would destroy reverence for the word of God, remove the fear of sin and overthrow the integrity of the character of God. These are the major targets in Genesis 3.

TAMPERING WITH GOD'S WORD

It is interesting that the man and woman had already opened up a chink in their armour by tampering with the word which the Lord God had spoken. They had imposed on themselves the additional requirement of not touching the forbidden tree (Gn. 3:3) and had given their own regulation the status of divine revelation. But God said no such thing: as far as his word was concerned they could touch at will, climb if they wanted, set up their home under the shade of the tree of the knowledge of good and evil – so long as they did not take and eat. It is no wonder that, with a telling inclusio, the Bible ends with a warning to those who would add to the words of the book (Rev. 22:18; *cf.* Mt. 15:3–9). At the end, it invites the condign judgment of God; at the beginning, it opened an avenue to the tempter with his 'Oh yes, of course God did say, didn't he, that you can't eat of any tree in the garden?' (3:1). There is nothing truer to the portrayal of Satan than a determination to undermine the word of God,[13] to get people to live on any other basis than revelation. Coupled with this is his attempt to deny the reality of divine judgment:[14] sin can be committed with impunity for 'there is no way you are going to die!' (3:4, lit.).

THE FINAL ASSAULT

The stage is now set for the final assault. If the woman has come this far with the serpent, registering some mini-assent to the proposition that life in the Garden is restrictive rather than free and that the sanction of death can be discounted, then maybe she will nod also to the possibility that God is not all he purports to be; that posing as bountiful he is actually niggardly, that claiming to be truthful he may be bluffing, and that his care of the man and the woman is a mere pretence, a cover for the fact that he is really denying them their proper status as his equals. If the first hurdle for the serpent was the word of God, the final one is the character of God. E. J. Young summarizes the situation aptly by saying:

In Genesis 3 . . . the serpent has left its proper sphere and is placing itself on a par with man. More than that, it is placing itself on a par with God indeed, even above him.[15]

All this is exactly the character of the devil as exposed in his temptation of the Son of God (Mt. 4:1–11), when he came to challenge the word of God in its affirmation of the Sonship of Jesus, to set himself up as able to put Jesus right about the Scriptures, and finally to usurp the right of God alone to be worshipped.

THE PARAMETERS OF TEMPTATION

Our study of 'the Fall' narratives in Genesis 2 and 3 have so far conducted us through two major truths. First, that the act of taking the forbidden fruit involved flouting the whole stated will of God. The law of God was condensed into one precept and the man and woman disobeyed it. Secondly, the way in which the temptation was presented involved accepting a slur on the character of God: an assault on the veracity of what he had said, a questioning of his benevolence, the calling into question of his motivations and the imputation to him of corrupt self-concern. Such was the downward progress of sin in the woman: self-awareness became self-concern and finally self-centred grasping after a different selfhood; and at the very heart of sinning all this is imputed to the Lord God himself! 'Adam,' remarks John Calvin, 'when carried away by the devil's blasphemies, as far as he was able extinguished the whole glory of God.'[16]

The third and final stage of the foundational act of sin must now be considered: that this total rejection of the law and character of God was an act implicating the totality of human nature. Genesis 3:6 offers a remarkable, perceptive and detailed analysis of sin from the point of view of the agent. In turn, three dimensions of the psychology of sin are brought before us.

The emotions

The first of these dimensions is that there was an emotional response to the temptation: 'The woman saw that the tree was good for food and that it was an attractive thing to the eyes' (3:6a, lit.).[17] Was there any essential sinfulness in this emotional reaction as such? Possibly not: in the halcyon days (if there were such) before the tempter came, it is not unthinkable that the man and his wife noted how attractive the tree was and how good its fruit looked, but there is a world of difference between an appreciation resting on the basis of good (a simple continuance within the will of God) and an appreciation that is beginning to be based on the possibility of disobeying.

At its deepest reality this is the difference wrought by 'the Fall' – on what basis is human progress to rest? Oswald Chambers said somewhere[18] that it was the divine purpose that humankind should 'transform innocence into holiness by a series of moral choices', *i.e.* that progress should always be made from the standpoint of commitment to the will of God, that progress should be from the good into the good, that humankind should know the good by direct personal knowledge and experience and the evil only as an external and theoretical contrast. With this enticement to the emotions, progress is coming to rest on a different foundation: advancement from incipient rebellion into rebellion. Every epistemology must reckon with this horror: that henceforth the serpent's forecast will hold true: 'you will be . . . knowing good and evil'. There will be progress in knowing but, because it sets out from the base of evil and rebellion, all knowledge will henceforth be – in whatever measure – skewed. From now on immediate, personal knowlege will be of the evil, and the good will only be known by contrast. The Fall stood the divine purposes on their head.

The emotions provided, then, the entrance-point for temptation. They did nothing inevitably sinful, but this 'new-look' at the tree arose from the satanic denials of the veracity of God's word, the questioning of his goodness and the denigration of his character. Therefore it was no longer a look savouring beauty but a questioning stirring of desire to experience the forbidden.

The mind

Secondly, and hard on the heels of the emotions, came the mind: 'the tree was to be desired to acquire wisdom' (3:6b, lit.).[19] There is a logic at work here, and it has every appearance of soundness: the name of the tree and its effects must surely match each other. If it is indeed the 'tree of the knowledge of good and evil', then surely it must result in the right management of life and conduct, and so it must 'make wise'.[20] It would seem so – but only if the woman is prepared to back the human mind against the divine, for God's wisdom has already revealed that the consequences which this tree will bring do not match its name: it seems to promise wisdom, but actually it brings death (Gn. 2:17). Once more, it is not the use of the mind or the operation of logic that is at fault, but the autonomy that is beginning to be claimed for human mental processes. As we have seen, the man had used his mind, with true philosophical discernment, in categorizing the animals, discerning their distinctives, matching like with like and apportioning names. But this was the mind operating in response to a God-given status and responsibility. Its foundation was obedience and its intent was to do the will of God. Governed by such a submissive mind, the progress to mature holiness sketched by Chambers would have gone forward. But in the temptation presented to the woman, an autonomy of mind is incited; the mind is no longer submissive to the divine word. It is using God-created faculties in an anti-God mode. Consequently, the reasoning is impeccable (for the faculty is God-given) but the result is erroneous (for it contradicts the mind of God).

The will

Hard on the heels of the emotions and the mind comes the will. In the deepest sense of all, no sin is committed until the will takes a hand in it. So far there has been a highly dangerous toying with a possibility, but the possibility is not yet an actuality. Toying with something is far from actually trying it out. Yet we are integrated beings, and the emotions and mind effect an inevitable pre-disposition of will so that the decision is made with frightening ease and simplicity: 'and she took some of its fruit and ate' (3:6c, lit.).[21] She chose what God withheld, did what he forbade, trespassed where he had issued warnings: sin had entered human experience.

Genesis 3:6, in this way, brings together the emotional, the intellectual and the conative. There is nothing else – saving to add that 'eating' brought the physical into the equation, and sharing with the man extended sin into the social dimension. The Fall involved the rebellion of the total person against the total law.

CONSEQUENCES

The stone has been dropped into the pool: now watch the widening circle of ripples and its effects become plain.

PERSONAL BREAKDOWN (GENESIS 3:7–10)

In these verses, three things happen in turn. First, the wording of Genesis 3:7 looks back to 2:25 and 3:5. What the serpent said proves to be all too true, but the world at which they now look with newly opened eyes is tragically different from the world that they found and have now left. If their nakedness simply reflected their sharing of the Creator's pure joy in his creation, just as he made it, now the created state is not enough. They must be clothed. Having come to knowledge on the basis of sin (instead of on the basis of holiness/obedience), no knowledge is now pure. Everything suggests a corruption. The old openness with which they had lived with each other, literally 'naked and unabashed', is replaced by a secretive awareness of self, and a desire to retire from the other, to hide, to retreat from the old unself-protective mutuality. The man and the woman have previously turned naturally to the other: they were the conjoint sides of the same reality, mutually finding wholeness. But now the secretive individual has come into being, the inward-turned person. Innocence has changed, but not into the God-intended holiness, rather into fear, as each with 'urgency and desperation'[22] seeks protection from the gaze of the other. The world seen on the basis of disobedience and evil is very different from the world seen on the basis of obedience and good.[23]

Secondly, in Genesis 3:8 there is an inadequate awareness of the seriousness of sin, moral perceptions are clouded, and the self-centred view of values is well beneath the God-centred view. Hearing the approach of the Lord God, the man and woman hide, but within the Garden. They cannot meet and keep company with the Lord God as before, but neither do they see that the consequence of sin is loss of paradise (3:22–24). The blindness of sin is beginning to take effect, bringing atrophy of moral alertness, an inability to face the holy, and yet an equal inability to appreciate what holiness is. Of course, in using the vocabulary of holiness we are reaching forward from Genesis 3 into the ensuing Scriptures, yet the actions of the man and woman speak louder than words and justify the attribution to them of those characteristics which remain true of sinful humanity: on the one hand (for those who think about it at all) an unfitness to appear before God but, on the other hand, the question 'Why not?' It is natural to us as sinners to say both 'I am unworthy of God's presence' and 'I am not so bad that he should banish me from it'. Thus, like the man and woman we acknowledge sin but, by nature, we cannot grasp its seriousness. From the moment of the Fall, humankind has suffered from moral schizophrenia: neither able to deny sinfulness nor to acknowledge it for what it is.

Then, thirdly, in Genesis 3:9–10 there is the matter of a bad conscience. We are not told how the man and the woman greeted the Lord's earlier visits to them. However, the air of easy delight that breathes through the narrative in Genesis 2 suggests that, when God spoke to the man about his place in the Garden and the law under which he was to live, and when he shared with the man and woman the divine ideal of marriage, they stood in his presence with open-minded pleasure. Now, however, that fear of God which is henceforth to mark human reactions to his appearing – that mortal fear which cries out 'I have seen him; I will die'[24] – has entered the world. Never again can humans stand unafraid before God. Yet it is not the awesomeness of his presence that warned the first couple of this, but the inner voice of conscience: it was now natural for them to be afraid of God.

Genesis 3:7–10 lays the groundwork for all humans ills in a fallen world: we are dislocated within ourselves, dislocated from each other, dislocated from God. Personal fragmentation, social tension and spiritual alienation are now the parameters of life on earth.

MARITAL BREAKDOWN (GENESIS 3:12, 16, 20)

The division between man and woman, signalled by their flight from nakedness, runs deeper than that significant act could by itself have revealed. The protection of the self from the other now (3:12) takes the form of self-exculpation at the expense of the one who was but recently hailed as 'bone of my bones and flesh of my flesh', my matching alter ego (2:23). If the one-flesh solidarity were still a reality, it would involve standing together in sin and guilt, whether in repenting or brazening the situation out, but the man chose to brazen it out alone, isolating and deserting the woman.

This is henceforth to become the grim truth, not just for the couple but for the institution of marriage within which they stand. For the gender-relationship of the man and the woman has been altered by the advent of sin. Possibly the most obvious sense of 3:16b is that henceforth woman's longing for marital oneness and fulfilment will be met only by domination. F. D. Kidner puts this with typical succinctness: '"To love and to cherish" becomes "To desire and to dominate".'[25] In favour of this understanding is its suitability to 3:20, literally: 'The man called his wife's name, Eve, for she was the mother . . .' In 2:23, the passive 'she shall be called . . .' is less the giving of a name than the recognition of a fact: the man (*'îš*) has at last found his co-equal and fully corresponding counterpart (*'iššâ*). They are the perfectly intermeshing unit; neither is complete without the other and in their completeness they are 'one flesh'. But now, the active form 'he called her name' matches 2:19–20. Note the threefold use of 'called': '. . . to see what he would call . . . and whatever the man called a living entity, that was its name. And he called names to all . . .' (2:19–20, lit.). Woman is now as much a possession and a chattel as a beast, and the name she receives is antipodean to 'Woman/*'iššâ*. For now she is not described as an equal but named for a function. No longer is it what she can *be* to the man but what she can *do* for him. A cow for milk, an ox for ploughing, and a wife for offspring! In relation to her husband she is not a person but a function.[26]

An additional interpretation is also possible, and indeed adds into the Genesis narrative an observation not unknown in Scripture and all too evident in the unfolding of history. Wenham quotes Susan Foh, who argues that 'the woman's urge is not a craving for her man . . . but an urge for independence, indeed a desire to dominate'.[27] This interpretation draws on the use of the same word in 4:7, literally 'at the door sin lies in repose but its desire is for you . . .'. Sin is ever present; it may seem as unalert and innocuous as a beast in repose, but it is ever waiting to pounce and to dominate, to have as its own.[28] Though this interpretation is not as likely to be in the forefront of Genesis 3:16 as the former suggestion, it cannot be denied its place.

ECONOMIC BREAKDOWN (GENESIS 3:17–19)

Turning to the man in his sin, the Lord's word is that the old economic order has disappeared. From now on, life will rest on the precarious basis of wringing a hard living out of a recalcitrant environment. The implied change from the Garden with its abundant fruits is dramatic. 'Work' is a creation ordinance,[29] but the lot of sinful man is to labour at the soil as woman labours in childbirth (Gn. 3:16–19),[30] and he has to work in this way because 'cursed is the ground because of you' (3:17), that is to say, the substantial creation itself has been infected with sin and now partakes of the oppositions which sin creates. The man is at odds not only with himself and with his wife but with his environment, and it is at odds with him.

THE MORAL VITALITY OF THE ENVIRONMENT

Adam entered the Garden as a beneficiary and left it as a plunderer. The key to a proper integration between him and his environment was the law of God.[31] As long as he kept the law, the world around him seemed to run to meet him with good and plenty. When he broke the law, the world became his antagonist, productive of thorns and thistles, grudging a livelihood to the law-breaker. On the one hand, the law makes him a beloved cousin to the 'forces of nature' as both he and they subserve the will of the Creator.

In this way, the Old Testament does not see the environment simply as a 'thing around' human life. The vitality in the soil and in its plants is the divine life (for there is no other life than the life of God). It is his life that 'made all kinds of trees grow out of the ground' (2:9), and this holy life naturally turns to be the enemy of the one who contradicted its Creator's will. On the one hand, this is because the infection of sin cannot be contained but brings the creation itself under the divine curse (3:17). Thus Isaiah can proclaim the downfall of every high thing in creation as being itself a manifestation of the ungodly pride of humankind (Is. 2:12–17). On the other hand, therefore, creation always sides with its Creator, subserving his purposes, reflecting his attitudes, yielding up its forces to do his will. Its thunder and hail are at the ready to scatter his foes, its mightiest uniformity yields to his greater requirement (Jos. 10:11–14) and its testimony is available to support his voice of judgment (*e.g.* Is. 1:2).[32]

YAHWEH AND BAAL: CONTRASTING PROGRAMMES

The Old Testament offers a striking application of this fundamental relationship between man and environment in the entry of Israel into Canaan and the provoking of a contest between the 'resident god' Baal and the incoming Yahweh. The owner had come to challenge the squatter. This contest was to be fought out on the battle ground of economic prosperity.

One main element in the Conquest traditions is of the sweeping away of Canaanite culture before the invaders. W. F. Albright notes that 'excavations show a most abrupt break between the culture of the Canaanite Late Bronze Age and of the Israelite Early Iron Age in the hill country of Palestine'.[33] But, by its own admission, the Conquest was not all quite like that: in some places Israel settled for a pluralist society (*e.g.* Jdg. 1:19–30) and Canaanite Baalism was to some extent domesticated into Israelite life – often apparently innocently, as David's use of 'Baal' for 'Yahweh' in 2 Samuel 5:20 suggests. The result, however, was that Israel became exposed to the 'theology' of Baalism.

The title 'Baal' means 'lord' and Baal was in particular 'lord' of earth and of its forces. Canaanite mythology saw the cycle of the seasons as a reflection of the supernal experiences of Baal: his death at the hands of Death, the god Mot, manifested itself in the dying of vegetation and the onset of winter; Baal descended to the underworld but, en route, contrived to fertilize the cattle: life continues and animals breed; Baal's 'body' was winnowed and strewn on earth by his sister/consort Anath; spring began, growth started; the revival of Baal 'produced' fruitfulness and harvest. This parallel between the essential life of man on earth and the mythology of the gods constituted the heart of Canaanite religion, an interpenetration of two integrities.

The contrasts between Baalism and Yahwism are plain to see. The Canaanites found their gods in the life of the farm; Israel was found by Yahweh in the land of Egypt. Yahweh came in love to his people but the forces of nature are impersonal and are not motivated by love. The God who came to deliver is a God of compassion: hence the social norms of care, justice, respect, kindness and concern sprang from the soil of Yahwism but there was no corresponding reality in pagan religion. The great agricultural regularities spoke to Canaan of a supernatural counterpart of warring 'gods', intrinsically absurd events, contrived results, but the same events spoke to Israel of what Yahweh had done for them, historically and before human onlookers: at the barley harvest (Ex. 12:17, 34; 13:3; Dt. 16:3), the wheat harvest (Lv. 23:15; *cf.* Ex. 19:1–2; Dt. 16:9–12) and the Harvest Home (Ex. 23:16;

34:22; Dt. 16:13–17; Lv. 23:42–43) they remembered their redemption. All their agriculture was exodus-orientated; it was rooted in history, not transmuted into mythology.

The practical result of these differences was dramatic. Since Baal was understood through the forces of nature, 'he' was understood in non-moral terms, and the main avenue of approach to 'him' was sympathetic or imitative magic: to do visibly on earth what they wanted 'him' to do in heaven, stimulating 'him' by example.[34] It was for this reason that the worship of Baal was located in 'high places'[35] securing visibility, and required the performance of human sexual acts of fertility[36] because the fertilization of humans, animals and land was what was desired from Baal.

Israel, however, entered Canaan armed with a fertility religion for, consonant with his own holy nature, the Lord promised prosperity upon the condition of obedience to his law (Lv. 26:3–13; Dt. 28:1–14).[37] The curse of Eden could be countered by the obedience of the Lord's people, in response to which he would bless them in home and work. The conceptual background to this is, of course, first of all, redemption: they were the purchased people of the Holy God, and within the life of grace the rewards of grace operated. Called to be like him through obedience to his law, they would receive the benefits that only obedience could bring. But there was also a background in creational thinking. Just as the forces of creation rounded on Adam when he flouted their Creator, so those same forces would rush to enrich Israel when they committed themselves to the Creator's will. On the other hand, should they turn their back on him – why, those very same forces would themselves turn and be their enemy (Lv. 26:14–41; Dt. 28:15–68), and not only would poverty ensue but, in a most dramatic personification of the moral vitality of the created order, the land itself would 'vomit them out' (Lv. 18:25).

THEOLOGY AND THE ECONOMIC ORDER

In this as in everything, the Old Testament is the Word of God. It exists not to record, for our patronizing amusement, the quaint notions of ancient man but, for our learning, imperishable principles of divine truth. In economics its foundation truth is Deuteronomy 8:18: 'He it is who gives you the ability to make wealth' (lit.). Prosperity is a divine blessing not a human contrivance, and its enjoyment is the result not of successfully playing the market but of being right with God.

Haggai and the Lord's house

What was thus succinctly stated in Deuteronomy became the heart of Haggai's message. The building of the Lord's house was the turning-point in the national economy.[38] His analysis of the current situation was searching (Hg. 1:6): the economy was in poor shape ('You have planted much, but have harvested little'); the people were not satisfied ('You eat, but never have enough. You drink, but never have your fill. You put on clothes, but are not warm'); inflation was rampant ('You earn wages, only to put them in a purse with holes in it'), and it was all due to the reality of divine hostility (1:9, 11): 'What you brought home, I blew away . . . I called for a drought . . .', and all (1:9) 'because of my house, which remains a ruin'. On the contrary, the two 'Consider your ways' oracles in 2:15–17 and 18–19 declare that even the laying of the foundation stone of the house marks a dramatic change: 'From this day on I will bless you.'

Why is the Lord's house so important? Is it for the reason that R. H. Pfeiffer gives?

> Haggai . . . had little in common with the great prophets of the preceding centuries. His great concern was not with the moral and religious wickedness of the people, but adherence to the rules of Levitical purity and the fulfillment of ritual acts.[39]

But the function of the house as a locus of cultic activity – large as this loomed – was secondary and derivative from its primary purpose, namely, to provide for the Lord's dwelling among his people.[40] Had this indwelling Lord been, *per impossibile*, of like nature with the people among whom he had come or they like him, his dwelling-place would have needed no special arrangements, but since he is the Holy One, his house must be segregated and their approach governed by stated requirements and procedures. The cultus is a spin-off from the holiness of God. This brings Haggai's concern into focus: the unbuilt house spoke of the people's lack of concern whether the holy Lord was among them or not. They had acquiesced in a practical atheism: they were managing nicely[41] without him; when circumstances and inclination coincided they would get round to providing his house. But Haggai knew that in the Creator's world 'all things betray thee who betrayest me'[42] and that his people were caught in a grip they had forgotten, the moral vitality of the environment.

Messianic abundance

The same principle is exemplified in those passages which see the messianic day as marked by unusual fertility and prosperity:[43]

> The . . . bounty of the Messianic day . . . indicates that the curse has ended and is gone. Adam was king in Eden (Gn. 1:28), heir and monarch of the abundance implied in the permission to eat of every tree of the Garden save one (Gn. 2:16–17). But when sin came, liberality dried to a hard-won trickle. When, however, its rightful king returns to Eden (*e.g.* Is. 11:6–9), all the energies, pent up while sin abounded and death reigned, will explode in an endless burgeoning as creation itself hastens to lay its tribute at the feet of him whose right it is to reign.[44]

ORIGINAL SIN

Opinions differ whether the Genesis narrative points to what later theology has called 'original sin':

> . . . the fault and corruption of the Nature of every man, that naturally is engendered of the offspring of Adam: whereby man is very far gone [*quam longissime distet*] from original righteousness, and is of his own nature inclined to evil.[45]

Such high-flown theological language stands at a great remove from the Genesis story, and N. P. Williams, for example, does not hesitate to scorn all possibility of a connection:

> There is not a word in the narrative to suggest that the first sin produced a reflex psychological effect upon Adam and Eve, or infected them with an interior corruption or infirmity capable of being transmitted by physiological heredity to their descendents . . . not a word which implies the theological doctrine of 'Original Sin'.[46]

Ludwig Koehler appears to agree – and to make the disclaimer wider than Genesis:

> The formulation of a systematic doctrine . . . and the statement that all men are evil, that man is depraved, that this depravity originated in the

Fall of his original parents . . . that through this Fall the whole creation was distorted – all this is quite foreign to the Old Testament.[47]

Much of the material already explored in Genesis 2 – 3 shows how baseless some of these contentions are: for example, that the first sin produced no interior corruption or distortion of creation. But it is worth noting, briefly, that writers like Williams and Koehler have not commanded the assent of other main writers on Old Testament Theology. Th. C. Vriezen points out, on the assumption that 'the Yahwistic narratives' of Genesis 2 – 11 'are by the same hand', that 'there must be a connexion between the views of this author in Gen. vi.5, viii.21 and the Paradise-narrative'.[48] If so then 'the Christian interpretation of the Paradise-narrative as the story of man's fall . . . is not unsound'. Genesis 2 and 3, he notes, stress the link between human misery and sin; Genesis 4 'makes it clear that . . . sin, which started with the first man, continued in his descendents'. Indeed 'the author is fully aware that, once man has admitted sin into his life, it spreads . . . and is transmitted by one generation to the next'. W. Eichrodt follows suit. He notes that Genesis speaks of

> . . . a decisive event by which God's plan for man in his creation, was frustrated . . . *This event has the character of a 'Fall', that is, of a falling out of the line of the development willed by God*, and, as the subsequent narrative shows, exerts a determining influence on the spiritual attitude of all men . . . The Yahwist narrator does little or nothing to develop this idea dogmatically, because, like all good story-tellers, he leaves it to the reader to draw his conclusions; but his whole composition hammers the message home inescapably, and his distinctive hand is clearly to be seen in God's judgment of the evil character of human nature in Gen. 6.5 and 8.21.[49]

THE NARRATIVE FLOW

Whilst Williams was dreadfully unperceptive to fail to see the 'psychological reflex effect' of the first sin, he is correct that Genesis does not theologize about sin and its consequences. It is in the events recorded, in the juxtaposition of incidents and in the overall flow of the narrative – where it starts and where it concludes – that doctrinal truth is found.

Genesis 4 is told with marked correspondences to Genesis 3 –

with, however, one major exception. There is no objective tempter in Genesis 4. It would seem that humankind no longer needed a talking serpent; the promptings are all inward, the acts are those that come 'naturally' to the agents.

Disobedience (Genesis 4:2b–7)[50]

The story of Cain and Abel and their respective offerings raises two possibilities. First, it is possible that the will of God regarding sacrifices had already been declared – and Genesis 3:21 offers itself as the moment of revelation: that animals must die if sinners are to be 'covered'. In this case, Cain acted in self-will and open disobedience. The second possibility is that the Lord revealed his will in the context of the offerings which the two men brought. This would have involved a sharper test for Cain, but the end result would be the same, that faced with a plain 'Not that but this' from the Lord his pride and self-will would not allow him to obey.

Broken relationships (Genesis 4:8–9)

It is typical of the sinful self to refuse correction – even from the voice of God – and to react with jealousy, malice and murder, springing out of wounded pride. By his parallel reaction (3:12), Adam killed off his marriage and destroyed society in the only form in which it then existed. Cain lived within the developing society of family and made his deadly assault on it. Sin is not only isolationist but also anti-society. In 3:12 Adam backed away from his wife, but he did not disown her (3:20). Cain went further in his denial of brotherly obligation.

The deceitfulness of sin (Genesis 4:9)

Adam prevaricated (3:12), but Cain spoke the first outright lie – one of a series of 'firsts' in Genesis 4: the first murder, the first lie, the first reaction of self-pity (4:13–14), the first polygamy (4:19), the first act of vengeance (4:24). When Paul speaks in Ephesians 4:22 of 'the old self' ever growing in corruption through 'the desires of deceit' (lit.), he might well have come fresh from reading Genesis 4 where, without any overt tempter, humankind is being drawn on by the inner reality of a destructive magnetism.

The curse extended and reaffirmed (Genesis 4:12)

In Genesis 3 the Lord God stops short of cursing the man and the woman. They live in a cursed environment (3:17) and in ceaseless conflict with the cursed serpent (3:14), but now the same word of the curse falls on Cain, and the dislocation between him and his environment goes a step further: on its part, the environment will not support Cain's life, and on his part, Cain will not be able to settle anywhere in the environment. Cain's only recourse (4:17) will turn out to be the appropriation of part of that environment as his exclusive preserve.[51] Adam was left with sole responsibility for his livelihood in a hostile world (3:17–19); Cain has to be responsible also for his own security: the building of the city is the outward and visible sign of the self-sufficient man – but also of the reclusive man: Adam hid himself behind fig-leaves; Cain behind stone walls. Significantly, he names his new-found security after his son (4:17): *i.e.* both these together, the city he has built and the son he has fathered, are the guarantors of his continuance. Sin has moved humankind much further than a single step away from the position of faith. And Cain's city-building will yet reach its climax in the building of Babel (11:1–9), the decisive rejection of the way of faith in favour of a do-it-yourself salvation through technology.[52]

The fallen world (Genesis 4:10–16)

The structure of Genesis 4 centralizes these verses:

A¹ The devaluation of Yahweh (4:1)[53]

  B¹ Murder (4:2–8)

    C¹ The denial of social unity: no brotherhood (4:9)

      D Environmental dislocation, inability to find rest, animosity/ xenophobia, alienation from the Lord (4:10–16)

    C² The attempt to create social unity and security (4:17–18)

  B² Murder (4:19–24)

A² Return to Yahweh (4:25–26)

Like all the other sections in Genesis 1 – 11 this is not without its note of hope (4:25–26), but its central focus is on what can only be called a 'fallen world'. The first man was sent to care for the soil (2:15); his son is driven from it (4:11). In Eden the Garden was richly watered (2:10ff.); now it is defiled with the blood it has soaked up (4:11). Eden was open to the presence of the incoming Lord God (3:8); that presence is now lost and the intuitive compulsion to hide from God (3:8) is now the recognition of a judicial sentence, 'I will be hidden from your presence' (4:14). Eden was a bountiful home; Cain will find no rest in the world (4:14) and the society that he and his parents disrupted will now itself be characterized by the sin of murder which he was responsible for introducing (4:14). Adam and Eve went out from the Garden (3:22–24); Cain went from the Lord (4:16). Eden/'delight' has been exchanged for Nod/ 'wandering'.

Lamech: the brutalizing of life and marriage (Genesis 4:19–24)

There is a sad consistency about Lamech. His boastful disregard for the life of the young man he murdered is matched by his arrogant disregard for the dignity and speciality of woman expressed in his bigamy. Adam's sin reached new proportions and expressions in Cain; Cain's sin increased in Lamech. The marital breakdown of Genesis 3 becomes marital destruction in Genesis 4. Adam, the sinner, no longer saw his wife in and for herself (2:23ff.), within the exclusive and all-absorbing union of marriage as God meant it: she is a chattel and a function (3:20). Lamech simply increased his breeding herd.

The reign of death (Genesis 5)

The note of hope sounded in Genesis 4:25–26 is seriously intentioned and leads to the fresh beginning of 5:1, 'This book is the emergent story of Adam . . .', that is to say, emerging from, begotten by the birth of Seth and the return to Yahweh. It too records its signs of hope: the ongoing life of humankind, illuminated by such examples as Enoch and his three-century walk with God, or another (and this time a godly) Lamech, nourishing the hope of the promised seed (3:15) and incarnating it in his son Noah. Life, faith and hope remain, but over all alike death is king, for no matter how they bid for immortality in their colossal life-spans[54] the ante-diluvians all had one epitaph: 'and he died', and, as we shall presently note, death was the most spectacular consequence of the first sin. If we ask why the death consequent upon the first sin should thus become the common denominator of all Adam's descendants, the answer is given at the start of chapter 5, the place where 'the book of the emergent history' begins: 'He begat a son in his image, according to his likeness' (5:1b, lit.). The glory of man, the image of God, now has the corrupting intermixture of the image of a sinful progenitor. In this way, the account comes as near as it ever will to a precise articulation of the doctrine of original sin.

Universal corruption, judgment and death (Genesis 6:1–8)

We have already noted above[55] the stress on universality throughout Genesis 6:5–7 and there is little need to say more. These verses constitute the reflective climax to the 'book of the emergent story of Adam' (5:1) and they both summarize and justify the contention[56] that Genesis charts the progress of sin inwards in the first sinners (3:1–24) and then onwards (4:1 – 6:7) in their offspring. The result is unflattering: the outward (6:5a, 'wickedness on the earth') and inward (6:5b, 'the thoughts of his heart') evidence of sin is the story-line of human history, collectively and individually (6:5c, 'only evil all the time'). Humankind is therefore a grief to God (6:6) and ripe for judgment (6:7). 'In Adam all die' (1 Cor. 15:22).[57]

PSALM 51

Throughout the books of the prophets there are scattered references which are most easily interpreted in line with an assumption of 'original sin'. According to Eichrodt:

> This conception is strikingly noticeable in the fact that the prophets bring not only their own contemporaries before God's judgment . . . but see them linked with all previous generations in a unitary entity, for which the sins of the fathers are also the sins of those now alive, and will be required of them.[58]

This is as clear, by implication, in Ezekiel 18 as anywhere else.[59] The prophet is contending against a spirit of false fatalism in his people: knowing that they inherit a sinful entail from the past, they feel themselves entangled in a web of sin which their fathers spun. This Ezekiel denies. It is not so. He does not deny the entail, but applauds the significance and effectiveness of repentance leading to reformation.

This leads directly into Psalm 51:1–5[60] where sin, repentance and original sin are the warp and web of the poem. Not all commentators, of course, would agree that Psalm 51 teaches original sin:[61] Calvin found it 'a striking testimony in proof of original sin', but W. O. E. Oesterley is blunt, saying that to find original sin in Psalm 51 'is a mistake'. However, his reason for this is sweeping and unimpressive – that 'Judaism has never taught this; the idea that Adam's sin is any way affected . . . the human race is quite alien to Jewish teaching'. Among the older commentators, C. A. Briggs cannot find original sin in the psalm but again the comment is unconvincing: the 'mother' is Mother Israel. This rather unlikely view, of course, solves nothing: it merely poses the question in a new form, for even if it is from Mother Israel that sin is inherited, it is still 'original'! A. A. Anderson appears to side with A. Weiser, who contended that 'it is the tragedy of man that he is born into a world full of sin'. A. F. Kirkpatrick, however, affirms that the confession teaches a 'natural perversity and liability to error'.

Whatever may be the truth about verse 5, Psalm 51:1–5 is one of the Old Testament's profoundest statements about sin. The first three verses contain no less than nine key words, three about sin, three about the nature of God and three about forgiveness. In measure the whole Bible vocabulary of sin is here. 'Sin' (51:2) expresses the basic reality of mistake or failing. It is a 'failure to hit the target/a missing of the mark/a short-coming' whether in thought, word or deed. It is the specific thing that has to be confessed.[62] The word translated 'iniquity' (51:2) goes deeper. M. Tate[63] approves of John Goldingay's translation 'waywardness' with its suggestion of a fault of character lying behind the fault of conduct. This is agreeable to the root meaning of 'distortion', a twisting out of shape, misdirecting, perverting.[64] The picture which these two words have begun to build up is completed by 'transgressions' (51:1). Its meaning is 'wilful rebellion', as of a subordinate against the known will of his overlord.[65] If the actual sins we commit were only the product of a warped nature which we have inherited, perhaps we could plead helplessness before God. Perhaps. But since it is also an act of will, knowingly and deliberately undertaken, we are hopelessly guilty and condemned.[66]

The full treatment

Three words now detail how God can deal with our sin: 'blot out . . . wash away . . . cleanse'. Of these, the first implies that sin leaves a mark on our lives and characters (*cf.* the expression 'a black mark') which God can see – and can also wipe away.[67] The second, 'wash away', is a launderer's verb: in our terminology, it indicates how a strong detergent can reach right into the fibres of a garment and deal with ingrained dirt. The figure here is of sin as a deep-seated defilement which only the Lord knows how to launder out.[68] Finally, verb number three is in its majority use concerned with achieving ceremonial purity, the purity which fits the sinner for the presence of God.[69] Thus sin, which marks the sinner (verb 1), and is a deep-seated defilement of the person (verb 2), also separates the sinner from God (verb 3).

The Lord: the divine ground of forgiveness

Finally, in Psalm 51:1–3, there are three words which describe the divine character in relation to the appeal for forgiveness: '. . . mercy . . . unfailing love . . . compassion . . .' 'Mercy' corresponds to the 'grace'-vocabulary of the New Testament. It is the same root as the 'grace/favour' in Genesis 6:8,[70] the free, unmerited outreach of divine forbearance. 'Love' and 'compassion' balance two aspects of love: the former is the love which makes a commitment and holds to it come wind, come weather, the 'ever-unfailing' love of the Lord for his people,[71] pledged by covenant, love rooted in the will of the lover; the latter is the surging passionate love of the heart, the love of 'being in love'.[72] Thus, because the Lord's love is free to the undeserving, constant and passionate, appeal can be made to him – even by that hopeless, deliberate, lustful sinner David – with an assurance of being heard.

Repentance: the human gound of forgiveness

Psalm 51:1–3 encourages us to ask the question: If sin is really like that – defiling, ingrained, separating – and the Lord is like that – gracious, unchanging, loving – can I too enter into benefit, and how? 51:4 provides the answer with glorious simplicity: by repentance, acknowledging that I am a sinner (verse 3), that sin is, above all else, an offence against God and an offence to God (verse 4ab) and that he has a proved right to exercise judgment (verse 4cd):

I am the sinner; I am the offence; I am in dire straits under judgment. This is what repentance is, and in response to repentance – so says the 'for' with which verse 3 opens – all the benefits of verses 1 to 3 are mine!

Without excuse

Verse 5 of Psalm 51 adds the final element in the recipe for true repentance: to recognize oneself to be without excuse.

The verbs used in verse 5 are not the customary verbs for conception, pregnancy and birth. NIV, 'at birth', conceals the main verb of the first line. It is the verb 'to writhe', used – though not exclusively – of the pains of childbirth.[73] The psalm uses a passive formation, 'I was writhed with', that is to say, it carries David's story back to the moment of emerging from the womb. In line two, 'conceived' means 'to be hot' and is used by extension to refer to the sexual passion of the moment of conception – though only here of human conception (Gn. 30:38–39, 41; 31:10). Literally, therefore, 'my mother was hot/passionate for me'. The intention of this unusual expression is to trace David's story further back still, to the very moment when he was conceived.

It should hardly need to be said that, in all this, the psalm is casting no slur whatever on the sexual intimacies of David's parents as though sex were the specific Edenic sin and marriage an inevitable participation in a sinful way of life.[74] It would be utterly contrary to the Bible to entertain such a thought. No, NIV correctly makes it clear that it is the child, indeed the embryo at the very split-second of conception, that carries the infection of sin. The sexual union of father and mother is itself pure and holy, yet it is the means of transmitting the reality of the fallen human nature to the next generation.[75]

The fact of original sin is here more distinctly expressed than in any other place in the Old Testament. But it is expressed as an additional culpable fact and in no way as an excuse. The purpose of the verse is to reveal that as far back as the personal entity, David, can be traced, he has been (lit.) 'in iniquity' (51:5a), 'in sin' (51:5b). Sin is undeniably a fact of life and experience, but it is also a fact of inheritance and of personality. It is part of our inheritance, part of the price of being human, and an issue where we have to be even more careful than usual to keep our thinking square with biblical revelation. For, once more, our logic and the Bible's logic are moving in opposite directions: to our way of thinking, an adverse moral inheritance would act as an excuse. This way of thinking is as old at least as Ezekiel 18, but it is as modern as the bland assumption that criminal behaviour is 'society's fault'. In the Bible, however, while no-one is locked fatalistically into an entail of evil, for the door of repentance and redirection of life is open, each generation stands in a place of mounting guilt, under the accumulating sins of the fathers. So the Lord Jesus himself taught in Luke 11:47–51. The outward ripples of sin embrace and encase the world we live in; the inward reality of sin binds us in a dead solidarity with a whole fallen race; and sin's entail reaches back to the man and woman in the Garden.

◇ AVENUES INTO THE NEW TESTAMENT

Since, self-evidently, John 1:17 cannot mean that Moses' law is devoid of grace and truth, it must mean that all the grace (*i.e.* the atoning efficacy, *etc.*, of the sacrifices) and truth (of the law as divine 'teaching') came to full flower in the Lord Jesus. Such an understanding makes the verse a gateway to the New Testament, where we are both 'not under law' (Rom. 6:14, *i.e.* as a way of redemption, *cf.* Rom. 8:1–2; Gal. 3:13) and yet 'under law' (1 Cor. 9:20) as a divinely authorized pattern of life. For law-obedience is our characteristic (Rom. 3:21; 7:22; Gal. 5:13–14; 1 Jn. 2:3, 5:3), and evidence of our reality (Jn. 14:15; 15:10).

The Lord Jesus is the perfectly obedient Son (Jn. 8:29; Rom. 5:19; Gal. 4:4; Phil. 2:8; Heb. 10:7). As such (*cf.* Ex. 12:3) he is qualified both to be our substitute (2 Cor. 5:21), and also to cast over us the robe of his righteousness (Rom. 3:21; 1 Cor. 1:30; Phil. 3:9). He is the 'end' of the law and that in two senses: first, he silenced its condemnation (Rom. 8:1–3); and secondly, in his person, life and teaching, he gave a full exemplification of the law for us to follow.

Furthermore, while, objectively, Christ's death silenced the law's condemnation by paying the wage it demanded (Rom. 6:23) and by clearing us of all debt (Col. 2:13–14), subjectively his saving work included the creation of a new heart shaped and designed for obedience (Heb. 10:15–16), so that the heart-obedience (Dt. 5:29; 6:5) that the law requires can be fulfilled.

In addition, as to the law itself, released from its ceaseless obligation to condemn, it is free in Christ to become the means of grace it was also intended to be (Lv. 18:5; Dt. 4:1; Ps. 119:45). Thus, Peter can speak of 'the Holy Spirit whom God has given to those who obey him' (Acts 5:32), for in Christ the law becomes a minister of life to those who set their feet in its paths. The prohibitory 'Thou shalt *not* . . .' becomes the promissory 'Thou *shalt* not . . .'.

CHAPTER SEVEN

Christ our life (2):
The theme of death

'What are we to think of life and death?' asks G. Pidoux:

> Was the first man mortal or immortal by nature? The sin resulted in denying man access to the tree of life whose fruits would allow him to nourish the life-force. Man was not created immortal. He had to return to the earth whence he had been drawn, but his earthly condition was suspended during the period when he was able to live near the tree of life.[1]

Leon Morris would concur with this.[2] In his monograph *The Wages of Sin*, he starts by approving of the observation of A. M. Stibbs,[3] who pointed out how marriage in humankind differs qualitatively from mating in animals and saw an analogy with the differential character also of death for man.[4] Then Morris continues:

> Is it too much to imagine that this closeness to God and this primacy over nature found expression in forces of a spiritual character which kept the natural tendency to bodily decay in check? The entrance of sin so radically altered the situation that fleshly dissolution could no longer be held at bay, and thus death became inevitable . . . Viewed in this way physical death is perhaps the most spectacular consequence of sin.[5]

If, however, death is a spectacular consequence of sin, the fact of ongoing life, notwithstanding the edict of death, is equally spectacular. N. P. Williams asked, 'Why did not the threat of instant death take effect?', and he could only reply that Genesis 2 and 3 must be a fusion of more than one stream of tradition![6] The truth is both more obvious and more striking, namely that life did indeed continue, but also that the edict did indeed take instant effect!

THE MYSTERY OF THE PROMISE

In the post-Fall world, two principles operated in tension with each other: the element of promise, and the reign of death. It was argued earlier[7] that Genesis 3:15 may allowably be understood as a protevangelium, but, even if this should not be the case, it is still manifestly a promissory statement, a declaration of divine intent that human life will continue and that humanity, as constituted in and through the first pair, will triumph over the serpentine opponent. This is the third supreme mystery in the early chapters of Genesis: why did God create at all? Where did evil originate, and why did he tolerate its entrance into the world? And now, since evil has entered and corrupted creation from its crown downwards, why did God bother to continue? The silence surrounding these questions seems impenetrable – and even where occasionally the silence possibly seems fractionally less than total, the whisper bids us to remember that God is God, that he must be left in sole command of his deity, that he does all things, does them well and does them for purposes internal to his own nature.

William Temple's characteristic way of expressing this was his concept of 'the sacramental universe'.[8] He wrote:

> God is God in the activity which sustains the process and directs the history. If He did not create He would still exist, for He is not dependent for existence on His creation. But if He did not create, He would not be what He is, for He is Creator . . . If he had no creatures to redeem, or if He had not redeemed them, He would not be what He is. Neither does his historical achievement *make* Him eternally Redeemer, nor does His eternal redemptive love simply express itself in history while remaining unaffected. But each is what it is in and through the other, like spirit and matter in the sacramental rite, yet so that the eternal and spiritual is first and last, with the historical and material as its medium of self-actualisation . . . God . . . is His eternal self in and through the historical process of creating a world and winning it to union with Himself. His creation is sacramental of Himself to His creatures; but in effectively fulfilling that function it becomes sacramental of Him to Himself – the means whereby He is eternally that which eternally He is.[9]

What Temple achieved, however, was a philosophical construct, and Bible passages do not come flooding into mind to support his conclusion in the precise way he stated it. In some ways the verb 'to create'[10] has a wide ambience; in another way it reveals very little. It is, of course, always 'God's verb', but it tells us more of the work of the Creator than of his mind. For the most part it is an unelaborated statement of what he did,[11] consonant with the general meaning of the verb seen in its total use: something was done which by its newness or greatness or both required a cause outside human capability. Since this is true of the commencement of all things, it is also true of the creation of the new heavens and earth in the eschatological 'day' (Is. 4:5; 65:17–18; Je. 31:32). Furthermore, between these two points, the Creator remains in full executive charge of his world in all its aspects, darkness and light (Is. 40:26; 41:20; 45:8; 48:7; 54:16). Birth is his creation (Ezk. 21:30<35>) and so are future generations (Ps. 103:18<19>). The Creator is the God of providential care (Is. 43:1, 15), of individual and natural renewal (Ps. 51:10<12>; 104:30) and of spiritual responsiveness (Is. 57:19). But, in all this, only two verses go on from 'to create' to indicate the purpose in the Creator's mind: the earth was created 'for inhabitation' (Is. 45:18) and the Lord's people were created 'for my glory' (Is. 43:7).

The Creator's glory is displayed in his creation and it is for his glory that the creation exists, but the Old Testament falls short of saying that the Creator needs his Creation or is in any sense incomplete or unfulfilled without it. It is the object of his love, not the fulfilment of his person.[12]

THE QUESTION UNANSWERED

The question 'Why?' thus remains unanswered. Just as the Creator does not explain himself to us at the beginning of all things, nor at the entrance of sin, neither does he explain why he made a promise of continuance – even though we know that in the outworking of that promise marvels of divine love and grace would be revealed that could not, as far as we can see, have come to such manifestation under other circumstances.[13]

DEATH DEFINED: THE THREE-SIDED REVELATION[14]

The promise of God was the word that pledged the continuance of the race, but the nature of death also, understood biblically, requires that the race should continue in life.

We need, at this point, to anticipate by reviewing one aspect of the Old Testament position as a whole. The uniform testimony of the Old Testament is that the dead are alive. Interpreters differ in their estimate of the sort of life they experience, but the fact that the dead live on cannot be questioned. The infant (2 Sa. 12:23), the young man (Gn. 37:35), the wicked (Jb. 21:13) and the grey-headed (1 Ki. 2:6), all alike leave this earth at death and enter Sheol,[15] the abode of the departed. The dead, first of all, experience a change of 'place'.

Secondly, there is an altered state, for while life continues, death effects a fundamental change because the body-soul unity of the person is sundered and 'the dust returns to the earth as it was and the spirit returns to God who gave it' (Ecc. 12:7, lit.). Important consequences arise from this sundering, but all we need to note at present is that death effects a fundamental change in the human state.

The third element in the biblical definition of death is that the individual person continues. Abraham 'was gathered to his people' (Gn. 25:8, lit.); David expected to meet with his dead infant son (2 Sa. 12:22); Samuel, 'disturbed' by the mediumistic activities of the witch at Endor, was the same Samuel who had spoken to Saul in his lifetime on earth – recognizable, speaking of himself in personal terms, unchanged in sentiment from the Samuel of old (1 Sa. 28:14–17).[16]

THE REIGN OF DEATH

Now, in principle, this threefold definition of death is what happened to the Adam and his wife in Eden. They experienced a change of place, moving from the Garden to the outside world. They experienced a change of state: inwardly in conscience and spirit; in the nature and basis of their moral perceptions; in their relationships to each other, to their environment and, above all, to

God. But they continued as the same persons in and through all this change: Eve, as she now became, used the birth of Cain to affirm the equality with God she had grasped after;[17] they are still Adam and his wife (Gn. 4:25 – 5:5), 'Mr and Mrs Man'. It is this perception which Paul expresses in Romans 5:14,[18] where he notes that 'death reigned from Adam to Moses'. In that period there was no itemized law of God exposing humankind to the detail of their sin, but the reality was there: the very life they lived from the Fall onwards was a death-life.[19]

AFTER DEATH[20]

Life on earth, therefore, is but a half-life, compared with the divine intention for man in the image of God and contrasted with the innocent bliss of Eden. The cynic who, when asked if there was a life after death, replied by asking 'Is there a life before death?' was unwittingly expressing and confirming what the Bible reveals. Even the happiest life on earth is but 'a vale of tears' by comparison with what life was meant to be; even the brightest and most lightsome life is still shrouded in the darkness of a sinful world. It is no wonder that the Bible foresees the approaching eschaton as the night passing and the day at hand.[21]

But if life before death is a half-life, the Old Testament sees life after death as even less still. David Stacey, with only slight exaggeration, memorably says that 'for most of the OT, Sheol is literally "a dead end"'.[22] It is not fair, however, to go on to criticize Old Testament folk by saying that 'one's best hope was to keep away from it for as long as possible' for, even with the full glory of New Testament hope, we continue to delight in life and to try to live as long on earth as possible – and rightly so! Paul, who thought in Philippians that it was better by far to depart and be with Christ, also, in the same letter, considered the prolongation of earthly life a notable mercy (Phil. 1:23; 2:27). There are, in fact, three dangers in dealing with death and Sheol in the Old Testament: one is painting the dark scenes too dark; the second is failure to take the light scenes at their face value; and the third is to omit to bring the sentiments of Old Testament saints into comparison with those of the New Testament, for, in both Testaments, death is a dread enemy (1 Cor. 15:26; *cf.* Is. 25:7–8; Jb. 18:14).

Isaiah 14:9–12 is, of course, high and imaginative poetry, but the reality it expresses is a factual truth. The king of Babylon is envisaged as arriving in Sheol, and the scene is depicted as one in which earthly distinctions are reflected and continued. Kings still sit on thrones and, according to protocol, are expected to rise from their thrones to greet this superior king coming among them. This picture of grandeur and status is deliberately contrived[23] in order to juxtapose the pretension of power and the reality of weakness, for, rising from their thrones, their greeting to the newcomer is (lit.) 'You too have become as flabby as we! Are you to be compared with us!' (14:10). And for all their pretence to royalty, the speakers are 'the shadowy ones' (14:9).[24] The irony is redoubled by the fact that in the same verse 'leaders' translates a word meaning 'he-goats',[25] leaders of their herd, 'macho', famed for potency! Such they once were but now, in Sheol, how very diminished! Sheol is not, of course, 'the grave', yet there is an identity between the condition of the spirit and of the body: the corruption of the body has its testimony to bear to the diminished state of the soul (14:11). 'In general', says H. W. Wolff, 'the Old Testament sees death in all its hideousness. It is surrounded by no halo of any kind.'[26]

REALISM

It has to be so. It is commonplace to criticize this diminished life of Sheol as simply the Old Testament's failure to develop a robust doctrine of the life to come – and this, if true, would be a considerable criticism when one considers, on the one hand, the pretty vivid after-life that ancient Egypt foresaw for at least its great ones, and, on the other hand, the Old Testament's much more forceful and insistent presentation of Yahweh as the Living God. The criticism, however, is misplaced. The Old Testament is not being less than realistic but rather precisely realistic and true to its own doctrine of creation. The Creator made man a unity with two aspects or foci: the body and the soul, the outer and the inner, the physical and the psychic. Both are equally the person: all humankind can be described as 'all flesh' (*e.g.* Gn. 6:12–13, Lv. 17:14, Is. 40:5–6). The spirit or soul has no 'edge' over the body as if it were the 'more real' person. This is plain, for example, in Ezekiel 36:26, where the regenerating work of God is equally 'a new spirit' and a 'heart of flesh'.[27] The consequence is that, if the unity is sundered, neither focus of personality can now be what it was before: without the spirit the body decays back into the dust; without the body the spirit is a 'half person': it lives on but cannot live fully.

GOD AND SHEOL

Where is God in all this? It is probably true that most writers on this subject would agree with R. Martin-Achard that the Old Testament offers us a 'multitude of testimonies', one of which is that:

> Death is ... an absolute separation from the Living God ... the creature ... becomes the prey of Sheol, and falls into a sort of nothingness, over which Yahweh is certainly sovereign, but in which He seems, in the last resort, to be disinterested.[28]

Martin-Achard has, of course, more to say than this in the course of his very powerful study, but this 'testimony' as such derives from a handful of verses in the Psalms. Thus we read (lit.) in Psalm 6:5<6> that 'in death there is no remembrance of you', and in 30:9<10>, 'Shall the dust praise you? Shall it declare your truth/faithfulness?' Psalm 88:10–12<11–13> appears to concur, but it also raises the question of how Yahweh may or may not relate himself to those in Sheol: 'Will you work supernaturally for the dead? ... Will your supernatural activity make itself known in the darkness?' According to these references, the dead do not remember or praise Yahweh, and he does not act in wonder and faithfulness on their behalf. The old two-way relationship is gone (cf. Ps 115:17; Is. 38:18).

J. H. Eaton speaks typically about Psalm 6:5 in his generally helpful (though all too brief) commentary:

> As generally in the Old Testament, the state of death is imagined as complete negation ... outside the sphere of God's action ... the opposite of all the living effects of God's presence and power ... for most of their course, the Old Testament people had to suffer and trust without a hope of future life ...[29]

We reach back to the older commentators and find F. Delitzsch lamenting that Sheol is 'secluded ... from the light of God's presence'.[30] Or we move forward to the more recent work of W. Van Gemeren and find him hopefully clutching at a straw:

> What is man when he is dead? This is not to say that the OT denies life after death but rather that it puts the emphasis on the present life as the most important stage in man's relationship with God.[31]

Cold comfort indeed!

The Psalms, of course, contain opposite statements: in the great psalm of 'No escape, no regrets' (Ps. 139),[32] not even finding oneself in Sheol would constitute separation from the divine guardian presence. Must we therefore simply affirm with Martin-Achard *et al.* that the Old Testament offers a multi-faceted testimony and leave it at that – even though, when the book of Psalms reached its present form and became the national hymn-book, people would find themselves singing contradictory songs?[33] Or is there possibly some profit in looking again at the disputed verses?

CONTEXTUALIZING IN THE PSALMS

Take an example that touches a different point altogether. In Psalm 7, David pleads (lit.), 'Judge me, O Lord, according to my righteousness . . . my perfection/integrity . . .' (7:8<9>), and he appears to mean it seriously for he goes on to speak of how the 'righteous Lord' acts in judgment (7:9<10>) and how he is 'a righteous Judge' (7:11<12>). In Psalm 18, he rejoices that 'the Lord paid me in full according to my righteousness, according to the cleanness of my hands . . .' (18:20<21>). The alternatives of interpretation are plain: on the one hand, knowing David as we do, we could say that he was plainly two-faced, that he was very far from being the sinlessly perfect person he seems to claim to be; on the other hand we could allow the context to arbitrate. David is not speaking of his whole life and character but of one episode in which he knew himself to be wrapped in a clean sheet. The context makes all the difference. Both these psalms belong to the period of Saul's increasingly manic dread of David and, within that period, and in everything to do with his relationship to the king, David's hands were indeed clean. He had acted with righteousness and integrity; he had walked the Lord's way.

Context matters. It is very remarkable, then, that commentators should draw sweeping general conclusions from statements like Psalm 6:5 and others, without asking in what context they were spoken; whether they are credal affirmations about the future after death for all alike, or whether they arise from some narrower situation in which the psalmists face or think they face dying. The answer is the latter. *In all these psalms the person facing death senses himself to be under the wrath of God.*[34] David sets the scene in Psalm 6, with 'Rebuke me not in your anger' (6:1<2>). Were death to come to him now, he would die under divine disapproval. The same is true throughout the disputed verses (*cf.* Ps. 30:5<6>, 7<8>; 88 *passim*). There is no way in which psalms which limit themselves contextually in this way can legitimately be generalized to make credal pronouncements about the state of all the dead without exception. Indeed, we may allow Ezekiel to provide a comment on the idea of 'dying in sin'. The expression occurs in Ezekiel 3:18 of the unwarned wicked man, in 3:19 of the warned but unrepentant wicked, and in 3:20 of the unwarned apostate. The NIV translation 'for his sin' is, of course, a possible rendering of the words as such[35] but contextually it is unsuitable: what would it mean? That the unrepentant die quickly or die young? It is unlikely that the Lord meant Ezekiel to say anything so plainly contradictory to experience. Rather, just as the promise that Abram would die 'in peace . . . at a good old age' (Gn. 15:15)[36] points to his condition at death, so those who die 'in iniquity' die in a condition all unfit to stand accepted before God.

ALTERNATIVE DESTINIES

Far from shaping the general Old Testament view of death and the after-life, therefore, these disputed verses begin to shape Old Testament thinking towards the idea of moral distinctions and alternative destinies on the other side of the grave. The Old Testament has no doctrine corresponding to the New Testament – and primarily dominical[37] – doctrine of hell. It is, indeed, one of the many popular misconceptions of the Old Testament to think of it as a 'hell-fire' book. In the Old Testament there are, however, four verses which seem to link Sheol with wickedness of life. When Psalm 9 says that 'the wicked will return to Sheol' (9:17, lit.) it points to something more than the destiny after death that awaits all; it is as if some special appropriateness linked Sheol with wickedness. Similarly, in Proverbs 5:5, 7:27 and 9:18, sexual immorality, whether in the prostitute or her clients, is a downward staircase to Sheol and into the company of the 'shadowy ones', the dead in all their weakness. Maybe it is proper to include here Isaiah 14:15 and Ezekiel 32:23, which speak of 'the inner extremity of the pit'[38] as a place reserved for special cases; Isaiah 14:19 refers to 'the stones of the pit' as a something of special abhorrence.

The use of 'the pit' as a synonym for Sheol is, in general, an aspect of that interweaving of the reality of the grave (with its corruption and loathsomeness) with the weakness and unattractiveness of the half-life that Sheol offers: the one a decay of the body, the other a decay of vital powers. Likewise there is the synonym Abaddon, a place-name developed from the verb 'to destroy, spoil'. Death is the great spoiler. The sufferer in Psalm 88 who never expresses hope and never gives it up laments that, dying as he is under divine displeasure, he will have no chance in Abaddon to enjoy the faithfulness of the Lord. Job 26:6 uses Abaddon as a measure of the Lord's power, but Proverbs 15:11 links it with divine moral discernment. In Job 31:12, it is the special lot of the adulterer.

The Old Testament therefore offers but the faint beginnings of a link between the life to come and the evil rewards of sin but never takes us beyond the broad statement in Daniel 12 that 'many asleep in the dusty earth will awake: some to eternal life; others to shame, to eternal abhorrence' (12:2, lit.). Significantly, the Revised Version, with its excellent cross-references, can only find New Testament passages to amplify Daniel 12:2.

SHINING HOPE

Alongside the general gloom of its depiction of Sheol and its broad suggestion of some link between Sheol or an aspect of Sheol and the eternal reward of wickness, does the Old Testament hold out a *hope* beyond the grave?

It would be an exaggeration to say that Old Testament specialists have advanced greatly beyond the position taken up by W. O. E. Oesterley – though possibly not all would wish to express it as he did. Proverbs 14:32 reads (lit.), 'In his calamity the wicked is thrust down, but (even) in death the righteous seeks refuge.' The order of words places a major stress on 'refuge' and an only slightly lesser stress on 'death'. Oesterley's comment is as follows: ' "In his death" . . . cannot be right, as it would imply hope in a future life, and such hope had not yet come into existence in Israel'.[39] Today's commentators are not so wedded to the doctrine of the evolution of religious ideas, but very many still hesitate to find any eternal hope in the Old Testament. It is, indeed, very hard not to feel that the sort of dogmatism expressed by Oesterley may still in measure be determining interpretation. Yet there are significant passages where the most obvious meaning seems to point to life, glory and fellowship with the Lord beyond the grave.

Psalm 16:9–11

Psalm 16 is a poetic meditation on trusting the Lord and the benefits that flow from such trust. It may be that the references at the end to death and Sheol suggest that David had had some sort of brush with potentially fatal danger.[40] We learn, however, from psalms which are furnished with historical titles, that their intent is not to provide a narrative poem of the occasion concerned but to probe the principles and draw out the lessons involved. In the present psalm, we may sense some danger lurking in the background, but it is not 'what the psalm is about' nor is it even a necessary pre-supposition to understanding the psalm. The prayer of 16:1a and the affirmation of 16:1b state the subject with which the psalm is engaged: divine preservation extended to the trusting one in answer to prayer.

The movement of Psalm 16 is plain enough: verse 1 (A¹) brings us into the heart of the matter with David's plea for the Lord's preservation, based on the trust-position he has adopted. In verses 2–8 (B) he rehearses the grounds which demonstrate the reality of this trust. These turn out to be three in number, expressed in parallel statements: (a¹, a²) the Lord means everything to him (verses 2, 5); (b¹, b²) the Lord's people and land are his delight (verses 3, 6); and (c¹, c²) his spiritual commitment is complete (negatively, verse 4; positively, verses 7–8). Consequently, David can now balance the plea for security (A¹, verse 1) with the affirmation of security in God (A², verses 9–11).

'Your holy one'

To take our study further, we must start by trying to pierce a little beyond the translation 'your Holy One' in Psalm 16:10. The word in question is *ḥāsîd*.[41] Here, and throughout the Psalms,[42] LXX represents this by *hosios*, a rendering endorsed by the apostles in the New Testament (see Acts 2:25–28).[43] Presumably influenced by this, translators, from the King James Version onwards, have opted for 'Holy One'.[44] As we shall see, the New Testament was unerringly right in finding the Messiah in Psalm 16 but, as in all the messianic psalms, the route to the messianic interpretation runs through the experiences and kingship of the current Davidic monarch – here, of David himself.[45] It is right to start therefore with the broad use of *ḥᵃsîd(îm)* as descriptive of the people of the Lord or of individuals within that people, and it is not necessary to decide whether, in Psalm 16:10, the appropriate translation should be 'the one you love' or 'your devotee'. David has taken up a position of faith (16:1, 2–8) and, for such a person, certain conclusions follow for the future (16:9, 'Therefore').

Hope, temporal or eternal?

The contents of Psalm 16:9–11 forbid us to write over them the words 'in the present instance', as if there were nothing more here than what P. C. Craigie describes as David's

> . . . assurance . . . that he was delivered from the immediate threat of death . . . the acute concern of the psalmist was an immediate crisis and an immediate deliverance.[46]

H. H. Rowley, however, takes a different view. He says that, in this psalm:

> There is no suggestion that he is in any danger or distress. Hence, when he says 'Thou wilt not abandon my soul to Sheol', there is no reason to suppose that he is thinking of deliverance from misfortunes, or recovery from sickness. He is cherishing the hope that in this life and beyond he may find in God his portion still, and so may be delivered from Sheol.[47]

Rowley's seeming hesitation, 'he may find', falls below what the psalm actually affirms. 'Heart . . . and flesh', the whole person, inward and outward, considered psychically and physically, is in a state of gladsome safety. Sheol for the soul and decay for the body may be the immediate prospect but not the ultimate state. Beyond, there opens a path to life, the divine presence and David at the Lord's right hand. 'Life', 'satiation of joy' and eternal security ('for evermore') lie ahead. We will find the same sequence precisely in Psalms 49 and 73, and there is no reason to resist the thought that Psalm 16 affirms hope, life and full personhood beyond Sheol. 'The Psalms', says W. Zimmerli, 'present us with sentences of audacious certainty which are not substantiated further but are ventured as affirmations of faith'.[48]

King and Messiah

All this eternal benefit awaits David because he is a true member of the people of God[49] as the key word *ḥāsîd* affirms: he is one of the Lord's beloved and he loves the Lord back. But it is possible also to interpret 'your beloved and devoted one' (LXX 'your holy one') as indicative of a particular status granted by the Lord. Thus Deuteronomy 33:8 speaks of Levi, not in his existential character but in his status as priest, as (lit.) 'your beloved/devoted one' (LXX 'your holy one'). Even when David spoke from within his membership of the people of the Lord he also spoke from his special position as king, and it is this aspect of Psalm 16 which the New Testament isolates and highlights. In order to do so without fear of misunderstanding, it accepts and endorses the translation 'holy'. According to R. C. Trench,[50] *hosios* in classical usage expresses 'the everlasting ordinances of right, which no law or custom of men has constituted, for they rest on the divine constitution of the moral universe'. Consequently, the person who is *hosios* 'is one who reverences these everlasting sanctities and owns their obligation'. Passing to 'sacred Greek', we find the word 'gaining in depth and intensity of meaning but otherwise true to the sense it already had in the classical language'. Trench offers Joseph in illustration who,

> . . . when tempted to sin by his Egyptian mistress (Gen. xxxix.7–12), approved himself *hosios* in reverencing those everlasting sanctities of the marriage bond, which God had founded, and which man could not violate without sinning against Him.[51]

Trench also points out that LXX characteristically uses *hosios* as its equivalent for *ḥāsîd* ('loved and loving') and *hagios* as its equivalent for *qāḏôs* ('holy') and never interchanges this usage. There is a difference between holiness as separation from an ungodly world (*hagios*) and holiness as belonging to God in a relationship of love and response. In this way, *hosios* is the strongest word in the Greek holiness-vocabulary, speaking of identification with the eternal moral principles and verities of God. Plainly such a word looked beyond David as the current holder of monarchic status, demanding from him responses and realities he could never achieve, to the One in whom all the monarchic ideals would at last be realized.

Psalm 49:14-15

In Psalms 49 and 73 the same problem is faced: life on earth seems so unjust and unfair. People of open ungodliness and spiritual carelessness so often prosper while those of consistent devotion do not! Why do the godless prosper and the righteous suffer?

In Psalm 49, the similar verses, 12 and 20, divide the psalm into two.[52] In the first half, the psalmist indicates that death as such brings no solution to life's inequalities: wise and foolish die alike; humans 'in spite of all their precious distinctiveness' (49:12<13>) die like cattle. But there is more to be said. The second half of the psalm brings us beyond the grave. The key verses (49:14-15<15-16>) can be set out as a series of parallel ideas (English versification):

a[1] Like sheep they are destined for Sheol (49:14a)

b[1] Death will be their shepherd (48:14b)

c[1] And the upright will rule over them in the morning (49:14c)

a[2] their form destined for Sheol to waste, far from the mansion it (once) owned (49:14d)

b[2] But God will redeem my soul from the grip of Sheol (49:15a)

c[2] for he will take me (49:15b)

This is the sort of extended parallelism found widely in the Psalms – both in the 'shape' of whole psalms, and in the internal development of sections. The a-lines are an amplificatory parallelism, the b-lines are contrastive and the c-lines explanatory. But more important than any such formal literary connections is the revelation of two sets of people, distinguished by their alternative destinies beyond this life. The one group (a[1], a[2]) is consigned to Sheol, where the old outward appearance which distinguished them is eroded and the old pomp of possessions is gone. Their unfortunate lot is determined by the fact that (b[1]) Sheol has them in its sole mastery, as a shepherd his sheep; but, by contrast, there is another possible mastery (b[2]), a redemptive transaction of God breaking Sheol's grip. The outcome is that no matter how the ungodly were top dogs on earth the situation is reversed beyond the grave (c[1]) and the reason is that the upright are 'taken' (c[2]) by God.

The verb 'to redeem'[53] in Psalm 49 has its distinctive price-paying emphasis. No amount of wealth can buy off death (49:6-9<7-10>).

The psalm says that such a transaction would prove too costly for human resources, even where brotherly love would gladly pay the price if it were possible. But God can and does pay the price (49:15<16>). The psalm offers no elaboration of this: it is an Old Testament thought left hanging in the air until it reaches its awesome New Testament explanation (*e.g.* Acts 20:28; Heb. 9:12, 14). But, because he pays the price, the ransomed soul passes into his possession and he 'takes' it. This is a very ordinary verb in itself with an enormous number of Old Testament instances, but it is used twice in a special context, giving it the particular force of being 'taken' to God in a way that cheated death: we read that 'Enoch walked with God; then he was no more, because God took him away' (Gn. 5:24). 'Then he was no more' is delightfully fresh and exclamatory in the Hebrew: 'and nothingness of him!'; 'Suddenly he wasn't there any longer!', He had been 'taken'. Likewise, in the case of Elijah, the verb rings through the narrative of his 'assumption' (2 Ki. 2:1, 3, 5, 9–10). Once more, quite suddenly he wasn't there any more: God took him! The context in Psalm 49 is too identical in its leading ideas not to require this very special and lovely meaning of a very ordinary verb.

This, then, in brief, is what the psalm says about death, Sheol and hope. The darkness surrounding the whole concept of death, the grave and the life to come (*e.g.* Ps. 88:6, 12, 18) is transformed to morning time (49:14b) – the time when joy comes (Ps. 30:5), and song (Ps. 56:16), and the delivering work of God (Ps. 46:5).[54] For 'the upright', as for the children in Narnia, 'term is over; the holidays have begun'.[55]

The word 'upright' has the sort of ambience one would expect,[56] but in verses like this it has its broadest meaning of membership of the people of God and of being 'right' with him: those who are acceptable to him, received into his fellowship and presence. In its use the word points to a straightforwardness of heart rather more than it is used of a straight way of life. Any idea of salvation by uprightness of conduct and character is as foreign to the Old Testament as to the New, though, of course, like the word 'righteous' applied as a general title to the Lord's people, the assumption is (as the references in note 56 indicate) that being right with God manifests itself in obedience to his 'right' and 'righteous' law and in conformity to right and righteous living in the world.

The particular force of the word in Psalm 49:14 is that the hope of triumph, morning-gladness, redemption and the Lord's presence await all the Lord's people, the whole company of the upright, after death. In this respect, the plural 'upright ones' is underscored by reversion to the singular 'me' in verse 15. The psalmist can only claim the hope as his own because it is the hope of the whole people of God.

Psalm 73:23–24

Our last dip into the Old Testament's hope of the life to come[57] is in a psalm which focuses on the same theme as Psalm 49, the inequality and unfairness of this life in terms of rewards and punishments, and which, interestingly, climaxes with the verb 'to take', which was so important in Psalm 49 also.[58] From the start, this psalm has taken death into its serious consideration. It is part of the psalmist's sense of the unfairness of life that the 'arrogant . . . wicked' (73:3) meet with (as MT stands) 'no fetters at their death'.[59] Their course of life was marked by 'prosperity' (verse 3); their death by painless ease! In this way they are, very literally, 'always at ease' (verse 12) by contrast with the poor old psalmist who, for all his moral and spiritual pains, lives a plagued existence and wakes to fresh trouble every morning (verse 14)! With a lovely concern for the welfare of fellow believers, he kept his problem to himself (verse 15) even though (verse 2) it was well-nigh the end of him. He knew that rarely is a problem shared a problem halved; much more truly is it a problem doubled, because now someone else has it too! So then, he took his perplexity to God (verses 16–17) where a new perspective dawned. His mind was directed no longer to the prospering lives of the wicked or even their pain-free death but to a closer considera-tion of their 'outcome', 'their afterwards' (verse 17, NIV 'final destiny'). By divine agency they are on a slippery slope (verse 18a), destined for 'ruin'[60] (verse 18b). The Great Terror[61] waits to sweep them totally away (verse 19). When the Sovereign God wakes[62] to judgment, they will be found – for all their solidity of health, possessions and supporters on earth – nothing but a hollow show, 'fantasies' (verse 20).[63]

It is apparent now why the thought of death was appropriate at the start of the psalm. It is going to be the very heart of the psalmist's solution to his problem: he had been preoccupied with earth, forgetful of eternity. Why should we not indeed surmise that it was in fact the painless death of just such a person, at the end of a life of unmerited prosperity, which brought the psalmist to his own slippery slope in 73:2? At all events, the thought of death, and its blessedness for the godly, now dominate the psalm. His real problem, he is prepared to admit, was within himself. He now thinks himself a 'brute beast'[64] (verse 22) not to have seen the truth – that is to say, what the New Testament would call 'a natural man' untouched by spiritual reality and regenerating grace, without the Spirit of God. But, alert to spiritual truth through the perspective granted in the sanctuary (verse 17), he now sees them as they are (verses 18–20) and himself as he truly is (verses 23–28). In particular, as to his present, he is in the Lord's company (verse 23a), gripped by the Lord (verse 23b); and as to his future, he is safe within the Lord's over-arching purpose (verse 24a) and 'afterwards' he will be 'taken' to 'glory'. God is the great bracket of reality round both heaven and earth (verse 25) and in God he has an eternal 'portion'.[65] The absurdity of the contention that the Old Testament knew nothing of hope after death is just this: that the heart of Old Testament religion is a fellowship union with the living God and, as the Lord Jesus himself pointed out, he is not the God of the dead but of the living (Mt. 22:31–32; Mk. 12:16–17; Lk. 20:37–38).[66]

LIGHT AND SHADE

The Old Testament, however, leaves us at a point of imbalance and without a final harmonizing of what it affirms. In a word, in relation to death and life after death, as in many other matters, it is on tip-toe awaiting the resolution of its conundrums. It is only Part One of the book with the answers at the back! But when Jesus comes, he will 'bring life and incorruption to light' with the spotlight of the gospel shining unwaveringly on both the glory of a blessed eternity and the darkness of a lost eternity, and with the dilemma of the sundering of the body-soul unity of the human person at death solved in the revelation of the resurrection body. So shall we be ever with the Lord.

◇ AVENUES INTO THE NEW TESTAMENT

In the New Testament revelation of 'life and immortality' (2 Tim. 1:10) in Christ, four truths open up.

(1) *The ultimate end of the sin-death nexus*. With sin came death (Rom. 5:12; 6:23; 1 Cor. 15:21–22), the judicial infliction of divine wrath (Lk. 3:14). This revelation pervades the New Testament but is prominently on the lips of Jesus (Mt. 5:29; 10:28; 13:42, 50; 18:8; 23:33; 25:41; Mk. 3:29; Lk. 16:23–28; Jn. 5:27–29. *Cf.* Rom. 2:5–8; 2 Thes. 1:7–9; Jude 13; Rev. 20:10, 15; *etc.*).

(2) *Eternal life*. By the victorious death of the Lord Jesus (Jn. 12:31), the long reign of death (Rom. 5:14; Heb. 2:14–15) was ended. Jesus is the giver of eternal life (Jn. 6:27; 10:28; 17:2; Rom. 5:21; 6:23) to all who believe in him (Jn. 20:31; 1 Tim. 1:16). Eternal means eternal – a concept which we, in our present condition, can only think of in terms of endlessness, but which essentially is sharing in the very life of God (Heb. 12:9–10; 2 Pet. 1:4).

(3) *The eschaton*, the second coming of Christ (Mt. 16:17; 24:30; 25:31; Acts 1:11; 1 Thes. 4:14–17; 2 Thes. 1:7–8): a personal return, visible, glorious, in the heavens.

(4) With and at his return, we enter into *the full reality of salvation*. In our present state, we labour under 'the body of this death' (Rom. 7:24; 8:23; 2 Cor. 4:7–18; 5:4). Furthermore, physical death sunders body and spirit, and while to depart and be with Christ is by far better (Phil. 1:23) yet it is incomplete from the point of view of redemption, for Christ died to redeem the whole person into the likeness of God (Eph. 4:24). At his return, the spirits of those who have previously died, who return with him and are united with their resurrection bodies (1 Thes. 4:14, 16), and we who are alive, will be caught up to meet the Lord, experiencing a total transformation (1 Thes. 4:17; 1 Cor. 15:35–38, 42–44, 51–57) and enjoying the presence of the Lord for ever (1 Thes. 4:17).

CHAPTER EIGHT

Christ our Hope:
The themes of creation and
consummation

The Old Testament gives an all-pervasive impression that 'everything is going somewhere'.

Genesis 1 sets the scene as its recurring refrain carries the reader forward as if on a journey of discovery: what will lie around the next corner? What will the end be? The creative process is presented as aiming at the foreseen good. The light is pronounced as 'good' (Gn. 1:3), so are land and seas when they are assigned to their respective spheres (1:10), the fruitfulness of earth (1:12), the establishment of the great heavenly luminaries (1:18), the advent of animate life (1:21) and the proliferation of animals (1:25). Thus we stand beside the Creator, learn his mind, and begin to sense in general where his creative work is heading. The advent of humankind in the complete duality of male and female crowns the good with the 'very good' (1:31), and all is now complete.

More particularly, of course, the sense of purposiveness is focused in the promise and fulfilment theme. While there is reason to understand Genesis 3:15 as a protevangelium,[1] it does not have to be understood in these precise terms in order to lay down the foundation building-block of the promissory aspect of the Old Testament. Without evangelic content it would, of course, be a meagre forecast, unworthy of the immensity of the issues raised in the context: 'wherever man and serpent meet, the meeting always involves life and death . . . It is a struggle of the species'.[2] Even so – even if the narrative is to be reduced to this banality – it is still to be remarked that, where the whole flow of the narrative from 2:4 – 3:15 requires a backward look to the threatened curse of death, the Lord points forward to ongoing life and a coming victory. In this, Genesis 3:15 is not only a foundation-stone but a paradigm: everything about fallen, sinful humankind proclaims that the end has come; it is in the Lord that the future is opened up and a contrasting end promised.

THE 'SHRILL DISSONANCE' OF BABEL

The major promise and fulfilment theme of the Bible can be seen most vividly by noting the development of the 'primeval history' to the Babel pericope and beyond. Von Rad perceptively points out that the Fall and Flood narratives hold in tension 'progressive divine punishment' and 'continued divine preservation'. The edict of death (Gn. 2:17) is held at bay by the Lord's prediction of ongoing life and his promise of a coming victory (3:15); the universal and just judgment of the flood (Gn. 6:5–7) embraces the divine component of grace (6:8) and covenant salvation (6:18). But, by contrast:

> This consoling preservation, that revelation of God's hidden gracious will, is missing . . . at one place, namely, at the end of the primeval history. The story about the Tower of Babel concludes with God's judgment . . . ; there is no word of grace. The whole primeval history, therefore, seems to break off in shrill dissonance.[3]

Yet this appearance of things is not the reality. Immediately following the Babel story, Genesis 11:10 backtracks to the fresh, post-Flood, start that God gave to humanity, the 'emergent history of Shem'. This turns out not to be a narrative of events but a list of names, a genealogy of the totally unknown, saving for where it begins and where it ends. For the point is not what happened but that, starting with Shem, the inheritor of Noah's blessing (Gn. 9:26), the patient, unforgetting, unremitting faithfulness of God persisted through generation after generation right up to the birth of a man named Abram, to whom the Lord will say 'all the families of the earth will be blessed in you' (Gn. 12:3, lit.).[4] From this moment onwards, the flow of biblical history will concentrate on this one line of development, but the particularity of Abraham and his family does not mean that God has abandoned the universality of his creation; the 'seed' of Abraham will be the blessing that the world lost through the Fall, the Flood and the scattering.

INTERIM FULFILMENTS

So the Old Testament, from the start, is a book-in-waiting. From the time of Abraham it awaits the promised 'seed'; presently the picture is filled out with the expectation of the prophet like Moses, the king like David, and in the subtle amalgam which we know as 'the Servant Songs', Isaiah brings king and prophet into the context of a priestly atoning sacrifice. As the expectation rolls forward it snowballs in richness.

In the meantime, the Lord sustained his people through minor but symbolic promises and fulfilments. Abram (Gn. 15) is promised a son and a land. The former promise was kept within fifteen years; the latter waited four hundred years, while the Amorites worked through and failed their centuries of moral probation. The Exodus and the Conquest alike gave evidence of the triumph that the Lord intends for his people over the forces of the world and of strengthened confidence that the larger promise would yet come. Isaiah is, as ever, the greatest exponent of the cream of Old Testament truth, and the greatest exposition of Davidic hope, for example, is in the colossal 'triptych' formed by chapters 13–20, 21–23 and 24–27.[5] But, lest his people should be in any doubt that such a grand vision would ever eventuate, he allows it to climax twice by using current powers as shadows of the true: Egypt, Israel and Assyria (Is. 19:24–25; 27:12–13). He then proceeds (chapters 28–35 and 36–37) to offer an interim fulfilment by showing the Lord's total mastery of exactly these powers in a particular historical sequence, as it were 'before your very eyes'. Interim fulfilments turn up the heat under the main promises of God; create and stimulate faith; validate hope by allowing it to cast its shadow before it.

THE CREATION QUADRILATERAL

The Old Testament, then, represents both creation and history as teleological. The promise is working itself out in history, but the creation itself too is 'going somewhere'. The Creator works with purposes in mind. In fact the Old Testament doctrine of Creation is a broader concept than usually springs to minds which, like ours, are conditioned by a century and a half of controversy between 'science' and 'religion', restricting attention to cosmogony as though there were no other question than who made the boat and pushed it out.[6] In fact, however, the Old Testament doctrine of creation is four-sided.[7]

1. ORIGINATION

The Creator God originates everything in the ultimate sense of 'origination'. The Creator's verb, √*bārā'*, is never used with any subject, stated or implied, other than the Creator himself, and it is never used of making something 'out of' something else. It is strictly inaccurate to say that before the work of creation there was 'nothing' for 'nothing' is a spatial and temporal concept: it implies space void of object, and time void of event. Before creation there was 'not even nothing', for it was with the material substrate of the universe that space and time sprang into being. Before that, there was only God. In Genesis 1,[8] the very material substrate – lifeless, without solidity or meaningful shape, shrouded in darkness – is the first act of the Creator. It lies, awaiting the word and Spirit of God to give it coherence, light and habitability. The sculptor can see the properties and possibilities inherent in the stone; the Creator built into his created material all that he would then shape into a meaningful world or leave to be discovered for the benefit and enrichment of his beloved humans. All alike – the ground we tread, the earth we probe, the life we enjoy, the air we breathe, the food we eat – owe their being and origin to the mind and hand of God.

2. MAINTENANCE

The Creator God maintains everything in existence. There is a moment-by-moment relationship of total dependence upon him. Isaiah 42:5 is an excellent verse in point, translated literally as:

> This is what the Deity, Yahweh has said –
> He who creates the heavens and stretches them out,
> who spreads the earth and its produce,
> who gives breath to the people upon it
> and spirit to those who live their lives in it . . .

This less than elegant translation is designed to allow the participial nature of the four main verbs to be seen: 'creates . . . stretches out . . . spreads . . . gives . . .' The Hebrew participle expresses the unvarying situation, here the relationship between the Lord and the created orders. He who created is still creating; he who extended the heavens and the earth is still extending them (not in the sense of increasing their size but of maintaining their extension); he who gave life gives life. Other passages speak of the divine Spirit as both the Giver of death (Is. 40:7) and the Giver of life, the Agent in the ongoing creative activity of Yahweh (Ps. 104:7). Just as that same Spirit awaited the divine fiat in the beginning (Gn. 1:2), so he goes out to maintain creation and all its processes in operation.

3. CONTROL

The Creator controls all things in their operation. Nothing happens by natural necessity; everything by creative oversight; nothing can spring into action without his word or run beyond the bounds he has set. According to Isaiah 40:26, the stars are in place, not by mechanical necessity, but by creatorial presidency. Vividly the prophet suggests that they are called by name like so many dogs coming out of their kennels at their master's voice.

Yahweh the omnipotent

Amos 5:8–9 spells the matter out at greater length. The Pleiades and Orion were used as seasonal markers, and here they indicate the Lord's sovereignty over the major changes from winter to spring to summer to autumn; deep darkness and morning, day and night, are the immediate, regular variations of life; the pouring out of the sea on the land is one of those occasional changes when the sea breaks its bounds and floods inland; the destruction of the strong is a historical, political change, a change within the realm of people and affairs. This passage is one where Amos may be quoting what seems to have been a hymn to God the Creator (Am. 4:13; 9:5–6; *cf.* Je. 10:12–16). The participial formation is best reflected in such a translation as 'There is One who makes . . .' *etc.*, but more important than form is content: the Lord presides over all changes – major and minor changes in 'nature', occasional changes in circumstances and history. He is 'Yahweh the Omnipotent/ Yahweh of Hosts'.

There seems to be no limit to the extent to which the Old Testament is ready to press divine overseeing control. Isaiah 54:16–17 teaches that, first of all, the craftsman and his craft are a creation of God; but then also the Lord has created 'the destroyer', who would take the craftsman's product and use it for hurt; yet at the same time, the power of the destroyer is within limits imposed by God so that the weapon can only reach to the extent that divine permission has been granted to it. In each case, the verb 'I have created' in 54:16 is strengthened by a free-standing personal pronoun: 'It is I myself who have created'. The intention of the verses is comfort: the Lord's people are secure within his sovereignty; the teaching of the verses is the way in which divine executive control reaches into the skill, productivity, malice and need of people on earth.

Created calamity

Isaiah 45:7 is a verse that has not infrequently caused difficulty to its readers with the assertion – which reached from the King James Version to the Revised Version – that 'I create evil'. NIV offers the alternative 'disaster' and JB 'calamity'. Etymologically, all this is possible for the word (*ra'*),[9] in its biblical usage, covers all meanings from nasty tasting to moral iniquity. One major meaning – almost half the examples – is 'trouble/ calamity', whether on the scale of individual life or in the affairs of men and nations. Thus, in Isaiah 45:1–7 with its major theme of the defeats and overthrows inflicted by the all-conquering Cyrus, verse 7 offers a summary overview: 'light' and 'darkness' comprise, metaphorically, all that life offers in pleasure and pain; 'peace' (rounded well-being) and 'ill-fortune/ calamity' are the realities of life. All alike are under the creatorial sovereignty of God. Isaiah 45:7 is emphatically a 'creation' verse, embodying all the significant verbs of Genesis 1 – 2: 'create', 'make' and 'form'. It is for our comfort that the major verb 'create' is used with 'darkness' and 'calamity'. If God were only sovereign in life's pleasantnesses, what an endangered species we would be! But the valley of deep darkness is as much a 'path of righteousness' – that is, a path that makes sense to the Shepherd – as is the green pasture (Ps. 23:3–4). Since, however, our more pressing need in life is to know how to look both personal adversity and the threats of world history in the face, we are invited to stand beside the Creator and see how all things are under his control[10] – or, rather, to know that he is standing by us.[11]

4. DIRECTION

The Creator directs all things to their appointed end, the goal he has set for them. Verses like Isaiah 65:17–18 express this in the grand manner. As we shall note presently, there is a particular significance in the fact that the ultimate perfection is a creative act of God – something that only he can do; something so great that he is required as an agent; something totally new. The threefold 'I am going to create' (17a, 18b and c) is surely designed to match the threefold use of the great verb in Genesis 1:27, save that here it covers the new environment (17b) and the new society (18c) as well as the new people (18d). The goal to which the Lord is moving all things matches and out-matches its starting-point; what was lost in the Fall is recovered and then transcended. 'By comparison, even the "very good" of Genesis 1:31 seems cool!'[12]

Isaiah 4:5 points us to the same combination of recovery and novelty in the new-creative work of God. The context is woven throughout on the loom of redemption. Isaiah has been focusing on 'the daughters of Zion', not because their wickedness was exceptional but because it was typical: they were the true daughters of their mother. They had identified themselves with materialism and would reap the reward of dereliction (3:16 – 4:1). Yet it is to this very point that the Lord directs his creative work of renewal: in his book a holy people have been recorded and destined for life (4:3), for he will wash away 'the filth of the daughters of Zion' (4:4, lit.), performing a work of new creation (4:5–6). The new-creation theme is a predestination theme. Things reach the goal that is set by the Creator (not a goal set by people or achievable by them), and that goal is accomplished by unique creatorial action.

This, then, is the 'Creation quadrilateral', the four-sided reality of the Creator's activity: originating, maintaining, controlling and directing. Our fixation with cosmogony limits our view to one quarter of what the Bible reveals, and it deprives us of the proper sense of security in God within his world.

GOD AND HISTORY

The directive control exercised by the Creator over the physical universe is matched in the prophets by their insistence that the whole movement of history is equally at the divine behest. No prophet differs from another in this, and Amos can speak for all. In his opening chapters he affirms a theodicy at work in history (Am. 1:4, 7, 10, 12, 14; 2:2, 5, 13–16).[13] The whole world, without exception – the Gentile nations guilty before the law of conscience, and the people of the Lord guilty for their disobedience to the revealed law of the Lord – all must answer *within history* to the world's Judge. The historical nature of the punitive calamities threatened betokens a detailed divine management of world events. The only God is both the guardian of universal morality and its enforcer.

In Amos 4 the doctrine of theodicy is widened to include natural disasters along with the action of victorious foes. In his determination to leave no stone unturned to save his people from the blight of self-pleasing religious punctiliousness, and to bring them to the spiritual and personal realities of repentance, the Lord used the tools so readily subservient to his sovereign will: famine, drought, blight, epidemic, foe and natural catastrophe (Am. 4:6–11) – each in turn serving the purpose of grace that Israel might 'come back right up to me' (Am. 4:4, 6, 8–11). Amplifying references could be supplied from the rest of the prophetic corpus but two utterances of Amos say it all: 3:6 makes a comprehensive assertion regarding circumstances, 'Or shall there be trouble in a city and the Lord has not done it?' (lit.), and 9:7 speaks identically about history, 'Did I not bring Israel up from the land of Egypt and the Philistines from Caphtor and Aram from Kir?' All variations in experience and all movements of peoples are alike the Lord's direct action. No trouble arises or national migration takes place apart from him.

THE AGENT AND THE AGENTS

It is typical of biblical thinking to seem to overlook or marginalize second causes and to attribute all directly to divine action. There is good reason behind this. As we shall note in a moment when we consider the workings of history more closely, it is not that the Bible discounts or is ignorant of second causes. Rather, the Bible wishes to inculcate a way of looking at life and a way of living it. It can be stated briefly like this: concentration on second causes leads to 'working the system'; concentrating on the 'first cause' leads to a life of acceptance and trust.

Consider Job's 'friends'. Their thinking was system-based: Job was in trouble, therefore Job had sinned; so, work the system: put the sin right by repentance and things would come right again. But the Lord's purpose for Job was quite different. At no point in the book does he allow us into his mind regarding Job's sufferings. The Prologue allows us to see a mechanism whereby suffering is inflicted but it offers no explanation, and, right through to the end, including the Yahweh-speeches, the sort of explanation that Job considered would have contented him is not offered. But, finally, the Lord stands in the whirlwind with Job (38:1); he comes down himself into the storm, and it is that face-to-face, personal encounter with a God who shares life's storms that brings to Job the comfort of trusting. He does not know anything at the end beyond what he knew at the beginning,[14] but he has been drawn into the fellowship of the 'first cause' and is at peace.

This is the wholesome and practical purpose served by the Bible's focus on the Lord as the direct doer of all. Theologically it is a derivative from its understanding of God the Creator; practically and pastorally it inculcates a response to the adversities of life expressed in acceptance as from God, in waiting upon God to draw near, and in trust in the all-wise, all-loving, all-powerful God who does and will do all things well.[15] This is all very far from the essentially 'Greek' modes of thought endemic in our world: it is yet another way in which the life of 'faith' challenges the life of 'works' and in which we are called away from a 'do-it-yourself' activism to personal and restful trust.

THE CARPENTER AND THE SAW

The arena of history is the proper sphere in which to see all possible agencies at work. The powers of nations and rulers are manifest and active for good and ill. They are real powers, effecting real changes, with consequences that go on and on making waves on the sea of life. The question has to be asked whether the Old Testament doctrine of the originating, maintaining, controlling and directing Creator leaves room for real actors on the stage of history, or whether the whole thing is an elaborate puppet show.

This problem is not exclusive to the relation between the Creator and, for instance, the imperialist state. It arises wherever eternity touches time. What, for example, is the relationship between the mind of God and the mind of the prophet in the matter of revelation and inspiration?[16] The insistence of the prophets on verbal inspiration might seem, at first blush, to invalidate human personality and to point to unacceptable 'models' like dictation, typewriters and tape-recorders. We need, of course, to be careful in case our inability to arrive at an acceptable 'model' should be allowed to call in question the substantial truth we are trying to illustrate. Rather, in the matter of inspiration, we should be guided by the fact that the Bible itself does not enter into the 'mechanisms' of inspiration, and thus it warns us against presuming to reduce one of God's unique operations to some measure that our minds feel comfortable with.

In the matter of the balancing of 'forces' in history, however, the Old Testament does venture into model-making. Isaiah 10:5–15 is a classic text on the subject and its shape displays its message:

A¹ The Lord's rod: Assyria in the Lord's purpose (10:5)

  B¹ The Lord and Assyria: motives (10:6–11)

    a The Lord's motive: punishment of Jerusalem (10:6)

    b Assyria's motive: world dominion (10:7–11)

  B² The Lord and Assyria: assessments (10:12–14)

    a The Lord's assessment: Assyria's pride and punishment

    b Assyria's assessment: ability and success (10:13–14)

A² The Lord's tools: Assyria under the Lord's sovereignty (10:15)

Expressed in the mighty poetry which only Isaiah could reach, here is a hard-headed and consistent wrestling with history in the light of both the doctrine of a sovereign Lord and the manifest super-power reality of Assyria. It is a study of ultimate reality: the Lord is sovereign, and even the colossal forces of the Great King of Assyria are but a punishing rod in the divine hand, an axe or a saw in the tool kit of the divine carpenter. The Lord takes full responsibility for the whole sequence of events. Jerusalem needed chastisement and the Assyrian was the appointed instrument.

But, equally, Isaiah offers a study of existential reality, for the Assyrian is safeguarded in his integrity as a person and we are allowed to see him thinking, deciding, planning – and culpable! All our models break down at this point. It is only a bad workman who blames his tools. How can the tool be blamed if it is in the hand of the perfect workman. There is no such thing as a culpable rod. It is, however, Sadduceanism of the worst sort to allow inadequate models to dictate truth, and the Sadducees deserved the trouncing they received at the hands of the Lord Jesus (Mk. 12:20–27).[17] On the one hand, then, Isaiah safeguards the sovereignty of God as required by the Old Testament doctrine of the Creator, but, on the other hand, there is no question about the validity of the Assyrian as a person and a power. The relationship between the Power and the power is not, as we shall see, symmetrical, but Isaiah does not call in question the existence and effectiveness of the earthly monarch and his armies. Divine sovereignty does not deny or diminish human efficacy. Nor does it call in question the more interior aspects of the human person. The Lord sent Assyria on a punitive expedition, but were we to ask the Great King why he attacked Judah, he would not have replied in terms of a divine commission but in terms of the standard imperialist assumption, 'a growing conviction of the right to rule'.[18] His banners display battle honours all the way down Palestine, and Jerusalem was as much rightfully his, as he saw it, as Calno and Carchemish. He had grown accustomed to taking what he wanted (Is. 10:13–14), and Jerusalem was his helpless prey along with the rest of the world. Here, in effect, is a real king in the real world playing the real game of power politics.

THE RIDER AND THE HORSE

It was in connection with this same Assyrian invasion that Isaiah sketched in another illustrative approach to the problem of the Creator and world history. To our loss it is no more than a sketch, but it says enough to say everything. In his oracle to Hezekiah about the Assyrian threat, speaking in the person of the Lord, he said, 'I will put . . . my bit in your mouth and I will make you return by the way you came' (Is. 37:29). The model is not now the carpenter and the saw but the rider and the horse.

Commentators on show-jumping often praise the rider for a clear round or the horse for being a good jumper. Neither statement, just in those terms, is true! The rider would not clear even the first fence without the horse, nor would the horse find its way over the fences without the rider. In a word, all the directive and management skill belongs to the rider and all the pent-up energy belongs to the horse. The rider determines the course, and the horse exerts its strength to complete it.

Taking care not to press illustrations beyond truth, we can, none the less, read off some of the plainer implications of Isaiah's model. The Lord is the all-deciding, all-controlling Rider. In holy judgment, he has determined to chastise Jerusalem and points his punitive agent towards that target. The horse with its energies is the Assyrian, with the powers that are at his disposal and also with his personal decision-making capacities, his world-ambitions, his pride of imperialism – all that makes him what he is. Thus, in assaulting Jerusalem the Assyrian is a responsible agent, gathering his armies, appointing his captains, planning his campaign and fixing his objectives; but in the Assyrian assault on Jerusalem, the Lord directs all this fearsome energy to his own moral ends.

EVEN SATAN

The Old Testament revelation of Satan follows the same course exactly. As with the whole Bible, the devil does not loom large in the Old Testament and, apart from Genesis 3, Job 1 – 2 constitutes the central text.[19] Three interwoven truths emerge: first, the Satan moves within the sovereignty of the Lord, whereby he is depicted as returning to the divine throne-room after a period of moving about the earth. The intended picture is of one 'reporting back' after one tour of duty and awaiting instructions for the next. Secondly, as the curmudgeonly opponent of humans, he does not operate at his own unfettered choice. It is not he who calls the Lord's attention to Job as a likely target for trials and temptations but, to the contrary, it is the Lord who invites the Satan to express an opinion about one so perfect and upright. In its way this is the very heart of the unexplained mystery of the book of Job. It was by divine intent that Job was tried, and the Lord never explains why it was important to him that this should happen. As ever, the Lord was 'coming down his own secret stair'. Thirdly, as well as calling the Satan's attention to Job and receiving typically malicious insinuations in reply, the Lord sets limits around the activities of the trial which the Satan proposes: in the first onset, Job will be tested domestically and circumstantially but himself remain unscathed; and in the second 'round', he will be tested with bodily affliction that stops short of death. Until the Lord has indicated the object at which the Satan is to direct his attention and has set out the 'rules of engagement', the Satan can only stand and wait. He is not a free agent.[20] The powers and the malignity which prompts and fills them are his. The directive and controlling agency is the Lord's.

The Old Testament, therefore, rejects all hint of dualism, whether in the ultimate sense of seeing Satan as an alternative supernatural agent alongside the Lord or in the less dramatic sense of thinking that powers at work in history have a free rein on earth. All such accommodations to theological dualism or practical deism are biblically unacceptable. A totally deistic system makes God an absentee. He pushes the boat out from one side of the pond and waits for it to make land at the other, but between those two points has no say or influence. Semi-deism thinks of him as the master chess-player, who is always at the board, always in command, even though he cannot tell in advance what move his opponent may make; he may be momentarily checked but must ultimately win. Each position falls short of the God of the Creation quadrilateral and the Old Testament's far more refined and subtle understanding of divine sovereignty.

TIME GOING SOMEWHERE

In the Old Testament both time and truth are going somewhere. Everything had a beginning and everything will have an end.

The Old Testament measures time in one way and understands it in another. Measurement is circular, understanding is linear. Like all others, the Hebrews watched the circling heavens and divided time up into years, seasons, months, weeks and days. Taking an observer's vantage-point, the Old Testament saw the sun rising and setting, the constellations appearing, moving across the heavens and disappearing only (predictably) to appear again. Abraham and Sarah's son will be born 'this time next year', or, as nearly literally as can be managed, 'about the (this) season living (again)' (Gn. 18:10, 14; *cf.* 2 Ki. 4:17).[21]

TIME BY COVENANT

Clock time comes round again, whether it is measured on the cosmic clock or by whatever domestic reckoning Abraham and Sarah employed, but even so it is not by natural or mechanical necessity but by the faithfulness of God. It is what the Lord promised: the regular agricultural 'round', the seasonal variations, and the alternation of day and night (Gn. 8:22). This concurs with the all-embracing doctrine of God the Creator: for, like, everything else, time is his creation; he is its originator, master and manager. Jeremiah puts the matter at the highest level by bringing into play the concept of covenant. In 31:35 he skilfully blends into his oracle what seems to be a snatch from the same hymn to God the Creator that surfaces in Amos 4:13; 5:8; 9:5–6. According to this, light and darkness are the Lord's 'gifts/appointments', and the stability of these 'ordinances' is a metaphor of the unchangeableness of the Lord's commitment to 'the seed of Israel'. In 36:20 and 25 there is a divine covenant regarding day and night and, just as this covenant lies beyond the hand of humans to touch or fracture, so it is with the Lord's covenant with David. It is secure within his determination that it shall be so.

This, of course, introduces a different view of time from the circularities of the observable heavenly bodies and earthly seasons. The hymn-writer is not sufficiently exact to envisage a time 'when with the ever-circling years comes round the age of gold'.[22] In the Bible it is not quite so. The month of May can come circling round and so can the season of Spring, but not the Day of the Lord! The Old Testament knows all about 'former days' and 'latter days', 'long ago' and 'far ahead' (using the same word, 'eternity', '*ôlām*, for each);[23] it has an ongoing, 'time like an ever-flowing stream', concept, with a point at which it arises and a great sea into which it will yet flow.

THE DAY OF THE LORD: AN INSTINCTIVE EXODUS ESCHATOLOGY

By the time of Amos (at least), the 'day of the Lord' was well established in popular expectation, for Amos can, without any introduction or explanation, challenge current and erroneous views of what the 'day' will involve (Am. 5:18). But how and where did it originate? S. J. DeVries suggests:

> Did it emerge as a foreign importation? Did it originate as a mythological element in Israel's cultus? Did it arise through spontaneous internal development? Or did it find its origin within the traditions of Israel's holy war?[24]

DeVries carefully documents all these views but allows that the question of origin is still vexed. Of them all, the idea of spontaneous internal development is the most likely, for the Old Testament is ineradicably eschatological in its view of life, time and history. The tiny event of the call of Abraham is pregnant with universal consequences yet to come to birth; the normative work of Moses as prophet will be outshone by that of the coming Prophet; the monarchy as an institution heralds the arrival of the perfect King. All this is more an aspect of Israel's psyche under God than the product of this or that event or catastrophe. It is very fruitful, therefore, to take note of the recurring expression 'the day I brought you up out of the land of Egypt',[25] for in very many ways that Exodus 'day' kept in step with the life of the Lord's people, and it also reached out to provide the imagery and the reality of the eschatological 'day of the Lord'. Just as the Exodus itself provided an eschatological model, so the Exodus 'day' sparked off the hope of a greater 'day' yet to come. .

This is a fruitful line of enquiry of which only a preliminary sketch can be given here. We may begin by noting the striking emphasis that Exodus 12:41 and 51 lay on 'this very day', stressing its exactness in the Lord's calendar, how it is to be 'observed' through all coming generations, and how it was marked by the divine work of Passover-redemption. Deuteronomy 16:3, therefore, contains no surprise as it embeds the remembrance of the Exodus 'day' in the cult, centralizing it in Israel's life and securing it in their memory; both David (2 Sa. 7:6) and Solomon (1 Ki. 8:16) looked back to the Exodus 'day' when they contemplated the Temple, whether in idea or in completion. The prophets merged history with expectation and eschatology: Isaiah took the journey of the Exodus 'day' as the pattern for the eschatological gathering (Is. 11:15–16; 51:9–11); Jeremiah related the distinctiveness of the new covenant back to the 'day' of the former covenant (Je. 31:32); Ezekiel and Hosea made the older 'day' the pattern for the new beginning, without blemish, which the Lord would yet engineer (Ezk. 20:5–6, *cf.* 35–36; Ho. 2:15); and Zephaniah took the darker aspects of the 'day of the Lord' directly from the Sinai pericope (Zp. 1:15–16). These references are all bound together simply by the incidence of the word 'day', but if we were to follow the core themes and motifs it would be seen how deeply and widely the Exodus had become the seed-bed of Old Testament 'end-time' expectations.[26]

THE DAY OF THE LORD: THE CONVEYOR-BELT OF TIME

Isaiah offers a particular perspective to this linking and balancing of the two 'days' when he notes that 'there is a day belonging to Yahweh the Omnipotent' (Is. 2:12, lit.; *yôm layahweh s^eḇā'ôt*). The very form of the expression parallels the Exodus comment that Passover night was 'a night of vigils belonging to Yahweh' (Ex. 12:42, lit.; *lēyl šimmurîm hû' layahweh*). Here indeed is a 'peep behind the scenes'. Outwardly, the circling universe, and in particular the setting and rising sun, brings night and day in ordered sequence; conceptually, this is no automatic, machine-like necessity but depends on the constancy of God's faithfulness to his pledge and covenant; but, efficiently, each day is, in its own right, the day that the Lord has made, a day reserved in his store and brought forth for his purpose and inserted, according to his judgment, in its proper place in the time-line. The month of May 'comes round' along with the season of spring through the faithfulness of God; but each day in May is there by divine appointment in its place on the conveyor-belt of time that reaches from creation to new creation.

THE DAY OF THE LORD: THE CLIMAX OF REDEMPTION

Standing back from the prophetic corpus, it is plain that there are two 'views' of the coming 'Day of the Lord'. On the one hand, there is the darkness of the coming Day, which Amos insisted upon in response to the eschatological complacency of his contemporaries (Am. 5:18–20);[27] but on the other hand, alongside the 'day of the great slaughter', Isaiah spoke (lit.) of 'the day when the Lord bandages the wound of his people', and he foresaw it as a day of almost unimaginable light (Is. 30:25–26). Throughout the prophetic books, these two expectations lie side by side. S. Mowinckel sketches in a very persuasive scenario when he writes:

> As the people hoped for the realization of the ideal of kingship, particularly when the reality fell furthest short of it, so, from quite an early period, whenever they were in distress . . . they hoped for and expected a glorious 'day of Yahweh'.[28]

The prophets rightly felt it necessary to challenge this view inasmuch as it reflected only a nationalistic and spiritually unreal complacency, but at the same time they never denied the vision of glory.

PROPHETS OF YAHWEH

Indeed, how could the prophets deny a vision of glory? They were prophets of Yahweh, the God who revealed himself in the double-sided activity of the Exodus: judgment on those who refused his word; redemption for those whom he chose to redeem. If Amos' people, for example, emphasized the second element in this revelation and forgot or marginalized the first, it would have been an identical sin against the truth if Amos were to have concentrated on the first and overlooked the second.[29] The 'logic' by which the prophets operated was the logic implicit in the divine Name, and this meant, first, that hope was always and intrinsically an element in their message; secondly, that when hope was realized, it was against the grain of events and contrary to deserving; and thirdly, that the glorious future would come, not by human progression towards the perfect, but by divine action consonant with divine justice.[30]

Isaiah summarizes all this by saying that 'Zion with justice will be ransomed, and her penitents with righteousness and at the same time the shattering of those who rebel – those who forsake Yahweh will come to an end' (1:27–28, lit.). What is striking is not that the 'shattering' is an act of justice and righteousness – this is taken for granted – but that the work of ransoming satisfied the righteous principles of God and is carried out in ways that his justice dictates. The same is true 'when the Sovereign has rinsed away the filth of the daughters of Zion by the Spirit of justice and the Spirit of burning' (Is. 4:4, lit.). The Spirit of God is the expression and executive of all that is true about him. In the coming work of cleansing, he will act in full accord with all that divine justice requires and as the full expression of the fiery holiness of the divine nature.

THE DOUBLE CLIMAX

It is in this sense that the message of hope – frequently even if not quite always – comes with a sense of intrusion, for it is not the way in which the grain of things is running. Thus Delitzsch speaks somewhere of 'the fringe of hope', as if a long black garment unexpectedly ended in a bright hem. For hope 'works' within the logic of God, not within the cause and effect of history. The Day does not come 'with the ever-circling years' as the terminus of evolution but rather as a climax of catastrophe which divine grace makes to be also the climax of divine redemptive purposes. On the one hand, it is the day that the Lord holds in store against everything exalted in pride; but also, in the very ruins of 'the city of meaninglessness', pilgrims sing as they pick their way to Zion and the messianic banquet. The day will come when the towers of human strength will fall, but the day of the slaughter is also the day of unparalleled light. Indeed, we can see in the Sennacherib pericope, itself an interim 'day of the Lord', a paradigm of the Day itself, for only when hope is gone is hope realized, or, as Isaiah shows later in his book, 'the day of vengeance' is also 'the day of my redeemed', and those who have access to 'my holy mountain' live in the awareness of the doom which they merited but from which they were saved.[31] The time of awesome judgment is the day of sure mercy, because the Lord's just retribution works according to the logic of covenant faithfulness.[32] In Ezekiel's vivid pictorializing, the promise of the Lord's tabernacling presence among his people and the fulfilment of the promise in the great Temple act as brackets around Gog and Magog, the last battle and the ultimate gathering of the Lord's people.[33]

TRUTH GOING SOMEWHERE

Matching the sense of history moving to a climax, there is the Old Testament's evidence that truth is a cumulative thing. In this area also there is a contrast amounting to opposition between the idea of humans searching after God – the 'evolution of religion' – and the biblical insistence that the initiative is always in the other direction: God comes to chosen individuals with an unfolding of the truth about himself. With evolution, ideas are disposable: the primitive and inadequate have to be rejected, exposed as false by the onward march of progress in knowledge. But in the Bible truth is cumulative – a better word than 'progressive', for while what is first revealed needs the completion which only further revelation will bring, yet the first revelation is indispensable as an eternal word of God, an essential contribution to the whole fabric of revealed truth.

THE SACRIFICES AND THE SERVANT[34]

There are many areas of Old Testament truth where we see the cumulative principle at work, that is to say, where the earlier statement requires some later amplification and where the two together look still further forward to a perfecton and fullness yet to be realized. One such area is that of the levitical sacrifices.

At the risk of seeming over-simple, it is easy to imagine a scenario on the model of Exodus 12:26. A father has just returned from presenting his sin-offering as prescribed in Leviticus 4:27–31. His family say:

> 'Why did you go to the temple today?'
> 'I wanted to make a sin-offering because I needed the Lord's forgiveness.'
> 'And have you been forgiven?'
> 'Oh, yes!'
> 'How do you.know?'
> 'Because I saw the goat die in my place.'
> 'But how do you know that it was dying in your place?'
> 'Because I laid my hand on its head and appointed it to be my substitute.'
> 'Why was it your substitute?'
> 'Well, this is what the Lord told us to do. He has taught us that he wants us to offer a sacrifice for sin and that when we lay our hand on the animal's head it becomes our substitute.'
> 'But how do you really know that when the animal died your sins were forgiven?'
> 'Because the Lord promised!'

This simple piece of imagination is no more than a conversational 'spelling out' of Leviticus 17:11.[35] All true religion must come to rest on a veritable divine revelation: 'He told us to do it', and all the benefits of true religion come to the worshipper on the ground of believing the promises of God. We could even dare to extend the conversation one step further and listen to what the eldest son says and what the father replies:

> 'Really, what you are saying is this: you believe the promise of God. You could say that you are "justified by faith".'
> 'Well, it's not an expression I've ever used. But, yes, that's the truth of the matter. "Justification by faith." I must tell Paul that when I see him. I know he intends to write something along those lines.'

Because the true religion rests on revelation and personal benefit comes by faith, the Bible is one book, united in its opposition to salvation by meritorious works, clear on salvation by faith in the promises of God. Abraham entered into the definitive experience of it; Paul ultimately framed the definitive statement.

THE OLD TESTAMENT WINDOW

We need to think very carefully about the Old Testament at this point, for we view its ordinances with hindsight and we know that Hebrews 10:4 says truly that the blood of bulls cannot take away sins. Are we to think, therefore, that Old Testament religion was unreal, its ceremonies without substance, its sacrifices without benefit?

The Psalms offer us a wide picture-window into the Old Testament church.[36] In them, we are privileged to watch our brothers and sisters of the old covenant facing the questions and answers of life, gathering for worship and thinking about God. We meet people with a real and positive spirituality. They were neither busying themselves with unrealities nor walking in the shadows. On the contrary, their worship was full of exuberance; their sense of God profound and reverent; and their enjoyment of the spiritual benefits of religion such as often puts us to shame who live in the light of full revelation and within a finished work of salvation. Psalm 103:2–5 offers a list of spiritual enjoyments, the standard 'benefits' of God: forgiveness, healing (*cf.* Ps. 107:20), next-of-kin redemption,[37] crowning experiences of ever-unfailing love and heartfelt affection,[38] satisfaction and renewal. These are all spoken of as present realities; they are not wishful thinking or even wistful expectations. Just as the promises were real and faith was real so the promises were kept and faith was confirmed.

The point is that it would be easy, in the light of the New Testament, to consign the Old Testament wholly to the realm of expectation: as if to say, Psalm 103:2–5 looks forward to what will be the case when the Messiah comes. It would be even easier to say – and indeed, there is reason in saying it – that the saints of the Old Testament enjoyed their spiritual benefits as a special act of divine grace which brought to them, proleptically, what Christ would yet achieve for them. Very likely this is as near as we can come to 'explaining' the reality of the spiritual good enjoyed in the Old

Testament, for was not the Lamb slain from the foundation of the world, and did not his death, when it came, demonstrate the justice of God in regard to sins earlier left unpunished (Rev. 13:8; *cf.* 1 Pet. 1:19–20; Rom. 3:25)?[39] This may be all well and good, however, as far as we are concerned, but if we stand inside the Old Testament, alongside the worshippers in the old covenant church, there is nothing to suggest that the levitical sacrifices were considered either prophetic or proleptic. They were the present way of God with his people, his provision for their enrichment. They did indeed believe his promises, obey his precepts and inherit his blessings.

THE HUMAN HEART AND THE HEART OF GOD

There is no rite so carefully ordered and safeguarded that it cannot be debased into ritual. This deterioration had taken place by the time of the pre-exilic prophets and provoked their unqualified opposition. Indeed, so unqualified were their words that it was once more fashionable than it seems at present to interpret the key passages (see Is. 1:11–15; Je. 7:21–22; Ho. 6:6; Am. 5:25; Mi. 6:6–8) as a rejection of the divine authorizaton of the cultus and a demand for an exclusively ethico-spiritual religion.[40] That their denunciations brought them within reach of this misunderstanding is itself an indication of the crusading spirit that those prophets brought to the task. We have already noted the Mosaic balance with which Israel's religion was instituted: divine grace, working through (the Passover) sacrifice brought the people to God; this redemption excites and looks to a response of obedience to God's law; and the ongoing round of levitical sacrifices provides for lapses from obedience and deficiencies in the human enjoyment and expression of redeemed status.[41] It was for this balance and priority that the prophets were contending, while at the same time the strength of their contention imposed the greater weight of importance on the spiritual verities of religion in the human and divine hearts.

Two passages in the Psalms bring this essential spirituality very prominently to the fore.

Psalm 40:6–8

Psalm 40 best yields up its meaning if it is kept in touch with the two Davidic psalms which precede it.[42] In Psalms 38 and 39, David was patiently waiting upon and for God throughout a crisis of sin

(38:3; 39:8) and maliciousness (38:16; 39:8). The waiting is now over (40:1–3) and trust has been vindicated (40:4–5). What then should be his response to such deliverance? David's reaction is to commit himself totally to doing the will of God as the written protocol of his coronation (the scroll of the book, 40:7b) demanded of him: to be whole-hearted in private devotion (40:8) and in public commitment (40:9–10). He even goes so far as to say that he has had a personal revelation from God ('my ears you have pierced', verse 6) to the effect that, given such a devotion, sacrifices are no longer relevant or sought (verse 6). Did David, however, consider himself capable of a devotion so complete that there would be no need for sacrifice? His realistic self-awareness as expressed in verses 11–12 suggests that he did not, but surely he was reaching out from the inadequate towards the perfect, and surely Hebrews 10:5–9 is moving with exactitude within Psalm 40 when it sees these verses fulfilled in the One who needed no sin-offering or burnt-offering for himself, but who voluntarily yielded himself to be the sin-offering and burnt-offering we needed.

Psalm 51:16–17

It is unfortunately commonplace to scout the psalm titles as merely late editorial irrelevances. The Hebrew Bible as we have inherited it does not, however, see them thus, but makes them an integral part of its text. Indeed, there is precious little ground for considering them as late insertions and, contrary to widely held opinion, much light is cast on the meaning of the psalms by considering them within the setting the title proposes. This is nowhere truer than in Psalm 51. It fits snugly into the context of David and Bathsheba and profits from the interpretative clues afforded by that setting. But if anyone were disposed to be contentious, it still remains true that the psalm is wrestling with the relationship between the spiritual reality of repentance and the limitations of the system of sacrifices that God has appointed. At the very least, the reference to David and Bathsheba in the title must be allowed to indicate that an editor thought that the psalm was raising the problem of sins which lay beyond the reach of the authorized sacrifices. What is the hope, for example, of the adulterer and the murderer for whom the levitical code holds nothing? Hope in plenty, replies the psalm!

This is the strikingly wonderful thing about Psalm 51. It

addresses 'no-hope' sins and reveals a way through to forgiveness. In a word, Psalm 51:1–4[43] is one of the Old Testament's profoundest statements about sin and its remedy (as discussed earlier in chapter 6, see pp. 130–134).

Though Psalm 51 looks to repentance as wholly and solely efficacious in dealing with sin, it should not, however, be read as denying the necessity of the sacrificial cult of Leviticus. Verse 16 is certainly not to be understood as a wholesale dismissal of the divine levitical ordinances but, like so much in the Psalms, it must be contextualized if it is to be understood correctly. The psalm is concerned with sins not covered by the existing ordinances, and it is in connection with these sins that no sacrifice acceptable to or desired by God has been revealed. Nevertheless, David uses the striking plea 'Purge [lit., "de-sin"!] me with hyssop' (51:7). In Exodus 12:22, hyssop is the instrument of the application of the blood of the Passover lamb, and throughout its biblical usage[44] it retains the symbolism of 'applied efficacy'. The plea, therefore, in Psalm 51:7, spelled out in the light of this symbolic quality of 'hyssop', would run like this: '*I* know of no sacrifice that can be applied to my need but *you* do.' In other words, there is in God the availability of a sacrificial provision beyond what is specified in Leviticus, and it is available to the sinner on the bare ground of repentance.

The Servant (Isaiah 52:13 – 53:12)

It fell to Isaiah to bring the principle of sacrifice to its Old Testament culmination by seeing clearly what a true substitution for sinners must involve.[45] The heart of our sinfulness lies in the will, which bows to temptation and consents to the sinful thought, word or deed. Until the will says 'Yes', no sin is committed. Yet this is the very thing that can never find its *alter ego* in an animal sacrifice. The beast is the unwitting victim, neither knowing what is afoot nor consenting to the transaction. It feels the touch of the sinner's hand but neither knows its significance nor voluntarily accepts its consequences. This, however, is the central thrust of Isaiah 53:7–9. 'Like a lamb . . . like a sheep' the Servant may very well be, but only because he consented that it should be so: 'He was maltreated but, for his part, allowed himself to be humiliated[46] and did not open his mouth . . .' (53:7, lit.), neither entering any plea or voicing any complaint. At last the age-long principle of substitution had reached its complete expression in a consenting sacrifice.

The principle of substitution is as old as Genesis 22:13, and from that time onwards was 'going somewhere'. Its truth accumulated until it climaxed in Isaiah 53, and from then onwards it awaited the sinless Person who alone could identify with sinners, meet the requirements of the holy God, and consent to die for others. As Isaiah looks forward, so Hebrews 10 looks back.

THE 'SEED' OF ABRAHAM AND THE WAY OF FAITH

Another whole stream of 'truth going somewhere' originates with Abraham and the promise that in his descendants ('seed') the whole world would come into blessing.

The implication of the Genesis narrative was perfectly expressed by Paul[47] when he explained Genesis 21:12 by saying:

> Not all who are descended from Israel are Israel. Nor are all Abraham's children also Abraham's seed ... it is not the physical children who are God's children, but it is the children of the promise who are regarded as Abraham's seed.
>
> (Rom. 9:6–8, lit.)

The Hagar-Ishmael pericope of Genesis 16 comes as a natural expression of impatience and a lapse from the position of expectant faith on the part of Sarai and Abram. That they acted within the legal norms of their day does not justify their sad, tragedy-bound attempt to help God keep his promises. For his part, Abraham would have loved it if the Lord would adjust his plans to make Ishmael the promise-bearer, but with both gentleness and reassurance the Lord set his request aside: 'To the contrary! Your wife Sarah is going to bear you a son ... but, regarding Ishmael, I have heard you. Behold, I will bless him ...' (Gn. 17:19–20, lit.).

Monergism

In this way, a principle of selection is introduced and subsequently followed through: the 'not Ishmael but Isaac' is replicated in 'not Esau but Jacob', notwithstanding that in each case it was the firstborn who was set aside. Likewise, though more unobtrusively, the narrative introduces 'not Reuben but Judah',[48] and, as far as the messianic line is concerned, goes on to 'not Jesse's elder sons but David'. In a word, the Lord will do his work his way. It is for him to say along what lines his promises will be kept, for 'it is not of him who wills or him who runs but of God who shews mercy' (Rom. 9:16, lit.).

Monergism and divine selection are at work. In the (mere) energy of the flesh Abraham produces a son, but the promise cannot be carried forward by the power of man; it has to be by the power of God. Neither can its course be traced by human logic or man-made custom: the Lord sovereignly imposes his principles of selection, over-ruling rights of primogeniture and bringing forward his own chosen candidates to carry the line of promise.

The genealogy of faith

It was a specific historical situation which compelled Isaiah to articulate the doctrine of 'the people within the people', the true within the (merely) professing. In the face of the Assyrian threat, the northern powers of Aram and Israel formed themselves into a sort of West Palestinian Treaty Organization and put pressure on Judah, under Ahaz, to join them. Unwilling to do this, Ahaz was faced with the question of achieving security for his tiny kingdom in a day of expansionist super-powers. He and his political advisers developed one doctrine of security (which, in fact, he adopted), the astute move of a link with the stronger of the competing giants. Isaiah had another political theory: there is no power mightier than the Lord. The soundest possible policy is to link with him.

In Isaiah 7:9 he enunciated this as the way of faith, and saw it as the *articulus stantis aut cadentis ecclesiae* – the truth on which the church stands or falls.[49] His words were addressed to Ahaz, but in context they embraced the whole dynasty of David and the people of Judah: 'If you will not trust you will not last' (Is. 7:9, lit.).[50] This brings to a point of definition the doctrine of the remnant. In his confrontation with Ahaz, Isaiah was instructed to be accompanied by his son, Shear-jashub, 'a remnant shall return' (7:3). No longer (if ever) does this mean that there will always be survivors to carry on the nation, but that there is a distinction between the secularized, politicized professing people of God, indistinguishable in principle and action from the nations of the earth, and, within them, those who turn to the Lord in repentance and faith, who look to his word and obey it. All this is close-packed into Isaiah 8:9–22, a passage of very diverse literary components, with a skilful editorial unity whereby its impact is clear and explicitly directed:

> A^1 International collapse (8:9)
>> B^1 Fruitless consultation (8:10)
>>> C^1 Isaiah set apart by the word of the Lord (8:11)
>>>> D^1 The fear of the ungodly (8:12)
>>>>> E^1 The fear of the godly (8:13)
>>>>> E^2 The privilege of the godly (8:14a)
>>>> D^2 The fate of the ungodly (8:14b, 15)
>>> C^2 Isaiah and his group separated to the Lord's word and patient faith (8:16–18)
>> B^2 Fruitless consultation (8:19–20)
> A^2 National collapse (8:21–22)

By its very shape the passage declares its meaning: there is a people within the people ($E^{1, 2}$ bracketed by $D^{1, 2}$), marked out by their reverence for the holy Lord (E^1) and his holy presence among them (E^2), and by hearing and treasuring his word ($C^{1, 2}$). Amid international turmoil they are secure (A^1, B^1) and when their own nation collapses, while not themselves immune from suffering, they hold on to what God has spoken (A^2, B^2).[51] The movement of Isaiah's thought in this passage consists of a progressive narrowing of focus. He starts by differentiating one people from the mass of the nations: the nations may gather their collective strength (8:9) and lay their best plans (verse 10), but they cannot succeed 'because God is with us'. But with whom? The focus narrows again: there is a people with a people. First, Isaiah personally testifies that he came under a particular divine pressure ('strong hand', verse 11) to distance himself from the people around him. He is, however, part of a separated group (verse 12, 'you'-plural) whose lives are, first of all, marked by peace amid the current turmoil of suspicion and fear (verse 12). Whatever 'conspiracy' may mean, the injunction separates off Isaiah's group from their angst-ridden contemporaries. Secondly, their religion is spiritual: they enjoy a personal relationship of reverent lowliness before the holy God and a direct access to him as being himself the 'sanctuary' in which he lives among them.

It is as if they were told: the professing mass of people may flock to the visible temple but the Lord is among you as an invisible temple to which you may resort in worship: this is the real 'God is with us' affirmed in verse 10. Thirdly, Isaiah and his group centre their lives as 'disciples' ('those under instruction') on the 'testimony' (what God bears witness to) and 'law' ('teaching') of the Lord. They are a fellowship of the Word – in contrast to the mass of the nation who have chosen a different word to follow (verses 19–20); and in the fourth place, they are called, with the prophet, to the patience of faith (verses 17–18). Others curse their God (verse 21), but the people within the people wait and trust. With the expression 'my disciples' (verse 16), the Lord lovingly and graciously claims the distinct, spiritual, word-centred and believing group as his very own.

In this connection, Isaiah 29:18–24 is worth more than the glance which is all it can now receive. The key thoughts of Isaiah 8 reappear in people hearing God's word (29:18), rejoicing in the Holy One (verse 19) and 'sanctifying' him with awe (verse 23). They belong to a people purged of every oppressive, hostile and malignant element (verses 20–21) and (by implication of verse 22) they are the people of Abraham. The Lord's providential care and self-identification with Abraham ('redeemed') ultimately issues in a spiritual, word-centred people, rejoicing and reverent before the Holy One of Israel.

The straight line

This Old Testament thinking is precisely what Paul took seriously in his description of the church of our Lord Jesus Christ as the children of Abraham (Rom. 4:13–18) and Gal. 3:26–29), 'the Israel of God' (Gal. 6:16) and 'the circumcision' (Phil. 3:3). The straight line out of the Old Testament runs into the New Testament. This is tragically confused when people speak or write of the New Testament church as the 'new Israel'. There is no such entity. There is only one 'Israel', and from the start it was the people within the people, the line within the line, the believing community within the professing body, the Israel within Israel – the 'Israel of God'.

REALITY AND FULL REALITY

Through these two examples of 'truth going somewhere' – the sacrifices and the seed of Abraham – we see what is true throughout the Old Testament: a true cumulative progression. There is no abandonment of the early in favour of the late, the primitive in favour of the developed, but a gathering and maturing body of truth which, by the end of the Old Testament, is also truth tensed up for its brilliant denouement. But neither do we find in the Old Testament an abandonment of the literal for the figurative. This is especially plain in the theme of the sacrifices and the Servant. In the delineation of the Servant, Isaiah is not consigning the sacrifices to the realm of 'figures of the true'. Rather, we suddenly see that this is *really* what they meant all the time. The true has become the really true, and the real has become the truly real. And the Messiah, when he comes, is the 'end', *telos*, the aim and consummation of the law, bringing righteousness to everyone who believes (Rom. 10:4).

THE TONIC OF HOPE

In conclusion, it is worthwhile to try to offer some sort of summary overview of prophetic expectation. In one sense, the expectation which began with God's promise to Abraham narrowed into messianic thinking, like a picture slowly coming into focus and finding its reality in a coming Person. But the model of a spring giving rise to a river is also appropriate. Abraham found himself to be the Creator's answer to the needs of the whole Creation: in him the blessedness – lost at the Fall, in the Flood and the scattering – would some day be restored to all the families of the earth and the created order would itself be transformed into new heavens and a new earth. Alongside their messianic view the prophets developed expectations on the grand scale. The following is just one attempt at a synthesis, notwithstanding the corners that must be cut and that richness that is inevitably sacrificed.

ABRAHAM AND THE WORLD

The left-hand line of the diagram takes up the world-wide emphasis in the Abrahamic promise and follows it through to the new creation. But the line runs through into judgment and darkness as well as into the light of the curse removed.

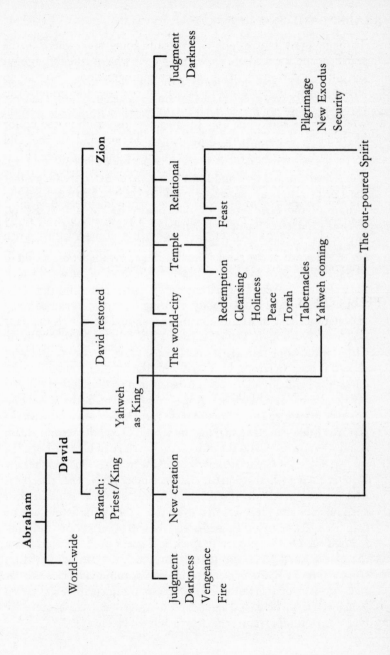

Jeremiah is a case in point, as he depicts the disaster of a whole world under judgment and yet bracketed with hope. Using the nations of his day as the building-blocks of vision (Je. 45 – 51),[52] his panorama begins with Egypt, the first would-be destroyer of the Lord's people, and ends with Babylon, the current destroyer. Between these two poles his arrangement is geographical: Philistia, Moab, Ammon and Edom stand for the Gentile nations near at hand; Damascus and Kedar reach out into the middle distance; and Elam represents the uttermost parts of the earth. In most cases the reasons for divine anger are analysed, in some cases a hope of Gentile restoration is held out, and time and again Jeremiah reverts to the theme that the Lord's action in the whole world is designed to safguard the welfare of the Lord's people. But, before he starts with Egypt, Jeremiah addresses Baruch, the scribe of the word of the Lord; and after he has finished with Babylon, he addresses Seriah, the messenger of the word of the Lord. Visually, therefore, the whole world in its day of judgment and hope is bracketed around by the word which the Lord has spoken. This is the governing principle of history.

Amos shows the impossibility of being over-neat in categorizing expectations, and this is, of course, as it should be, for all that falls under the heading of 'David' is itself a line flowing from Abraham. The Davidic hope is international (Am. 9:12; *cf.* Is. 9:1–7), and why should it not, therefore, be linked with the creational theme of the curse lifted and all the 'forces' of the created order released to pour out their immeasurable riches (Am. 9:13)? *Isaiah* made the same point when he juxtaposed the 'shoot of Jesse', *i.e.* David redivivus, with the restored Eden – in effect making the second David the second Adam – and went on to extend the thought to the stage of Gentile hope (Is. 11:1–5, 6–9, 10–16). His major vision of the new heavens and the new earth is likewise Zion-centred, and once more defies neat classification as between Abraham and David. It begins with a divine work of such novelty and greatness that everything that went before will be forgotten (Is. 65:17). Immediately, however, attention becomes focused on what is apparently the key element in the new creation, the new-created Jerusalem (65:18), in which joy is undimmed by sorrow (verse 19), life unblighted by lack of fulfilment (verse 20) or lack of security (verses 21–22) or disappointment of expectation (verse 23), and where God and people live together in close mutuality (verse 24) within a transformed environment (verse 25).

NARNIA LIKE WE NEVER SAW IT BEFORE

When C. S. Lewis finally allowed his privileged children to die (as they used to say in the shadowlands) and they found themselves at last in Aslan's Land,[53] why it was just Narnia on a hitherto unrealized scale of spaciousness and beauty! That is as far as the Bible too takes us into what both Old and New Testaments call 'the new creation' or the 'new heavens and the new earth'. Just as the prophets used the nations around them as the 'furniture' of vision, so also they used the cosmos around them as the motif of perfection. For there is no way in which we can think ourselves out of the framework concepts of space and time. The substantial point within all this motif-making, however, is this: that all that was ruined by sin will be re-created by redemption; not only us sinners but also our environment. If, as must surely be the case, the reality when we arrive 'there' will transcend all that we ever could imagine or foresee, it is still true that the only way we can make any approximation is through the envisaged perfection of what we know and love. Redemption rescues, transforms and irradiates all. Hence, God's future is full of light such as this world cannot offer (Is. 30:25–26; 60:1; Zc. 14:6; Mal. 4:2), and full of peace – full-orbed well-being in relation to God, society and self (Is. 2:2–4; 9:6 with Mi. 5:5; Mi. 4:1–5)[54] – such as was never known before.

DAVID AND ZION

The theme of David and his royal city is one of the leading Old Testament enigmas: that is to say, there are loose ends which only the New Testament will tie up. One main enigma is clear in the diagram on page 183: Who is the king? For on the one hand, 'David' is coming back[55] to reign, the 'golden boy' being a shadow cast before him by the truly golden king of the future. But, on the other hand, it is the Lord who will reign in Zion and to whom the kingdom will belong.[56] The Old Testament did not solve its enigma, even though Jeremiah pointed the way when he envisaged a king whose family-tree reached back to David but who would be 'The Lord our righteousness' (Je. 23:5–6).[57]

In the prophetic idealization of Zion there is a whole cluster of eschatological delights, including two which link the particularity of the city of David with the universality of the promise to Abraham. Of these the first is 'the world-city'.

The world-city

We owe to *Isaiah* today's commonplace of 'the global village'. Nowadays – as compared even with the end of the last century or the early years of this – little or nothing can happen in any part of the world without every other part being implicated. The world is one place: as can be said of many actual villages, when one catches cold, all cough. Isaiah's thought, however, went somewhat seriously beyond this pragmatic level. Possibly stemming from Genesis 4:17, 11:1–9, he saw the city as fallen man's chief attempt to make himself secure – to be his own salvation – in an environment no longer on his side,[58] and he used the motif of the city for the human attempt to organize the whole world without reference to God: the final throw of humankind to be its own saviour. The Isaianic eschatology of chapters 24–27, therefore, is in effect a 'tale of two cities': on the one hand, the merely human 'city without meaning' (see Is. 24:10),[59] and, on the other hand, the 'strong city' with salvation for its walls, righteousness for its animating principle, and faith and peace as the marks of its citizens (Is. 26:1–4).[60] This divine 'world-city' is both the culmination of Zion-expectations and also one significant way of understanding the new earth, the perfect society, in perfect security, the 'city which has foundations', the city 'whose builder and maker is God', the 'new Jerusalem' which does not owe its origin to earth or evolution but 'comes down out of heaven, from God' (Heb. 11:10; Rev. 21:10).

The new Temple: the Lord and his people

Some prophets very beautifully see the final state as a blissful relationship between the Lord and his people. *Hosea* expresses with great feeling how Israel will seek forgiveness, renounce all reliance on human deliverance and on man-made gods, and turn to the God in whom 'the orphan finds compassion'. He foretells how the Lord himself will heal their backsliding, love with generosity, and come like refreshing, life-giving dew to his people (Ho. 14:1–7). *Zephaniah*, too, makes his book leap to a climactic outburst of emotion as he looks forward to Zion on cloud nine with heartfelt joy in the Lord and the Lord dwelling among his people, lost for words in his silent adoration of them and singing their praises – just like a true Lover with his beloved (Zp. 3:14–17). *Isaiah*, as usual, has his own perfect gloss to put on this thought: Zion will be marked by a specially created cloudy-fiery pillar, the ancient symbol proclaiming 'God is here among you'. But now he is more than merely 'among', for the cloud forms itself into a marriage canopy, under which the divine bridegroom is at last united with his bride, and to which (unlike the Tabernacle of old) the Lord's people can fly for shelter (Is. 4:5–6). As Revelation puts it: 'He who sits on the throne will spread his tent over them . . . and God will wipe away every tear from their eyes' (Rev. 7:15, 17).

Under this heading of 'relational eschatology' – the eternal state seen as relationship – we must include the great messianic banquet for all nations with its consummation of long-awaited salvation (Is. 25:6–10a; *cf.* 55:1–2), and, of course, that second major link between David's Zion and Abraham's world: the Spirit poured out from on high, on the one hand the Agent in transforming people (Joel 2:28), and on the other hand, the Transformer of the world and of society (Is. 32:15–20).

THE LORD WILL COME TO HIS TEMPLE

The institutions of Israel were its experience of realized eschatology, and we have seen above how land, monarchy, covenant and marriage, for example, were all laid under contribution to express as best they could the glory that is yet to be. Central among these institutions was 'the Lord's house'. To this extent, the word 'temple' is a bad friend for, while it adds some emotive dignity, it obscures the fact that the 'house' was intended to provide the Lord with an 'address' on earth, a home among his people.

When the eschatological perfection comes, the Lord will indeed indwell his people, the shadow will become the substance. The Tent that Moses pitched and the House that Solomon built were places of cultic sacrifice, for only by atonement could sinners live in the presence of the Holy God; they were places too of the continual burnt-offering, morning and evening, for only thus could an erring people – however aspiring to true obedience – offer a perfect obedience to God. When the perfect comes, there will be perfect cleansing (Is. 4:4; Mi. 7:18–20), holy people (Is. 4:3; Joel 3<4>:17; Ob. 17; Zc. 14:20, Mal. 3:2), a perfect teaching of the Lord's Law from the mountain of his house (Is. 2:3), and a world-wide centre for pilgrimage, far outshining the glories of the first Exodus (Je.

23:7–8; 16:14–15), as the nations make their way to the worship of the King (Zc. 14:9).

'I wished myself among them,' said John Bunyan.[61] And well he might, for, far beyond any other glory, the Lord will have come to his temple (Mal. 3:1), the kingdom will be his (Ob. 21), and the city will be called 'Yahweh is There' (Ezk. 48:35, lit.).

◇ AVENUES INTO THE NEW TESTAMENT

The Scriptures are a beautifully rounded whole. The Garden in which human history opened and became permanently scarred (Gn. 2 – 3) is balanced by the eternal garden-reality of Revelation 22:1–5 with its river, its tree of life and its unmarred reign of the servants of the Lord. The work of creation (Gn. 1) is transcended in the work of new creation (Rev. 21:1–8). The divisiveness of sin at Babel (Gn. 11:1–9), reversed in principle in Acts 2, is gone for ever as nations walk harmoniously, securely, fearlessly, in the city that needs neither sun nor lamp (Rev. 21:23–27). The Exodus gathering of the Lord's people (Ex. 1 – 12) is exceeded by the world-wide exodus and gathering out of Revelation 7:9–17, and the tiny beginning of the 'seed of Abraham' (Gn. 21:2), flowing in the channels mapped out in Romans 4 and Galatians 3, at the last matches and even outruns the promises with which it all began (Gn. 15:5) – an innumerable, world-wide company of the redeemed.

Neither the Old Testament nor the New spells out the concept of new heavens and new earth (Is. 65:17–25; Rev. 21:1 – 22:7). Two truths suggest the parameters for our thinking. First, God's purpose is to 'sum up' (Eph. 1:10) and reconcile to himself (Col. 1:16–20) all things in heaven and earth in Christ. Just as sin infected the created orders (Gn. 3), so redemption rescues, purges and recreates them. The heavens and earth are not dispensable entities but part of the creative and redemptive purposes of God. Secondly, in our case, the wholly redeemed person bears the same relation to our present condition as a flower to its seed (1 Cor. 15:35–38, 42–44) and, by analogy, there will be the same observable continuity and unimaginable transformation of the created orders of heaven and earth, a perfect environment for perfected saints and for the dwelling-place of God the Holy One himself (Rev. 21:2–3).

Notes

INTRODUCTION

1. J. Buchan, *Witch Wood* (Nelson, 1948), pp. 21–22.
2. *Ibid.*, p. 407.
3. *Ibid.*, pp. 418–421.
4. H. Walpole, *Vanessa* (Macmillan, 1932), p. 114.
5. W. C. Kaiser, *Towards an Old Testament Theology* (Zondervan, 1991), p. 5.
6. W. Eichrodt, *Theology of the Old Testament*, 2 vols. (SCM, 1961, 1967). First German edition, 1933.
7. G. von Rad, *Old Testament Theology*, 2 vols. (Oliver & Boyd, 1962, 1965). First German editions 1957, 1960.
8. Kaiser, *op. cit.*, p. 5.
9. B. S. Childs, *Introduction to the Old Testament as Scripture* (SCM, 1979), explored the possibility that the Old Testament as it has been received, the canon, makes sense and bears its own distinct testimony. Undoubtedly, Childs allowed the literary and source criticism which was his own particular inheritance to intrude too vigorously between himself and the canonical form of the text and, seminal though his work is, he did not allow 'canonical criticism' to bear its full fruit. In many ways, when J. Muilenberg coined the expression 'rhetorical criticism' (in 'Form Criticism and Beyond', *JBL* 88.1, 1969) he launched a movement which is still gathering force. His insistence that the purpose of analysis is not fragmentation but synthesis – an appreciation, through literary analysis, of the wholeness that a book or pericope truly possesses – has pointed others in a most fruitful direction. *Cf.* R. Alter, *The Art of Biblical Narrative* (NY Basic Books, 1981); D. J. A. Clines, David Gunn and A. J. Hauser, *Art and Meaning: Rhetoric in Biblical Literature* (JSOT Press, 1982). In *The Unity of The Twelve* (JSOT Press, 1990), P. R. House remarks that 'there is room for

189

explorations of the anatomy of whole books and groups of books' (p. 12). Consult also J. Sailhamer, *An Introduction to Old Testament Theology* (Zondervan, 1995).

10. J. L. Mays, *Amos* (SCM, 1969) and *Micah* (SCM, 1976); C. Westermann, *Isaiah 40–66* (SCM, 1969) and many others offer examples of rich commentaries which none the less are wholly anthological in their approach to the prophetic texts. Contrast the analytic-synthetic approach in J. A. Motyer, *The Message of Amos*, BST (IVP, 1974); 'Amos', in *NBC*; *The Prophecy of Isaiah* (IVP, 1993); 'Zephaniah' and 'Haggai', in T. McComiskey (ed.), *The Minor Prophets*, vol. 3 (Baker, 1995).

11. Kaiser, *op. cit.*, p. 8.

12. T. Bradshaw, *The Olive Branch* (Paternoster, 1992), pp. 283–284, 289; also pp. 104, 151, 233, 292–295. Along with pp. 154–158, see J. Goldingay, *Approaches to Old Testament Interpretation* (IVP, 1981); *idem, Theological Diversity and the Authority of the Old Testament* (Eerdmans, 1987), and the review of this book by J. A. Motyer, *Churchman*, 103.1, 1989, pp. 78–80. See also, C. J. H. Wright, *Walking in the Ways of the Lord* (Apollos, 1995), pp. 14–26; V. Philips Long, *The Art of Biblical History* (Apollos, 1994), p. 37.

13. H. L. Ellison, *The Centrality of the Messianic Idea for the Old Testament* (Tyndale, 1953); C. J. H. Wright, *Knowing Jesus through the Old Testament* (Marshall Pickering, 1992).

1. THE MASTER THEME OF THE BIBLE

1. D. L. Baker, *Two Testaments, One Bible* (Apollos, 1990); M. Strom, *The Days are Coming: Exploring Biblical Patterns* (Hodder & Stoughton, 1989); G. Vos, *Biblical Theology: Old and New Testaments* (Eerdmans, 1963).

2. J. A. Motyer, 'Bible Study and the Unity of the Bible', in J. Job (ed.), *Studying God's Word* (IVP, 1972), pp. 11–23; J. Barr, *Old and New in Interpretation* (SCM, 1966); E. G. Kraeling, *The Old Testament since the Reformation* (Lutterworth, 1955), esp. chs. 13, 15 and 17; G. Hasel, *Old Testament Theology: Basic Issues in the Current Debate* (Eerdmans, 1975); C. Westermann (ed.), *Essays on Old Testament Interpretation* (SCM, 1963); J. Bright, *The Kingdom of God* (Abingdon, 1953), esp. chs. 7 and 8.

3. J. Bright, *The Authority of the Old Testament* (SCM, 1967). See also

A. J. B. Higgins, *The Christian Significance of the Old Testament* (Independent Press, 1949); A. G. Herbert, *The Authority of the Old Testament* (Faber, 1947); F. F. Bruce, *This is That* (Paternoster, 1968).

4. W. S. Churchill, from *Painting as a Pastime*, quoted by Denis Healey in *The Time of My Life* (Penguin, 1990), p. 147.

5. E. J. Bicknell, *A Theological Introduction to the Thirty-nine Articles of the Church of England* (Longmans, 1944), p. 127.

6. See J. W. Wenham, *Christ and the Bible* (IVP, 1972); J. I. Packer, *God has Spoken* (Hodder & Stoughton, 1979); C. H. Pinnock, 'The Inspiration of Scripture and the Authority of Jesus', in J. W. Montgomery (ed.), *God's Inerrant Word* (Bethany, 1974); M. A. Noll, *Between Faith and Criticism* (Apollos, 1991), s.v. 'Jesus, stance towards Old Testament'.

2. CHRIST AS FULFILMENT

1. *E.g.* C. A. Simpson, *The Composition of the Book of Judges* (Oxford, 1957).

2. See W. H. Schmidt, *Introduction to the Old Testament* (SCM, 1984), pp. 136ff.

3. B. G. Webb, *The Book of Judges: An Integrated Reading* (JSOT Press, 1987); L. R. Klein, *The Triumph of Irony in the Book of Judges* (Almond, 1988); R. D. Davis, *Such a Great Salvation* (Baker, 1990); D. Jackman, *Judges, Ruth* (Word, 1991); M. J. Wilcock, *The Message of Judges*, BST (IVP, 1992).

4. Webb, *op. cit.*, pp. 13, 29.

5. J. P. U. Lilley, 'A Literary Appreciation of the Book of Judges', *TynB* 18, 1967, pp. 94ff.

6. On this evidence, Judges must be dated very early in the monarchy. It could even be pre-monarchic, but its tone of complete optimism in what a king would mean for his people might just have survived David and Solomon but could never have survived Rehoboam! See further W. S. LaSor, D. A. Hubbard and F. W. Bush, *Old Testament Survey* (Eerdmans, 1982), p. 221.

7. A two-source hypothesis has long been favoured: an account favourable to monarchy (1 Sa. 9:1–10, 16, 27b; 11:1–15) has usually been held to be earlier and historically more reliable; a hostile account (8; 10:17–27a; 12) is supposed to be later and historically dubious. There are supposedly many other doublets, indicating some complexity of

original sources but, like the two-source hypothesis these, on examination, fail to support the weight imposed on them. For example, it is alleged that there are two accounts of David's introduction to Saul, but to make 16:14–23 and 17:55–58 diverse accounts of the same event fails to note that the point at issue in the second is not 'Who is this young man whom I have never met before?' (which the theory would require) but 'What is his father's name?' By this time word would have reached Saul of Samuel's secret trip to Bethlehem and that he had, so it was rumoured, anointed one of Jesse's sons. No wonder Saul was interested! J. G. Baldwin, *1 and 2 Samuel*, TOTC (IVP, 1988), ad loc.; V. Philips Long, *The Art of Biblical Narrative* (Apollos, 1994), pp. 216ff.

8. H. P. Smith, *Samuel*, ICC (T. & T. Clark, 1912).

9. W. McKane, *Samuel* (SCM, 1963).

10. J. Mauchline, *1 and 2 Samuel*, NCB (Oliphants, 1972).

11. S. Mowinckel, *He that Cometh* (Blackwell, 1959) is a notable example of the insistence of making hope a late arrival on the Old Testament scene. The very occurrence of the words 'in that day' were considered to be editorial additions and a sure proof of lateness. See, to the contrary, P. R. House, *Zephaniah: A Prophetic Drama* (JSOT Press, 1988), on Zephaniah 1:8: 'The phrase . . . "and it shall be on the day . . ." is considered an addition. BHS makes a similar judgment in 1:10. Apparently the editors believe most formulaic sayings of this nature are additions. No textual or contextual evidence supports this claim and it must be rejected' (p. 127).

12. The rejection of Saul is appealed to as another doublet in the narrative of the institution of monarchy, but in fact 1 Samuel 13:13–14 is a rejection of the possibility of a Saulide Dynasty and 15:23 a rejection of Saul in his personal kingship.

13. See J. A. Motyer, 'Psalms', in *NBC*, pp. 550–551.

14. For this messianic idea, see, for example, A. Bentzen, *King and Messiah* (Blackwell, 1970); H. Ringgren, *The Messiah in the Old Testament* (SCM, 1956).

15. P. and E. Achtemeier, *The Old Testament Roots of our Faith* (SPCK, 1964), p. 101.

16. J. A. Motyer, 'Messiah (OT)', in *IBD*, vol. 2, p. 989.

17. 2 Sam. 7:12 (NIV 'offspring'); *cf.* 22:51; Ps. 18:50<51> (NIV 'descendants'); Ps. 89:4, 29, 36 <5, 30, 37> (NIV 'line'). It is one thing for the editors of NIV to reject a concordant principle in translation but quite another to take a crucially important word like 'seed' and bury it under

a diversity of renderings, usually without any footnote to alert the reader.

18. Gn. 12:7; 13:15–16; 15:3, 5, 13, 18; 17:7–10, 12, 19; 21:12; 22:17–18; 24:60; 26:3–4, 24; 28:14; 32:12; 35:12; 46:6–7; 48:4, 11, 19. NIV renderings swing between 'offspring' and 'descendants' with an occasional footnote. Gn. 26:4 is notable for three different renderings of the single Hebrew word 'seed': 'descendants . . . them . . . offspring'!

19. 2 Sa. 7:12; Gn. 15:4 (of Isaac). *Cf.* of Absalom (2 Sa. 16:11), does David use the expression here almost as a technical description for the covenant heir?; of Solomon (2 Ch. 6:9); of Jacob's family, Gn. 35:11 and 46:26 use a slightly different expression, as does Ex. 1:5. *Cf.* 2 Ch. 32:21; Is. 48:19 for completeness.

20. 2 Sa. 7:9, *wᵉʾāsîtî lᵉkā šēm gādôl kᵉšēm haggᵉdôlîm*; Gn. 12:2, *waʾᵃgaddᵉlâ šᵉmekā*. There are similar references to Yahweh's Name, 2 Sa. 7:26 and 1 Ch. 17:21, but otherwise the expression of 'making the name great' is not found.

21. See J. A. Motyer, *The Prophecy of Isaiah* (IVP, 1993), pp. 453–454; 'Psalms', in *NBC*, pp. 543–545.

22. The word is *ḥesed*, a key covenant word referring to 'pledged love', love as an act of will and therefore free of the sort of fluctuations that beset the emotions. It is the 'ever-unchangeable' love of the Lord, though used also of the responsive love that he has a right to expect.

23. Motyer, *Isaiah*, pp. 453–455.

24. G. von Rad, *Genesis* (SCM, 1961), p. 90.

25. *E.g.* N. P. Williams, *Ideas of the Fall and Original Sin* (1927); see further pp. 113–115 below.

26. G. J. Wenham, *Genesis*, vol. 1 (Word, 1987), p. 80.

27. H. Blocher, *In the Beginning* (IVP, 1984), p. 180.

28. *Cf.* W. Vischer, *The Witness of the Old Testament to Christ* (Lutterworth, 1949): 'The Protevangelium . . . proclaims the victory of the race born of the woman' (p. 225).

29. 'Seed' (*zeraʿ*) is used of progeny of indeterminate number (Gn. 19:32; *etc.*); of descendants in the plural (Gn. 9:9; *etc.*); of animal kind (Gn. 7:3); of human semen (Lv. 15:16; *etc.*); of conception (Nu. 5:28); of belonging to a family (1 Ki. 11:14; *etc.*); also to express 'a generation' (Ps. 22:30<31>); or the 'holy seed' (Is. 6:13); or Israel as vine (Je. 2:21).

30. Motyer, *Isaiah*, pp. 121–124.

31. *Ibid.*, pp. 445–446.

32. *Ibid.*, pp. 436–441, 492–493.

33. NIV translates 'seed' in Is. 53:10 as 'offspring', and in 59:21 as 'children . . . descendants').

34. *Cf.* Am. 9:11–15; Mi. 5:1–5a; Hg. 2:20–23; Zc. 3:8; 6:12.

35. J. A. Motyer, *The Revelation of the Divine Name* (Tyndale, 1959), 27–28.

36. A. R. Johnson, *Sacral Kingship in Ancient Israel* (University of Wales Press, 1955), pp. 31–53.

37. The NEB translated Is. 9:6 as 'in battle God-like' but *the identical words* in 10:21 as 'God their champion'. Why is there this hesitancy in recognizing that the OT foresaw a divine Messiah? This was precisely the point that the Lord Jesus sought to make the Pharisees face in Mk. 12:35–37.

38. Motyer, *Isaiah*, pp. 170, 367.

3. CHRIST AS CLIMAX

1. See G. A. F. Knight, *Law and Grace* (SCM, 1962); T. McComiskey, *The Covenants of Promise* (IVP, 1985); W. J. Dumbrell, *Covenant and Creation* (Paternoster, 1984); D. J. McCarthy, *Old Testament Covenant* (Blackwell, 1972); D. R. Hillers, *Covenant: The History of a Biblical Idea* (Johns Hopkins, 1969); J. G. McConville, *Grace in the End: A Study in Deuteronomic Theology* (Paternoster, 1993); *idem*, *Law and Theology* (JSOT Press, 1984).

2. G. J. Wenham, 'History and the Old Testament', in C. Brown (ed.), *History, Criticism and Faith* (IVP, 1976), not least pp. 13–73; J. Bright, *Early Israel in Recent History Writing* (SCM, 1956).

3. H. G. Guthrie, *God and History in the Old Testament* (SPCK, 1961); C. R. North, *The Old Testament Interpretation of History* (Epworth, 1946); *cf.* the significance of Is. 36 – 37 in the schema of Is. 12 – 37, J. A. Motyer, *The Prophecy of Isaiah* (IVP, 1993), pp. 227, 276.

4. From Francis Harold Rawley's hymn 'I will sing the wondrous story'.

5. M. Weinfeld, in *TDOT*, vol. 2, pp. 253–255 (and 256–279). See also McComiskey, *op. cit.*; Dumbrell, *op. cit.*; McCarthy, *op. cit.*; W. Dyrness, *Themes in Old Testament Theology* (Paternoster, 1979), pp. 113–126.

6. NIV inexplicably alters its translation to 'mankind' in Gn. 6:7 and thus destroys an important identity of wording. The Hebrew is '*ādām* in each case and therefore should be 'man/mankind/humankind' in each verse. The stress on universality is crucial to the passage.

7. Gn. 6:8; 18:3; 19:19; 30:27; 32:5<.6>; 33:8, 10, 15; 34:11; 39:4; 47:25, 29;

50:4; Ex. 33:12–13, 16–17; 34:9; Nu. 11:11, 15; 32:5; Dt. 24:1; Jdg. 6:17; Ru. 2:2, 10, 13; 1 Sa. 1:18; 16:22; 20:29; 25:8; 27:5; 2 Sa. 14:22; 15:25; 16:4; 1 Ki. 11:19; Est. 5:8; 7:3, 8:5. Readers without Hebrew would be well advised to follow these references through in some such translation as the RV, because the NIV rendering is so variable that it is not always possible to trace the presence of the formula sufficiently precisely.

8. KJV's 'grace' is precisely correct here.

9. U. Cassuto, *A Commentary on the Book of Genesis: Part One, From Adam to Noah* (Magnes, 1961), p. 307. Also J. H. Sailhamer, 'Genesis', in F. E. Gaebelein, *EBC*, vol. 2 (Zondervan, 1990): 'In . . . vv. 9–12 the author explains why God found Noah an exception' (p. 81); W. C. Kaiser, *Towards an Old Testament Theology* (Zondervan, 1991): '. . . "Noah found grace" . . . for he was "a righteous man" . . .' (p. 80).

10. Gn. 5:1; 6:9; 10:1; 11:10, 27; 25:12, 19; 36:1, 9; 37:2.

11. Nouns of the same formation as *tôlᵉdōt* uniformly express 'the verbal idea in action': from hiphil √*yādāh*, 'to give thanks', *tôdâh*, 'thanksgiving'; from hiphil √*yākāḥ*, 'to arbitrate', *tôkēḥâh/tôkēḥat*, 'adjudication'; from hiphil √*yāṣa*, 'to go out', *tôṣā'âh*, 'an outgoing' *etc.*

12. The OT has a rich covenant vocabulary which ought to be observed. We read that the Lord 'inaugurates' (√*kārat*, 'to cut', *e.g.* Gn. 15:18; Ex. 34:10, 27; Dt. 4:23; 5:2), 'implements' (hiphil √*qûm*, lit. 'makes to rise up', *e.g.* Gn. 6:18; 9:9; 17:7; Ex. 6:4), 'places' (*i.e.* sets the covenant between himself and the covenant person so that it determines the abiding relationship between them: √*nātan*, to [give] put, place, appoint, Gn. 17:2; Nu. 25:12). Preparatory to covenant action the Lord 'remembers' (√*zākar*, *e.g.* Gn. 9:15; Ex. 2:24) or 'has regard' ('looks upon', hiphil √*nābat*, Ps. 74:20).

13. Hebrew has no word for 'rainbow' as such. It uses simply the word for the weapon, a 'bow'. In the Noah-narrative this, of course, has a special significance. After the divine hostility revealed in the Flood, the Lord hangs up his weapons for all to see: the war is over, peace has been declared.

14. E. Jacob speaks for many when he says that 'the institution of circumcision is recorded three times (Exod. 4.24ff.; Josh. 5:2ff.; Genesis 17) and ascribed to Moses, to Joshua and to Abraham' (*Theology of the Old Testament*, Hodder & Stoughton, p. 200). *Cf.* G. A. F. Knight, *A Christian Theology of the Old Testament* (SCM, 1959), p. 238. This view of three institution accounts is only possible by scouting the veracity of the three accounts as they stand. *Cf.* J. A. Soggin, *Joshua*

(SCM, 1972): 'MT tries to harmonize this rite with that described in Gen 17' (p. 70). Whatever else may be said about Ex. 4:24ff. and Jos. 5:2ff., one thing is clear: neither, taken as it stands, lays any claim to recount the origin of the rite of circumcision. Joshua 5:2, indeed, says 'again . . . the second time' (see RV; according to its customary conflationist principle, NIV simply says 'again' and thus loses the emphasis). The purpose of the Joshua passage is to record the recovery of a lost status as the circumcised people – for (5:5) those who left Egypt were circumcised. In Ex. 4 it would be impossible to explain how Zipporah intuited what must be done to save Moses' life if the practice of circumcision in his family were previously unknown. By its own confession, Gn. 17 is the only passage which registers a claim to record the introduction of circumcision in the family of Abraham, and once this is accepted the other two passages fall into place in a coherent scheme.

15. J. A. Motyer, 'Circumcision', in *IBD*, vol. 1, pp. 288f.; *cf.* J. P. Hyatt, 'Circumcision', in *IDB*, vol. 1, pp. 629–631; J. B. Payne, *The Theology of the Older Testament* (Zondervan, 1962), pp. 391–394.

16. See note 12.

17. Genesis does not explain the meaning of the sacrifice which Abram prepared at the Lord's command. The lack of direction and explanation means that it was a rite with which he was familiar and, from our point of view, the lack of explanation is intended to focus our attention on the 'bare' truth that the divine covenant must be inaugurated in sacrifice. As to its meaning, light is cast by Je. 34 where those who (lit.) 'enter into . . . covenant' (34:11) 'cut [a calf] in two and walked between the pieces' (34:18–19) and, having broken the covenant, will be treated themselves like the severed calf (34:18). The ceremony was thus one of oath-taking, its terms possibly being 'I swear that . . . and should I break my oath, so may it be done to me'. Since Abram was a deliberately immobilized onlooker (Gn. 15:12) the Lord alone is the oath-taker – and, ultimately, though he was ever faithful to his covenant, yet took on himself the whole penalty of the broken covenant. The 'smoking brazier with a blazing torch' (more literally 'an oven (earthenware pot) with smoke and flame of fire') which symbolizes the divine presence (15:17) is an unexplained 'pre-view' of the pillar of cloud and fire of Ex. 13:21 and the colossal cloud and fire on Sinai (Ex. 19:18).

18. Exodus says three things about Pharaoh's heart: (1) the Lord hardened it (Ex. 4:21; 7:3; 9:12; 10:1, 20, 27; 11:10; 14:4, 8; *cf.* 14:17); (2) Pharaoh

hardened his heart (Ex. 8:15<11>, 32<28>; 9:34; *cf.* 7:23; (3) his heart became hard (Ex. 7:13, 22; 8:19<15>; 9:7, 35; *cf.* 7:14. All three statements are true, and all must be held together for every act of disobedience is a deliberate hardening of the heart, results in the heart becoming harder than it was before, and does so in accord with the moral procedures which the Creator God instituted. But he alone knows at what point it is in the ongoing process of disobedience and hardening that eternal justice requires that the point of no return has been reached and that the heart must be judicially declared irretrievably hardened. He decreed such a point for Pharaoh. See in principle, B. S. Childs, *Exodus* (SCM, 1974), pp. 170–175.

19. See NIV margin. The Hebrew is *l*^e*ratson*, 'unto favourable acceptance', *cf.* Lv. 19:5; 22:19–21, 29; 23:11. *Cf.* Ex. 28:38. For the verb √*rāṣāh*, see Lv. 1:4 with 7:18; 19:7; 22:23, 25, 27. The idea of the Lord's delighted acceptance is foremost throughout the usage of both noun and verb.

20. Ex. 12:10 is the ultimate stress on exact equivalence. Should anything remain of the lamb it must be totally destroyed. Its function is for these people alone, to feed and shelter them.

21. This supposition is confirmed by Nu. 3:11–13.

22. Lv. 1:4; 3:2; 4:4, 15, 24, 29.

23. The qal (simple active) of √*kāpar* only occurs in Gn. 6:14, of Noah 'covering' the ark with pitch. Otherwise, piel and pual (intensive active and passive) are found about 100 times, 'to make atonement/pardon/ have mercy/purge' *etc.* in Lv. 1:4, *etc.* Secularly the intensive verb occurs in Gn. 32:20<21> of Jacob 'pacifying/appeasing/propitiating' Esau's anger with a gift-payment.

24. *E.g.* Ex. 21:30; 30:11–16; Nu. 35:31–32; Ps. 49:7<8>; Pr. 13:8; Is. 43:3 (see Motyer, *Isaiah*, pp. 331–332).

25. L. Morris, *The Apostolic Preaching of the Cross* (Tyndale, ³1965), pp. 24, 26.

26. *Ibid.*, pp. 161f.

27. *Ibid.*, pp. 166, 170.

28. It is usually thought that the intensive form *kippēr* ('to make atonement/cover by an exact price') is a 'denominative' verb – *i.e.* it derives from the noun *kōper*. The process can be illustrated: the verb 'to be white' (√*lāban*) produced the noun 'a brick' (*l*^e*bēnâh*) which in turn produced a verb (√*lāban*) 'to make bricks'; the verb 'to pluck' (√*ḥārap*) produced the noun 'autumn/winter' (*ḥôrep*) which in turn led to the verb 'to over-winter' (√*ḥārap*). According to GKC 52h, denominatives

formed in the piel 'generally express a being occupied with the object expressed by the noun, either to form or to make use of it'. Hence $\sqrt{k\bar{a}par}$, 'to cover' → $k\bar{o}per$, 'a covering price' → $kipp\bar{e}r$, 'to pay a covering price'.

29. S. R. Driver, 'Propitiation', in J. Hastings (ed.), *Dictionary of the Bible* (T. & T. Clark, 1898–1904).

30. For examples of what is called the 'Beth of price or value' (*i.e.* prefixing the preposition b^e to a noun to express cost), see, *e.g.*, 2 Sa. 21:3 (lit., 'At what cost am I to pay a ransom price?'); 23:17 (lit. 'at the cost of their lives'); 1 Ki. 2:23; Pr. 7:23; La. 5:9.

31. A. M. Stibbs, *The Meaning of the Word 'Blood' in Scripture* (Tyndale, 1947).

32. See Dt. 19:21, where 'for' is the preposition b^e expressing the exact equivalence required by the legal principle, the Lex Talionis. Also 2 Sa. 14:7; Jon. 1:14.

33. See note 22.

34. M. Noth, *Leviticus* (SCM, 1965), p. 22. *Cf.* H. H. Rowley, *The Faith of Israel* (SCM, 1956), p. 96.

35. The preposition *tahat* is often used to express the exact balance between one thing and another. *E.g.*, in Is. 53:12, the exact balance between the Servant's work and his recompense; Gn. 4:25, the replacement of Abel by another child, or of a new king replacing a dead king, 1 Ki. 11:43; the Levites 'instead of' the firstborn, Nu. 3:12, 41, 45; 8:16.

36. Lv. 16:21 (RV) contains the three main components of the OT vocabulary of sin: 'iniquities' (*'āwôn*, from $\sqrt{'\bar{a}w\hat{a}h}$, 'to bend, twist', hence the perversion of human nature giving rise to sin); 'transgressions', better 'rebellions', wilful revolt against a superior, *cf.* the 'secular' use in 1 Ki. 12:19; 2 Ki. 3:7; *etc.*; 'sins', actual misdemeanours, from $\sqrt{h\bar{a}ta'}$, 'to miss the mark', *e.g.* Jdg. 20:16.

37. Heb. 10:4 rightly says that 'the blood of bulls and goats' cannot take away sin, yet we must be careful to note that 'the old Fathers did' not 'look only for transitory promises' (Article 7 of the Thirty-nine Articles of Religion of the Church of England). The Psalms reveal people living in the enjoyment of the forgiveness of sins, peace with God, *etc.*, and, as we have seen, promises of actual forgiveness and atonement were attached to the sacrifices. Like ourselves, the 'old Fathers' – our dear ancestors in the Old Testament church – took the promises of God seriously, trusted them, were justified by faith and, in God's mercy, received the promised benefits. Equally like us, they

received the promised benefits in ways that made them long for and cry out for the coming full realization of the mercies of God.

38. Th. C. Vriezen, *An Outline of Old Testament Theology* (Blackwell, 1960), *e.g.* p. 300. See U. E. Simon, *A Theology of Salvation* (SPCK, 1953), pp. 212–214.
39. See Motyer, *Isaiah*, pp. 430–431.
40. For this translation of Is. 53:12, see Motyer, *Isaiah*, pp. 442–443.
41. √*gā'al* occurs for the first time in Gn. 48:16 where NIV translates it 'delivered'(!). Jacob's point is that he was accompanied through all his life's pilgrimage by a kinsman-God who identified with and undertook for him in every need. The verb has a wide secular use which offers a rich background to its religious and spiritual significance. Thus, for example, property which has become alienated from its ancestral owners must be 'redeemed' by purchase (Lv. 25:26; Ru. 3:3). If someone vows to God something which in the nature of the case cannot as such be given to him (a house, for example) he must 'redeem' it by paying the equivalent market value (Lv. 27:13–31). But specially the 'redeemer', the *gō'ēl*, of an injured or murdered person is the one who has the right to exact payment (in the case of murder, life for life) (Nu. 35:12–27; Dt. 19:6, 12; Jos. 20:3, 5, 9). The price-paying conception is especially clear also in the related noun meaning 'the opportunity to buy back' (Lv. 25:24, lit. 'you shall provide an opportunity to buy back . . .'), 'redemption price' (Lv. 25:51–52), and 'the right to buy back' (Je. 32:7). There is another verb translated 'redeem/ransom', √*pādâh*. For the most part it can be considered synonymous with √*gā'al* but it seems to have its own individual emphasis: its secular use is entirely devoted to the idea of redemption *price* (*e.g.* Lv. 27:27; Nu. 18:15–17; Ps. 49:7). Thirteen out of thirty-nine occurrences look back to the Exodus (*e.g.* Dt. 9:26; 2 Sa. 7:23). Redemption is linked with divine mercy and love (*e.g.* Ps. 26:11; 44:26), and achieved by divine power (*e.g.* Dt. 7:8); in one verse it is connected with the righteousness of the Lord (Is. 1:27) and with the forgiveness of sins (Dt. 21:8; Ps. 130:8). √*padah* lacks the personal associations of √*gā'al*. In a word, it focuses on *the price of redemption* while √*gā'al* also stresses the person of the redeemer.
42. *E.g.* Ex. 6:6; 15:13; Pss. 74:2; 77:15–20; 106:10; Is. 43:1–4.
43. *E.g.* Is. 48:20; 51:10–11; 63:16; Je. 31:11.
44. See L. Morris, *Ruth*, TOTC (IVP, 1968); D. A. Leggett, *The Levirate and Goel Institutions in the Old Testament with Special Attention to*

the Book of Ruth (Mack Publishing Co., 1974); R. L. Hubbard, *The Book of Ruth*, NICOT (Eerdmans, 1988); M. D. Gow, *The Book of Ruth: Its Structure, Theme and Purpose* (Apollos, 1992).

45. Against most commentators. See Motyer, *Isaiah*, p. 331.

46. The word in question is *ḥesed*. As distinct from both *aḥᵃbâh* (e.g. Gn. 29:20) and *raḥᵃmîm* (e.g. 1 Ki. 3:26), which express aspects of the emotional quality of love, *ḥesed* is 'love in the will', the love which commits itself in marriage vows 'till death do us part'. This is the characteristic OT word for the divine love, found over 200 times, of which only thirteen are in the plural.

47. Prepositions used with the verb 'to make a covenant' mostly express the idea 'with' of a person/people brought into the covenant relationship; less frequent is the preposition 'to/for' which, in its distinct usage (as here), means 'to make a covenant in favour of', *i.e.* to covenant specified blessings to someone.

48. *E.g.* J. A. Thompson, *Jeremiah* (Eerdmans, 1980).

49. See note 36 above.

50. *Cf.* Is. 34; Am. 9:12. See Motyer, *Isaiah*, pp. 268–269.

51. See J. A. Motyer, *A Scenic Route through the Old Testament* (IVP, 1994), pp. 33–34.

52. See pp. 49–50 above.

4. CHRIST AS REVELATION (1)

1. J. Pedersen, *Israel, its Life and Culture*, vol. 1 *Israel I and II*, vol. 2 *Israel III and IV* (OUP, 1926, 1940).

2. Pedersen, *Israel III and IV*, pp. 646–648.

3. *Ibid.*

4. U. E. Simon, *A Theology of Salvation* (SPCK, 1953), p. 56 (and see pp. 54–58).

5. P. Craigie, *The Book of Deuteronomy*, NICOT (Hodder & Stoughton, 1976), on Dt. 4:15ff. On the same passage, see J. A. Thompson, *Deuteronomy*, TOTC (IVP, 1974); A. D. H. Mayes, *Deuteronomy*, NCB (Oliphants, 1979); R. Brown, *The Message of Deuteronomy*, BST (IVP, 1993), pp. 68–70. Also H. Frankfurt, *Before Philosophy* (Penguin, 1949), pp. 28f.

6. The verbs used in the two passages differ – the general verb 'to see' (√*rā'âh*) in Dt. 4:12, and the possibly more pointed verb 'to look at' (√*nābaṭ*) in Nu. 12:8. The noun is the same, *tᵉmûnâh* from √*mānâh* 'to

count, number, reckon up' – as if to suggest that the Lord had 'vital statistics'.

7. J. Calvin, *Institutes*, I.iv.3 (SCM, 1955): 'True religion ought to be conformed to God's will as to a universal rule . . . God . . . is not a spectre or phantasm to be transformed according to anyone's whim . . . All who set up their own false rites . . . worship and adore their own ravings . . . No religion is genuine unless it be joined with truth' (pp. 49–50). See also *Institutes*, II.vii.17–21, where Calvin makes additional comments on the second commandment. Section 17 ends 'As soon as idols appear true religion is corrupted' (p. 384).

8. Y. Kaufmann, *The Religion of Israel* (George Allen & Unwin, 1961), pp. 20, 147f., 236f.

9. J. A. Motyer, *The Prophecy of Isaiah* (IVP, 1993), pp.76–77.

10. G. von Rad, *Genesis* (SCM, 1961), p. 47; E. J. Young, *Studies in Genesis 1* (Baker, 1964), p. 27.

11. G. J. Wenham, *Genesis 1–15*, vol. 1 (Word, 1987), pp. 1–14; H. Blocher, *In the Beginning* (IVP, 1984), pp. 60–66; D. Atkinson, *The Message of Genesis 1–11*, BST (IVP, 1990), pp. 20–22.

12. J. Calvin, *Institutes*, I.xv.3: '. . . all the excellence in which the nature of man surpasses all other species . . . And though the principal seat of the Divine Image was in the mind and heart, or in the soul and its faculties, yet there was no part of man, not even the body, which was not adorned with some rays of glory'; G. C. Berkouwer, *Man: The Image of God* (Eerdmans, 1962); J. Orr, *God's Image in Man* (Hodder & Stoughton, 1907) – possibly more dated than others of Orr's books but still worth reading; D. F. Payne, *Genesis One Reconsidered* (Tyndale, 1964), pp. 23–26; D. J. A. Clines, 'The Image of God', *TynB* 19, 1968; D. Atkinson, *op. cit.*, pp. 36–41; N. Porteous, 'Image of God', in *IDB*, vol. 2; Bibliography in Wenham, *op. cit.*, p. 26.

13. 'Image', *selem*, occurs thirty-three times in the OT: twenty-five refer to physical replicas of gods, men or things (*e.g.* 1 Sa. 6:5; Ezk. 23:14; Dn. 2:31); Ps. 39:6<7> (NIV 'phantom'), an outward shape without substance; Ps. 73:20 and Dn. 3:19, outward appearance indicative of inward state. 'Likeness', *demût*, occurs twenty-four times in the OT: nineteen refer to physical resemblance or identity of appearance (*e.g.* 2 Ki. 16:10; Ezk. 1:5; Dn. 10:16); Ps. 58:4<5> and Is. 13:4 use the word of a non-material simile. U. Cassuto, *A Commentary on the Book of Genesis* (Magnes, 1961), on Gn. 1:26, speaks of 'the corporeality explicit in the statement'.

14. H. H. Rowley, *The Faith of Israel* (SCM, 1956), pp. 75f.

15. See Clines, *op. cit.*, pp. 70–80.

16. On 'seeing God', Gn. 16:7–15; 32:24–30; Jdg. 6:11–23; 13:3–23; *cf.* Ex. 19:21; 3:20.

17. Rowley, *op. cit.*, p. 66.

18. J. J. Von Allmen, 'Marriage', in J. J. Von Allmen (ed.), *Vocabulary of the Bible* (Lutterworth, 1958), pp. 253–258.

19. G. A. F. Knight, *A Biblical Approach to the Doctrine of the Trinity*, Scottish Journal of Theology, Occasional Paper 1 (Oliver & Boyd, 1953), pp. 21–22.

20. H. Ringgren, *Israelite Religion* (SPCK, 1966), pp. 124–125. See also E. Jacob, *Theology of the Old Testament* (Hodder & Stoughton, 1958), p. 167. See 1 Sa. 15:12.

21. On Gn. 2:4–25, see p. 111 below. But see also D. J. A. Clines, *What does Eve Do to Help?* (JSOT Press, 1990), pp. 23–48.

22. Note this kingly element in Ps. 8:5–6.

23. In connection with discussions of 'headship' in relation to the respective positions of men and women, the fact that the imperatives in Gn. 1:28 are plural means that, as far as this passage is concerned, there is no 'male headship' in creation. Regarding 'headship' in marriage, the key idea in Gn. 2:18ff. is expressed by 'a helper suitable for him' (2:18, NIV). The Hebrew is '*ēzer lᵉnegdô*. The word 'helper' points to a function but not necessarily to a status – for the Lord is the Helper of his people (*e.g.* Pss. 10:14; 30:10<11>) but not their subordinate. Regarding 'suitable for him', the idea is best expressed by thinking of a two-piece jig-saw puzzle, each piece the perfect match and complement of the other, each co-equally important for the whole picture. This meaning of the words expressing the divine intention is confirmed by the 'man/woman' '*iš*/'*iššâ* relationship of 2:23. On 'headship' in the NT, see S. Motyer, *Ephesians: Free to be One*, CBG (Crossway Books, 1994), pp. 123–124, 151–152, 155–156, 160–164.

24. Wenham, *op. cit.*, p. 33.

25. *Cf. ibid.*, pp. 71–72.

26. W. Temple, *Nature, Man and God* (Macmillan, 1940), pp. 362, 397, 513–514; C. E. M. Joad, *Guide to the Philosophy of Morals and Politics* (Gollanz, 1944), pp. 262–264, 428–429; A. Flew, *An Introduction to Western Philosophy* (Thames & Hudson, 1989), ch. 3; T. C. Hammond, *Perfect Freedom* (IVF, 1946), pp. 84–88; C. F. H. Henry, *Christian*

Personal Ethics (Eerdmans, 1971), s.v. 'Good'; R. A. P. Rogers, *Short History of Ethics* (Macmillan, 1937), s.v. 'Good'.

27. S. R. Driver, *A Treatise on the Use of the Tenses in Hebrew* (Oxford, 1892), pp. 84–88, sought to make out a case that Imperfect with Waw Consecutive cannot introduce a pluperfect. He did not reason on linguistic grounds but based his case on the examination of instances. Closer and further examination shows that he is far from proving the point. NIV is undoubtedly correct in translating Gn. 2:19 as pluperfect.

28. Gn. 9:6 indicates that, notwithstanding sin, the image of God has not been obliterated. F. Delitzsch, *New Commentary on Genesis* (T. & T. Clark, 1888), vol. 1: '. . . the inviolable majesty of the Divine image, which even after the Fall is fundamentally the *character indelibilis* of mankind and of each individual' (p. 287). Atkinson, *op.cit.*: 'Every living human being bears the image of God. If our discussion of the divine image . . . [see *ibid.*, pp. 36–41] is on the right lines, it is the relationship God has with such beings – their history before God – rather than any capacity they have within themselves, in which the image of God is seen. And that should lead us to very great caution with respect to those youngest members of the human species – the human embryos. For whatever else we may believe about their "personality" – their capacities or abilities – they are without doubt living members of the human species, and so in the image of the personal God . . .'(p. 160). Calvin is, of course, correct in speaking of the 'image' in the post-Fall race as 'confused, mutilated and disease ridden' (*Institutes*, I.xv.3), yet the image remains humanity's uniqueness and, in Gn. 9:6 as in Jas. 3:9, it is the basis of our mutual relationships in deed and word.

29. G. A. F. Knight, *Law and Grace* (SCM, 1962); W. C. Kaiser, *Towards Rediscovering the Old Testament* (Zondervan, 1991), esp. pp. 147–155; G. Vos, *Biblical Theology* (Eerdmans, 1963), pp. 141–159; J. A. Motyer, *Law and Life: The Meaning of Law in the Old Testament* (Lawyers' Christian Fellowship, 1978); *idem*, *The Image of God: Law and Liberty in Biblical Ethics*, Laing Lecture (London Bible College, 1976); T. E. McComiskey, *The Covenants of Promise* (IVP, 1985), s.v. 'Law'; W. Dyrness, *Themes in Old Testament Theology* (Paternoster, 1979), chs. 7, 10.

30. See Lv. 19:2–4, 10, 12, 14, 16, 18, 25, 28, 31–33, 36–37.

31. J. A. Motyer, *The Revelation of the Divine Name* (Tyndale, 1959), pp. 21–24.

32. See the Services of Baptism in *The Book of Common Prayer*.

5. CHRIST AS REVELATION (2)

1. W. Temple, *Nature, Man and God* (Macmillan, 1940), p. 317. (See pp. 311–322.)
2. See J. I. Packer, 'Contemporary Views of Revelation', in C. F. H. Henry (ed.), *Revelation and the Bible* (Tyndale, 1959), pp. 89–104.
3. Temple, *op. cit.*, p. 314.
4. *Ibid.*, pp. 315, 318. See also G. E. Wright, *God Who Acts* (SCM, 1952); *idem*, 'Reflections concerning Old Testament Theology', in *Studia Biblica et Semitica* (Wageningen, 1966), pp. 376–388; J. Bright, *The Authority of the Old Testament* (SCM, 1967), pp. 130–131, 136–140, 147, *etc.*; G. J. Wenham, 'History and the Old Testament', in C. Brown (ed.), *History, Criticism and Faith* (IVP, 1976), pp. 13–66; J. Goldingay, '"That you may know that Yahweh is God": A Study in the Relationship between Theology and Historical Truth in the Old Testament', *TynB* 23, 1972, pp. 58–93; W. C. Kaiser, *Towards Rediscovering the Old Testament* (Zondervan, 1991), pp. 61–79; H. D. McDonald, *Theories of Revelation* (George Allen & Unwin, 1963), s.v. 'History and Revelation'; W. Pannenberg, 'Redemption Event and History', in C. Westermann (ed.), *Essays on Old Testament Interpretation* (SCM, 1963), pp. 314–335.
5. J. H. Hayes and E. F. C. Prussner, *Old Testament Theology: Its History and Development* (SCM, 1985), pp. 216–218. *Cf.* S. Herrmann, *Israel in Egypt* (SCM, 1970): 'It is not events themselves and their often insignificant radius of actions that are capable of releasing far reaching consequences; it is the depth of experience of the man who experiences these events. This depth of experience is set down in the biblical account' (p. 65).
6. G. von Rad, *Old Testament Theology*, vol. 1 (Oliver & Boyd, 1962), p. 108.
7. *Ibid.*, p. 109.
8. *Ibid.*, pp. 110–111.
9. J. A. Soggin, *Joshua* (SCM, 1972), p. 6.
10. S. J. DeVries, *1 Kings* (Word, 1985) is a case in point. For a sensitive and much deeper understanding of 'deuteronomic' thinking, see B. G. Webb, *The Book of Judges: An Integrated Reading* (JSOT Press, 1987).
11. G. von Rad, as quoted in G. Hasel, *Old Testament Theology: Basic*

Issues in the Current Debate (Eerdmans, 1975), p. 57.

12. W. C. Kaiser, *op. cit.*, pp. 66–79. See also R. de Vaux, 'Method in the Study of Early Hebrew History', in J. P. Hyatt (ed.), *The Bible in Modern Scholarship* (Abingdon, 1965); G. W. Ramsay, *The Quest of the Historical Israel* (Knox, 1981).

13. J. Barr, *Old and New in Interpretation* (SCM, 1966), pp. 65–102.

14. *Ibid.*, pp. 72–73.

15. J. I. Packer, *God has Spoken* (Hodder & Stoughton, 1979), pp. 77–80.

16. Packer, *ibid.*, quoting C. H. Dodd, *The Authority of the Bible* (SPCK, 1960), p. 83.

17. Barr, *op. cit.*, p. 20.

18. R. W. Dale, *The Atonement* (Congregational Union of England and Wales, 1905), p. 52.

19. See Am. 7:14–16 where, for the second time, Amos asserts his authority as a prophet and in an identical context.

20. See, *e.g.*, Elisha's surprise when he was not wise before the event, 2 Ki. 4:27. This is the key also to understanding the weight that Isaiah reposes on the argument from prediction and fulfilment in chapters 41–48, and in particular his insistence (44:24 – 45:7) that Cyrus possessed all the evidence needed to know that Yahweh alone is God. See J. A. Motyer, *The Prophecy of Isaiah* (IVP, 1993), pp. 353–359.

21. U. E. Simon, *A Theology of Salvation* (SPCK, 1953), p. 25. I owe the expression 'occupational hazard' (if my memory is correct) to N. H. Snaith but I cannot trace the reference. On the changed climate regarding emending texts, P. A. Verhoef, *The Books of Haggai and Malachi*, NICOT (Eerdmans, 1987), p. 18.

22. Je. 1:4, 2:1; 7:1; 11:1; 13:3, 8; 14:1; *etc.*; Gn. 15:1, 4; 1 Ki. 6:11; 12:22; 13:20; 16:17; 17:2, 8; 18:1; Ezk. 1:3; 3:16; 6:1; 11:14; *etc.*; Ho. 1:1; Joel 1:1; Jon. 1:1; 3:1; Mi. 1:1; Zp. 1:1; Hg. 1:1, 3; 2:1, 10, 20; Zc. 1:7; 4:8; *etc.*

23. Barr, *op. cit.*, p. 22.

24. Notwithstanding that NIV makes them identical (contrast RV), Ezk. 2:7 and 3:4 are significantly different. 2:7 lays down a basic requirement that a prophet 'speak my words', whereas 3:4 affirms the word as the sole and sufficient instrument for the prophet's task: 'speak with my words'.

25. It is an elementary error to mock the 'typewriter' model. If Almighty God were to come and say, 'Will you be my typewriter?' the proper and true reply would be, 'I would be honoured.' The integrity of the creature can truly be left in the hands of the Creator; the dignity of the

Creator merits the glad submission of the creature. On verbal inspiration and the typewriter model, see D. A. Carson and J. D. Woodbridge (eds.), *Hermeneutics, Authority and Canon* (IVP, 1986), pp. 11–14; in ch. 5, D. J. Moo puts the true position with covetable exactness: 'The words of Scripture are viewed as the product of a "concursive" operation whereby the human author freely wrote what he wanted while the divine author at the same time superintended and guided that writing' (p. 187). For some of the huge literature that this theme has attracted, see the notes attached to Carson, 'Recent Developments in the Doctrine of Scripture' (ch. 1), and Moo, 'The Problem of *Sensus Plenior*' (ch. 5). See also J. W. Montgomery (ed.), *God's Inerrant Word* (Bethany, 1974) *passim*, but note C. H. Pinnock, 'Limited Inerrancy' (pp. 143–158) and, more especially, R. C. Sproul, 'The Case for Inerrancy' (pp. 242–261), with notes and bibliography in each case. Also P. Feinberg, 'The Meaning of Inerrancy', in N. L. Geisler (ed.), *Inerrancy* (Zondervan, 1979). C. J. H. Wright, *Walking in the Ways of the Lord* (Apollos, 1995), addresses the question of 'the hermeneutical issues involved in discovering [the Scriptures'] authority and relevance for the modern world'. See especially pp. 47–116.

26. See F. D. Kidner, *The Message of Jeremiah*, BST (IVP, 1987), p. 92; J. A. Thompson, *Jeremiah*, NICOT (Eerdmans, 1980), pp. 497f.; J. Guest, *Jeremiah, Lamentations*, The Communicators Commentary (Word, 1986), pp. 170–175. Nowhere did Jeremiah solve the problem of the criteria of true prophecy by reference to technique. The stresses in Je. 23 fall on personal holiness, a fundamental message about sin and its seriousness and an intimate relationship with the Lord.

27. Kidner, *op. cit.*, p. 92.

28. Guest, *op. cit.*

29. See pp. 86–87 above.

30. Thompson, *op. cit.*

31. It is often and erroneously said or implied that the Bible is 'the church's book', that the church settled the content of the canon and gave the Bible to the world. Thus Archbishop George Carey in *The Meeting of the Waters* (Hodder & Stoughton, 1985) writes: 'Protestants too easily cry *sola scriptura* without acknowledging that apart from the church we would not have the book we call the Bible. Apart from the church there would be no well-defined canon . . .' (p. 63). Put like that, the words can only mislead. The fact is that, on the model of Jeremiah and the rest of the prophets and of the apostles after them, chosen individuals were

the Lord's agents in giving the Bible to the church. If anything belongs to anything, then it is not that the Bible is the church's book but that the church is the Bible's people. As to the canon, historically the church did not select and authorize the canon but recognized it and sat down under its authority. When a patient returns to a doctor and says, 'Yes, that medicine is exactly what I need', the patient does not authorize the medicine but recognizes its inherent authorization.

32. It is still debated whether the base-meaning of 'holiness' is 'separation' (*e.g.* N. H. Snaith, *The Distinctive Ideas of the Old Testament*, Epworth, 1944, pp. 24ff.) or some other concept like 'brightness/awesome splendour' (*e.g.* T. C. Vriezen, *An Outline of Old Testament Theology*, Blackwell, 1960, pp. 149ff.). H. Sebass, 'Holiness', in C. Brown (ed.), *NIDNTT*, vol. 2, holds that 'the basic idea is not that of separation . . . but the positive thought of encounter which inevitably demands certain modes of response' (p. 224). Such a vague definition hardly offers a precise enough encapsulation of the biblical evidence. Certainly the use of 'holy woman' (*qᵉdēšâh*) for what NIV calls the 'shrine-prostitute' of Gn. 38:21 hardly falls within Sebass' terms, and is much more favourable to the idea of one separated off for and belonging to the sphere of existence of the god she served. By contrast with such a god, what makes the God of Israel distinct and what dominates his sphere of reality is ethical holiness. See J. A. Motyer, *A Scenic Route through the Old Testament* (IVP, 1994), pp. 135–136; W. Dyrness, *Themes in Old Testament Theology* (Paternoster, 1979), pp. 51–53; G. A. F. Knight, *A Christian Theology of the Old Testament* (SCM, 1959), pp. 88–94; J. Pedersen, *Israel III and IV* (OUP, 1940), pp. 198–263. When the Lord says that he has 'sanctified' Jeremiah (1:5) while still in his mother's womb, the idea of being set apart for Yahweh and for holiness is foremost. Commenting on the juxtaposed ideas of 'consecrated' and 'appointed/given' in Je. 1:5, Kidner (*op. cit.*, p. 25) notes how the former relates Jeremiah to the Lord and the latter relates him to the world, and how well they are illustrated by what the Lord says of the Levites in Nu. 8:16, 19: 'I have taken them for myself . . . given them as a gift to Aaron . . .' (RSV). He notes how 'giving' 'completed God's act of taking or consecrating his servant' and how this corrects a too-introspective definition of holiness.

33. On human error in relation to inerrancy, see Carson, *op. cit.*, pp. 26–28; for essential further discussion of the nature of biblical propositions, the relation of 'propositional revelation' to the varieties of literary genre

in the Bible, and various suggested 'adjustments' to the notions of infallibility and inerrancy, see K. J. Vanhoozer's brilliant essay 'The Semantics of Biblical Literature', in Carson, *op. cit.*, p. 52–104.

34. Pedersen, *Israel III and IV*, p. 167.

35. J. A. Motyer, 'Curse', in *IBD*, vol. 1, pp. 348–349; J. Pedersen, *Israel III and IV*, s.v. 'Blessing', 'Curse'; H. Aust *et al.* 'Curse, Insult, Fool', in C. Brown (ed.), *NIDNTT*, vol. 1, pp. 413–418; J. B. Payne, *The Theology of the Older Testament* (Zondervan, 1962), pp. 201ff.; J. B. Lightfoot, *Galatians* (Macmillan, 1880), on Gal. 3:10 and pp. 152–154.

36. This is a noteworthy example of the idiom of 'indeterminateness for the sake of emphasis'. See GKC 125c. *E.g.* Jos. 3:10 ('a living God!'); Is. 31:8 ('flee from a sword'), *etc.*

37. Lit., 'By the word of Yahweh the heavens were made, And by the Spirit of his mouth all their host' (Ps. 33:6).

38. There is no good reason to deny a reference to the Spirit of God in Gn. 1:2. See J. H. Sailhamer, 'Genesis', in F. E. Gaebelein (ed.), *EBC*, vol. 2 (Zondervan, 1990), p. 25. C. Westermann translates and argues for 'God's wind' in *Biblischer Kommentar I* (Neukirchener Verlag, 1974, 1982). To the contrary, G. J. Wenham, *op. cit.*, has 'adopted the rendering "Wind of God" as a concrete and vivid image of the Spirit of God'. *Cf.* F. D. Kidner, *Genesis*, TOTC (IVP, 1967), p. 45. Understood thus, the Spirit of God has the same position as in the rest of Scripture: the mediating Agent between the Creator God and the rule of God over his world by his word.

39. G. A. F. Knight, *A Biblical Approach to the Doctrine of the Trinity* (Oliver & Boyd, 1953), p. 16.

40. *Cf.* Ex. 6:30 – 7:1, where the same arrangement is put slightly differently.

41. See Je. 42:1–7. 2 Ki. 3:15 is the only place which suggests the use of means to induce inspiration, and the tenses affirm that this was Elisha's custom ('It used to be that . . .'); Je. 42 implies that prayer occupied Jeremiah's waiting days. But the use of means to cultivate receptivity does not seize the initiative from the Lord: the word is still solely his to give (sometimes suddenly! Is. 38:4, *cf.* 2 Ki. 20:4) or to withhold (1 Sa. 28:6; Is. 21:11–12).

42. *Cf.* Am. 7:10–17.

43. G. A. Smith, *The Book of Isaiah I–XXXIX*, Expositor's Bible (Hodder & Stoughton, 1904), p. 74.

44. See Is. 28:9–10: scorn was levelled at the prophet by the sophisticates in church and state for the simplicity and clarity of his word.

45. See note 41 above.

46. Commentators (see note 26 above) appear to favour some such rendering as NIV, 'utter worthy, not worthless words', in Je. 15:19. This would imply that, through lack of care and discernment, even Jeremiah could become a false prophet: being Yahweh's mouth calls for conscious intellectual commitment and integrity. But √*yāṣā'* (hiphil) is never elsewhere used 'absolutely' of speech 'going forth': see, however, Nu. 14:36–37.; Ne. 6:19; Pr. 10:18; Ecc. 5:2<7> where the verb occurs with a 'speech' object specified. Neither 'worthy' (*yāqār*, 'precious') nor 'worthless' (*zôlēl*, 'vile') is elsewhere used of words – the sense in 1 Sa. 3:1 is different, 'rare/a rare thing'. The reference may well be, then, to Jeremiah's purgation of his own character/conduct, but, while this suits 'precious . . . vile', it is equally unexemplified for √*yāṣā* (hiphil). S. R. Driver, however (quoted in L. E. Binns, *Jeremiah*, Methuen, 1919), has 'If thou separatest, like a refiner, what is pure . . . in thee from the slag of earthly passion . . .'.

47. *Cf.* Elijah and Elisha in 1 Ki. 17:1; 18:15; 2 Ki. 3:14; 5:16.

48. Motyer, *Isaiah*, pp. 76–78.

49. J. Lindblom, *Prophecy in Ancient Israel* (Blackwell, 1963), pp. 178–182.

50. *Cf.* 1 Cor. 2:12. In the OT, of course, the history books that are considered as prophecy demonstrate the perceptive use of the mind in the whole selective and presentational process of historiography. This is particularly obvious in Chronicles, *cf.* M. Wilcock, *The Message of Chronicles*, BST (IVP, 1987); M. Selman, *1 Chronicles* and *2 Chronicles*, TOTC (IVP, 1994).

51. Jeremiah sees *šōqēd*, the almond shoot that heralds the wakening life of spring; the Lord says *šāqēd*, 'Wakeful (I am)' (Je. 1:11–12).

52. Amos sees *qayiṣ*, 'ripe fruit', and hears *qēṣ*, 'the end', *cf.* NIV 'the time is ripe' (Am. 8:1–2).

53. Any OT commentary in the ICC series will show the process at work. The present-day development of rhetorical criticism and 'integrated reading' is now working strongly in the reverse direction. There is, of course, no historical evidence for 'continuing "schools"' of disciples who conserved, developed, adjusted, re-applied and enlarged whatever core deposit they received from their 'master'. In the case of Jeremiah, see E. W. Nicholson, *Preaching to the Exiles* (Blackwell, 1970), and *cf.* J. G. McConville, *Judgment and Promise: An Interpretation of the Book of Jeremiah* (Apollos, 1993), pp. 16–19, 153–154, *etc.* We still need some fundamental work to establish criteria for the study of the prophetic books.

54. R. B. Y. Scott, 'The Literary Structure of Isaiah's Oracles', in *Studies in Old Testament Prophecy* (Edinburgh, 1950), pp. 175–186, quoted in C. Westermann, *Basic Forms of Prophetic Speech* (Lutterworth, 1967), pp. 44ff.

55. In considering how the prophets might have secured the transmission of their message to future generations, has sufficient weight been given to their conviction that they had been made vehicles of the very word/words of God? If they believed this – as they did – would they have been content to play 'Chinese Whispers' with divine truth by committing it to the uncertainties of oral tradition, or even leaving it without safeguard to an ongoing school of disciples? This is not the most obvious implication of Isaiah 8 or Jeremiah 36.

56. The view taken here is that the narratives in Ho. 1 and 3 refer to two stages in one marriage. F. D. Kidner, *The Message of Hosea*, BST (IVP, 1981); D. A. Hubbard, *Hosea*, TOTC (IVP, 1989); Lindblom, *op. cit.*, pp. 165–169.

57. Lindblom, *ibid.*, p. 172.

58. This is the meaning of the great passages of blessing and bane within the covenant: Lv. 26; Dt. 28; *cf.* Dt. 30:15–20. 'Credal' statements like Ps. 1, expressing confidence in the well-being of the righteous in the world of a holy and just God, arise from the same 'blessing and bane' basis within the covenant.

59. See pp. 51–53 above.

60. Lindblom, *op. cit.*, p. 172.

61. *Cf.* pp. 45–46 above.

62. See J. A. Motyer, *Baptism in the Book of Common Prayer* (Fellowship of Evangelical Churchmen, 1974). See also S. Motyer, *Remember Jesus* (Christian Focus Publications, 1995), ch. 9.

63. There are over thirty places in the NT where *estin* has the significance of 'means/signifies/stands for' *etc.* (*e.g.* Mt. 9:13; 23:16; Mk. 7:34; Lk. 8:9; Acts 10:17; 1 Cor. 3:7; 7:19; Gal. 3:16; 4:24; Rev. 5:8; 19:8).

6. CHRIST OUR LIFE (1)

1. For the 'generations formula', see pp. 43–44 above, and note 10 on p. 195.

2. C. Westermann, *Genesis* (T. & T. Clark, 1988), pp. 3–22.

3. *Ibid.*, p. 12.

4. *Ibid.*, p. 16.

5. See pp. 69–70 above, and note 23 on p. 202.

6. J. Orr, *The Christian View of God and the World* (Andrew Elliott, 1907), p. 172. *Cf.* W. Temple, *Nature, Man and God* (Macmillan, 1940), s.v. 'Sin, Original Sin, Evil'; C. Hodge, *Systematic Theology*, vol. 2 (Nelson, 1874), pp. 123ff., 280ff.; E. A. Litton, *Introduction to Dogmatic Theology* (James Clarke, 1960), pp. 109–177; J. O. Buswell, 'The Origin and Nature of Sin', and C. Van Til, 'Original Sin', in C. F. H. Henry (ed.), *Basic Christian Doctrines* (Holt, Rinehart & Winston, 1962), pp. 103–116.

7. See O. C. Quick, *Doctrines of the Creed* (Nisbet, 1951), pp. 206f.

8. Temple, *op. cit.*

9. C. S. Lewis, *Broadcast Talks* (Bles, 1943), p. 47; *cf.* H. Blocher, *Evil and the Cross* (Apollos, 1994).

10. N. P. Williams, *Ideas of the Fall and Original Sin* (1927), pp. 43ff. Though in many ways a mine of information, Williams' book is typical in that a determined denial of any historical worth to early Genesis seems to lead to an inability to take Gn. 2 and 3 seriously even as a parable requiring consistent interpretation. But see J. Murray, *The Imputation of Adam's Sin* (Eerdmans, 1959); B. A. Milne, 'Sin', in *IBD*, vol. 3, pp. 1456–1459; Blocher, *op. cit.*

11. Westermann, *op. cit.*, p. 22.

12. Possibly Gn. 2:25 offers a sidelight on the inner constitution of the first couple, especially when linked with the immediate post-sin sense that nakedness was a problem. In the post-Fall world, such exposure betokens moral obliquity in the person offering it and is recognized as a moral impropriety by those who witness it (Gn. 9:20–27). It sends the wrong signals (Ex. 20:26). It is $n^e\underline{b}\bar{a}l\hat{a}h$, moral insensitivity and carelessness (2 Sa. 5:20).

13. *Cf.* F. D. Kidner, *Genesis*, TOTC (IVP, 1967), p. 67; D. Atkinson, *The Message of Genesis 1–11*, BST (IVP, 1990), p. 84; H. Blocher, *In the Beginning* (IVP, 1984), p. 139.

14. Kidner, *op. cit.*

15. E. J. Young, *The Study of Old Testament Theology Today* (James Clarke, 1958), pp. 74–75.

16. J. Calvin, *Institutes*, II.i.4.

17. 'Attractive thing', $ta^{a}w\hat{a}h$. *Cf.* Nu. 11:4; Jb. 33:20; Ps. 78:29; *etc.*

18. Sadly, I have lost my copies of Oswald Chambers' books and have no recollection which volume contains these key observations. They are there somewhere, and I am glad to record my debt to a very great Christian writer.

19. √*sāka̱l*, in the hiphil mode: wisdom in the management of affairs, knowing what to do, making a success of things. *Cf.* (both in a good sense) Jos. 1:7; Is. 52:13.

20. For a review of the expression 'good and evil', see G. J. Wenham, *Genesis*, vol. 1 (Word, 1987), pp. 62–64.

21. Note especially the perceptive comment here in Kidner, *op. cit.*; Blocher, *In the Beginning*, pp. 135–195.

22. Wenham, *op. cit.*, p. 76.

23. Williams, *op. cit.*, is quite astray in proposing that the new-found knowledge is the knowledge of sex 'of which . . . they had hitherto been ignorant'. Such a proposal evidences the lack of serious exegetical and expository principle whereby, it seems, anything can mean anything. Even if a story is a myth, a legend or a parable, it must be treated steadily within its own terms. In the present case, since marriage is established in Gn. 2, how can sexual knowledge be reserved as a discovery in Gn. 3? And since marriage is essential to the 'good' (2:18) how can sexual knowledge now be the essence of sin? This is an inexcusable laxity of thought. But, as we have seen, the point at issue is much more far-reaching than merely this piece of knowledge or that: the basis on which all knowledge rests has been corrupted and changed.

24. See pp. 68–69 above.

25. Kidner, *op. cit.*, p. 71.

26. The dignity of motherhood as such is not in question. The topic in Gn. 3:16, 19 is the marital relationship. Negative conclusions must not be drawn about a subject that is not involved.

27. S. Foh, 'What is Woman's Desire?', *WTJ* 37, 1974–75, pp. 376–383.

28. 'Desire', *tᵉsûqâh*, only appears elsewhere in Song 7:11, evidence of how strong a word it is.

29. J. Murray, *Principles of Conduct* (Tyndale, 1957), pp. 82–106.

30. 'I will surely multiply your aching toil . . . By aching toil you will eat . . .' (Gn. 3:16–17, lit.): in each case, '*iṣṣābôn* is used.

31. J. A. Motyer, *Law and Life: The Meaning of Law in the Old Testament* (Lawyers Christian Fellowship, 1978), pp. 7–8.

32. See J. A. Motyer, *The Prophecy of Isaiah* (IVP, 1993), pp. 42–43.

33. W. F. Albright, *From Stone Age to Christianity* (Doubleday, 1957), p. 284; *cf.* Dt. 12:2–3; Jos. 11:1–23.

34. The incident of Baal Peor reveals the sexual and orgiastic nature of Baal-religion but the clearest instance of the practice of sympathetic or imitative magic in the OT comes in 1 Ki. 18. The volume of noise and

vigour of activity implied in 18:26–27 was designed to capture the attention of the 'god', make him look their way. Elijah's mockery was virtually a blow below the belt: their 'god' could be otherwise occupied (lit. 'musing', whereby 'his' people were less than central to his concerns), subject to a call of nature ('busy' or 'gone aside', a euphemism: subject to human limitations and needs), away somewhere else ('travelling', not an omnipresent God), tired out ('sleeping', subject to human weakness). So they shouted all the louder, and since what they wanted was the down-rushing of red fire they did their best, as they pranced, to simulate it with 'blood pouring out over them'. When Elijah's turn came, he set about a radical denial of imitative magic. Desiring an outpouring of fire he proceeded to pour out water (18:33–34)! The nearest we come to imitative magic is when we teach out tiny children to wipe their noses – which has to be done before there is much vocabulary in common: so we hold a tissue to the offending nose and make nose-blowing noises, hoping for an imitation. The whole Carmel contest, however, put the matter on a different plane: it was not the fire that mattered but that there was a God who hears prayer – only One, Yahweh: 'The god who answers . . . *He* is the *real* God' (18:24, lit.).

35. For the 'high places' of Baal worship, see, *e.g.*, Nu. 22:41; 33:52; Jos. 13:17 (Bamoth Baal = 'The High Places of Baal'); 1 Ki. 3:2; 11:7; 12:31–32; *etc. Cf.* Je. 2:20; 3:6; 17:2.

36. See Nu. 25:1–3, 6–8; Je. 3:2; Ho. 4:13–14; *etc.*, regarding the sexual acts of the fertility rites.

37. The apparently categorical statements of Psalm 1 ('whatever he does prospers', 1:3) are rooted in the basic moral principles of Israel's life. But, of course, they are 'credal' statements – in the same way that we say 'I believe in God the Father Almighty' in a world where often he appears neither God, nor Father nor Almighty. A true creed affirms dominant and ultimate truth; it is not intended to describe experience.

38. J. A. Motyer, 'Haggai', in T. McComiskey (ed.), *The Minor Prophets*, vol. 3 (Baker, 1996).

39. R. H. Pfeiffer, *Introduction to the Old Testament* (A. & C. Black, 1953), p. 603. *Cf.* W. S. LaSor, D. A. Hubbard and F. W. Bush, *Old Testament Survey* (Eerdmans, 1982): 'In addition to the messianic hope . . . the re-establishment of the cult was also essential' (p. 485); P. D. Hanson, *The Dawn of Apocalyptic* (J. Knox, 1975), pp. 173–175, 245–250; D. L. Peterson, *Haggai, Zechariah 1–8* (SCM, 1985): '. . . to

initiate work on the temple, and to have the appropriate rites of purification performed' (p. 96). For a different view, R. L. Smith, *Micah–Malachi* (Word, 1984): '. . . the temple must be rebuilt so that the glory of the Lord might return and dwell with his people' (p. 149); *cf.* J. G. Baldwin, *Haggai, Zechariah and Malachi*, TOTC (IVP, 1972), p. 33; D. R. Jones, *Haggai, Zechariah and Malachi* (SCM, 1962), p. 33.

40. See p. 60 above, with note 51 on p. 200.

41. It is wrong to think of Haggai's time as one of poverty and deprivation, and the relevance of his message to today is thereby missed: rather, the reference to 'pannelled houses' indicates times of some affluence (equivalent today to double-glazing and cavity wall insulation), but coupled with national discontent and an inflated economy.

42. From Francis Thomson, 'The Hound of Heaven'.

43. *E.g.* Is. 30:23–25; 32:15; Je. 31:12; Joel 3:18<4:18>; Am. 9:13; *cf.* Lv. 26:4–5.

44. J. A. Motyer, 'Amos', in *NBC*, p. 808; *idem, The Message of Amos*, BST (IVP, 1974), pp. 205–206.

45. Article 9 of the Thirty-nine Articles Of Religion (in *The Book of Common Prayer*), see the Latin original in W. H. Griffith Thomas, *The Principles of Theology* (Church Book Room Press, 1945), p. 155; *cf.* Hodge, *op. cit.*, p. 192.

46. Williams, *op. cit.*, p. 50.

47. L. Koehler, *Old Testament Theology* (Lutterworth, 1953), pp. 178–181.

48. Th. C. Vriezen, *An Outline of Old Testament Theology* (Blackwell, 1960), pp. 210–211. Vriezen's refusal to acknowledge that Genesis 2ff. 'teaches a general doctrine of original sin' seems to run counter to the way his argument has been proceeding. It arises from his assumption that the doctrine of original sin requires us to believe that all people are equally bad actual sinners. *Cf.* E. Jacob, *Theology of the Old Testament* (Hodder & Stoughton, 1958): 'a kind of congenital illness' (p. 283).

49. W. Eichrodt, *Theology of the Old Testament*, vol. 2 (SCM, 1967), pp. 406–409. The italics are Eichrodt's. Von Rad does not specifically address the question of original sin in early Genesis, but what he writes takes note of the narrative groundwork that such a doctrine requires. See *Old Testament Theology*, vol. 1 (Oliver & Boyd, 1962), pp. 157–160.

50. Discussion of 'I have acquired/created a man with Yahweh' in Gn. 4:1 would require too lengthy a treatment. See Wenham's careful note (*op. cit.*, pp. 99–100). But his opting for 'I have gained a man with the Lord's

help' is somewhat pallid. Why call a new-born baby a 'man' (*'iš*) unless Eve is comparing her achievement with that of the Creator? 'With the Lord', on any interpretation, requires elaboration beyond the actual words themselves – as Wenham's 'with the Lord's help' shows. U. Cassuto's suggestion 'equally with the Lord' (*A Commentary on the Book of Genesis, Part One*, Magnes, 1961, p. 202) builds on the implication of 'a man': 'I am as good as the Lord'. This would replicate the way in which the woman grasped after equality with God in the previous chapter: the act there is now an attitude.

51. See J. Ellul, *The Meaning of the City* (Eerdmans, 1973), *passim* and esp. pp. 3–9.

52. *Ibid.*, pp. 10–23. Linguistically, Ellul's suggestion that 'hunter' (Gn. 10:8) might be 'plunderer' is without exemplification in the Bible, but, of course, Genesis does single Nimrod out as symptomatic of a changed attitude to the environment: not content to live by what it would 'yield' but going to war on it. And he too was a city-builder. See also D. W. C. Ford, *A Key to Genesis* (SPCK, 1951), pp. 41–45.

53. See note 50.

54. On the question of the very long lives of the ten antidiluvians, see excellent notes in Wenham, *op. cit.*, pp. 130–134; J. H. Sailhamer, 'Genesis', in F. E. Gaebelein (ed.), *EBC*, vol. 2, p. 72. See especially the all-too-brief note in Kidner, *op. cit.*: it is not as if any interpretation is free from difficulty but 'as far as we can tell . . . the life-spans are intended literally' (pp. 82–83). To accept them as such involves no larger problems than attend other views and also gives primary weight to the plain testimony of Scripture.

55. See p. 43 above.

56. Contra Williams *et al.*

57. Regarding Gn. 6:1–4, the details and broad meaning have excited differences of opinion. Blocher, *op. cit.*, pp. 200–202; M. G. Kline, 'Divine Kingship and Genesis 6:1–4', *WTJ* 24, 1961–62, pp. 187–204; Murray, *op. cit.*, pp. 243–249. It seems to me to be decisively in favour of taking 'sons of God' as supernatural beings that (1) there is no Old Testament evidence in favour of any other meaning; (2) the counterpoising of a 'godly' Sethite line over against an 'ungodly' Cainite line lacks explicit support in Genesis; (3) the mere mingling of some godly with some ungodly humans is hardly the sort of climactic sin which Gn. 6 appears to require by its place in the narrative; (4) there is no reason why a mixed human marriage should produce the sort of

offspring that 6:4 implies; (5) an inruption of angelic beings, copulating with human girls, does provide a cosmic extension of sin and a suitable climax to the process started in Genesis 3; and (6) this interpretation suits the likely reference to Gn. 6 in 1 Pet. 3:19–20; 2 Pet. 2:4–6; Jude 6. See Kidner's as ever seminal note (*op. cit.*, pp. 83–84).

58. Eichrodt, *op. cit.*, p. 407.

59. *E.g.* Jacob, *op. cit.*: 'Jeremiah often speaks of the evil inclination of the heart (16:12; 17:9; 18:12) and looks on sin as a kind of congenital illness . . .' (p. 283).

60. Note that all verse references to Ps. 51 in this section are to the English text. For the Hebrew Bible (MT) add on two!

61. In the following references, the prefix '(p)' indicates 'in favour of the interpretation of original sin' and '(c)' indicates opposition to it: (p) J. Calvin, *Psalms* (Eerdmans, 1949); (c) W. O. E. Oesterley, *Psalms* (SPCK, 1955); (p) A. F. Kirkpatrick, *The Psalms* (CUP, 1910); (c) C. A. Briggs, *Psalms* (T. & T. Clark, 1909); (c) A. Weiser, *The Psalms* (SCM, 1962); (c) A. A. Anderson, *Psalms* (Oliphants, 1972); (p) F. D. Kidner, *Psalms* (IVP, 1973); (p) W. E. Barnes, *The Psalms* (Methuen, 1931); (p) J. Goldingay, *Songs from a Strange Land (Psalms 42–51)* (IVP, 1973); (p) F. Delitzsch, *Commentary on the Psalms* (T. & T. Clark, 1880). M. Tate, *Psalms 51–100* (Word, 1990) provides a thorough linguistic note on Ps. 51:1–5, but is curiously hesitant about verse 5 itself.

62. Sin derives from √*ḥaṭ'a. Cf.* 'secular' use in Jdg. 20:16 ('and not miss').

63. Tate, *op. cit.*

64. 'Distortion' is the noun '*āwôn*. For the verb (√'*āwâh*) in its root sense, see Is. 22:1 (NIV 'ruin', but see RV 'turn upside down'); Lam. 3:9 ('made . . . crooked').

65. √*pāša', e.g.* 2 Ki. 3:7; 8:20. Is. 1:2 excellently exemplifies the moral use: rebellion within a relationship of knowledge.

66. See how all the key words occur in Lv. 16:21.

67. √*māḥâh, cf.* Nu. 5:23 ('wash them off'); 2 Ki. 21:13 ('wipe').

68. √*kābas, e.g.* Ex. 19:10; Lv. 13:6; *cf.* Mal. 3:2.

69. *E.g.* Lv. 11:32; 12:7; 13:6; *cf.* Ps. 51:7<9>.

70. See pp. 42–43 above.

71. *ḥesed, cf.* Ps. 85:8; 90:14, where *ḥesed* is linked with forgiveness. Tate, *op. cit.*: 'God's willingly assumed and continued obligation' (p. 13).

72. √*rāḥam*, gives rise to *reḥem*, 'womb'. It is the rich maternal love which the Lord feels, without ceasing to be a father, Ps. 103:13. *Cf.* 1 Ki. 3:26.

73. √*hul*, see Is. 13:8; 23:4; 26:19; 66:7–8; Mi. 4:10.

74. Delitzsch's excellent comment contains the unfortunate aside that the verb 'to be hot' 'hints at the beast-like element in the act of coition'. See too Y. Kaufmann, *The Religion of Israel* (George Allen & Unwin, 1961), pp. 293–294.

75. This surely is the background to the obligatory purificatory rites after childbirth and even after nocturnal emission and menstruation (Lv. 12; 15:16–33). All these events involved contact with the mysterious sources of fallen human life. On another matter, it ought to be noted that David speaks not only of the infant at birth but of the embryo at the moment of conception as 'I . . . me', *i.e.* already a distinct, personal human being. See J. R. W. Stott, *Issues Facing Christians Today* (Marshalls, 1984), pp. 280–299, especially pp. 286–290 on 'the Biblical Basis', and see the statement of scientific evidence that 'It was only in the 1960s that the genetic code was unravelled. Now we know that the moment the ovum is fertilized by the penetration of the sperm, the twenty-three pairs of chromosomes are complete, the zygote has a unique genotype . . .' (p. 289); O. O'Donovan, *The Christian and the Unborn Child*, Grove Booklets on Ethics 1, 1973); D. MacKay, *Human Science and Human Dignity* (Hodder & Stoughton, 1979), pp. 98–102 (with Dr Stott's comments on both these authors, *op. cit.*, p. 292); L. Smedes, *Mere Morality* (Lion, 1983), pp. 135–153; N. L. Geisler, *Christian Ethics: Options and Issues* (Apollos, 1989), pp. 135–155.

7. CHRIST OUR LIFE (2)

1. G. Pidoux, 'Sin', in J. J. Von Allmen (ed.), *Vocabulary of the Bible* (Lutterworth, 1958), p. 407.

2. L. Morris, *The Wages of Sin* (Tyndale, 1955), pp. 13–15; and see especially J. R. W. Stott, *The Message of Romans*, BST (IVP, 1994), pp. 162–166.

3. From a private communication by A. M. Stibbs.

4. *Cf.* J. A. Motyer on Psalm 49 in *NBC*, p. 517.

5. Morris, *op. cit.*, p. 14. See also J. Denney, *Studies in Theology* (Hodder & Stoughton, 1900), p. 98.

6. N. P. Williams, *Ideas of the Fall and Original Sin* (1927), p. 74.

7. See pp. 33–34 above.

8. W. Temple, *Nature, Man and God* (Macmillan, 1940), pp. 473–495. *Cf.* M. A. Jeeves, *The Scientific Enterprise and Christian Faith* (Tyndale, 1969); D. M. MacKay (ed.), *Christianity in a Mechanistic Universe*

(IVP, 1965); P. Davies, *The Mind of God* (Simon & Schuster, 1992).

9. Temple, *op. cit.*, pp. 493–495.

10. See pp. 66–68.

11. Gn. 1:1, 21, 27; 2:3–4; 5:1–2; 6:7; Dt. 4:32; Ps. 89:12<13>; Is. 40:28; 42:5; 45:12; Am. 4:13.

12. W. Dyrness, *Themes in Old Testament Theology* (Paternoster, 1979), pp. 63–78.

13. Isaac Watts: 'In Him the tribes of Adam boast more blessings than their father lost' (from 'Jesus shall reign where'er the sun'). But all this only deepens the mystery, for Christ the Lamb was 'slain from the foundation of the world' (Rev. 13:8; *cf.* 1 Pet. 1:20; Acts 2:23).

14. On the 'three-sided' definition of death and related questions, see J. A. Motyer, *After Death* (Hodder & Stoughton, 1965; reissued Christian Focus Publications, 1996), pp. 44–46.

15. 'Sheol' must be considered to be a place-name. It ought not to be 'modulated' to 'grave' or (worse) to 'hell' (as RV sadly does). It is not where the lifeless body lies, but where the soul lives on; nor is it a place of torment. *Cf.* L. Koehler, *Hebrew Man* (SCM, 1956): 'Sheol . . . is really the "not-land", the "land which is not a land" . . . but this not-land was by no means the hell of later times' (p. 113); and G. E. Ladd, *A Theology of the New Testament* (Lutterworth, 1974): 'Sheol is the Old Testament manner of asserting that death does not terminate human existence' (p. 194).

16. 1 Sa. 28:14–17 disposes of any claim that the dead are privy to a superior knowledge to that which they possessed in earthly life – a spiritist claim evident in Is. 8:19 and implicit in all necromancy, Dt. 18:9–15.

17. See note 50 on pp. 214–215.

18. See Stott, *op. cit.*, pp. 148–154.

19. *Cf.* Heb. 2:15 for the same thought. Jesus delivered (lit.) 'all those who, in fear of death [*phobou thanatou*], through their whole life, were held in slavery'. Here *phobos* has the same meaning as in Rom. 13:7 – not 'being afraid of dying' but living under an overlord.

20. See Motyer, *op. cit.*

21. See Rom. 13:11–12; *cf.* Is. 24:23; 30:26; 60:19–20; Zc. 14:6–7; Rev. 21:23; *etc.*

22. D. Stacey, *Isaiah 1–39* (Epworth, 1993), p. 105.

23. For Sheol as the great leveller, see Jb. 3:11–19.

24. $r^e\bar{p}\bar{a}'\hat{i}m$, of uncertain derivation, probably $\sqrt{r\bar{a}\bar{p}a'}$ 'to sink down, droop'

(*e.g.* Jos. 12:4; Je. 6:24). The more obvious verb √*rāpa'* means 'to heal' and there is no other link than spelling between the words. See J. D. W. Watts, *Isaiah 1–33* (Word, 1985), p. 209.

25. '*attudîm*, 'he-goats', *e.g.* Gn. 31:10; Ps. 50:9. The metaphorical use, for human, assertive leadership, occurs elsewhere only in Zc. 10:3, and possibly Ezk. 34:17.

26. H. W. Wolff, *Anthropology of the Old Testament* (SCM, 1974), p. 102.

27. *Cf.* A. R. Johnson, *The Vitality of the Individual in the Thought of Ancient Israel* (University of Wales Press, 1949); *idem, The One and the Many in the Israelite Conception of God* (University of Wales Press, 1951), pp. 7–13; W. Eichrodt, *Man in the Old Testament* (SCM, 1951); Wolff, *op. cit.*, pp. 10–80.

28. R. Martin-Achard, *From Death to Life* (Oliver & Boyd, 1960), p. 46.

29. J. H. Eaton, *Psalms* (SCM, 1967), p. 40.

30. F. Delitzsch, *Commentary on the Psalms*, vol. 1 (T. & T. Clark, 1880), p. 134.

31. W. Van Gemeren, 'Psalms', in F. E. Gaebelein (ed.), *EBC*, vol. 5 (Zondervan, 1991), p. 99.

32. See Motyer, 'Psalms', in *NBC*, p. 578.

33. This is offered as a serious, practical observation. Suppose, on Easter Day, we were invited to sing, 'Hail the day he didn't rise! In the grave his body lies: But the church his glory hails, Telling most unlikely tales: Hallelujah!' We would have expected our hymnologists to have ironed out this sort of thing before publication, would we not? If ancient editors were as daring as commentators often suppose and as careful as they plainly were, would they inflict this sort of confusion and obfuscation on their worshippers?

34. The only case where this does not apply is in Psalm 115, 'It is not the dead who praise Yahweh, nor all who go down into silence' (115:17, lit.). By themselves, these words support the idea of death as the decisive end of fellowship with the Lord such as was enjoyed on earth. Contextually, the interpretation is not so simple for 'those who go down into silence' are at once contrasted with 'we' who look forward to 'blessing' the Lord 'from now and unto eternity' (*mē'attâh wᵉad 'ôlām*). This counters any thought that 'the dead' means 'all who die', for some, apparently, enjoy a far from silent eternity. Who 'the dead' are depends on the setting proposed for the psalm. Was it some specific pagan attack in which, carrying their idols, they scoffed at Israel's aniconic religion and invisible God? If so, the outcome showed that it is not them, 'the dead' (*i.e.* as

linked with the dead gods of 115:4–8, or as now lying dead on the field of battle) who are true worshippers with an eternal relationship to the true God. If the psalm is a poetic reminiscence of (for example) the invasion of Canaan, the interpretative result is the same. See Motyer, 'Psalms', in *NBC*. There is no more ground for drawing broad, apparently logical conclusions from Psalm 115 than there is for questioning the correctness, within its own limits, of William Cowper's 'when this poor lisping, stammering tongue lies silent in the grave' (from his hymn, 'There is a fountain filled with blood').

35. *ba⁽⁾wônô* (Ezk. 3:18–20).

36. *bᵉšālôm . . . bᵉsēbâh tôbâh* (Gn. 15:15).

37. E. B. Pusey, *What is of Faith as to Everlasting Punishment?* (London, 1880): 'Christ on Himself – considerate Master – took The utterance of that doctrine's fearful sound: The Fount of Love His servants sends to tell Love's deeds; Himself reveals the sinner's Hell' (pp. 50ff.).

38. *yarkᵉtê-bôr* (Is. 14:15; Ezk. 32:23).

39. W. O. E. Oesterley, *The Book of Proverbs* (Methuen, 1929), follows LXX (*te heautou hosioteti* – 'in his own moral perfection') and consequently alters *bᵉmoto* ('in his death') to *bᵉtummô* ('in his integrity'). See also W. McKane (*Proverbs*, SCM, 1970, p. 475) who adopts the emended text. He notes correctly that √*hasah*, 'to seek refuge', is not elsewhere used 'absolutely' (= 'to possess refuge') but he is wrong to discount an ellipsis, 'seeks refuge (in Yahweh, of course!)'. F. D. Kidner (*Proverbs*, TOTC, IVP, 1964), believes that the emendation makes for 'closer parallelism and easier sense' but urges that 'the Heb. text . . . must not be discarded merely as implying too advanced a doctrine of death'. Kidner notes that David in Psalm 31, believing himself about to be 'cut off' (31:22<23>), committed himself into the Lord's hand (31:5<6>) 'whatever the state of his knowledge'. D. A. Hubbard (*Proverbs*, Word, 1989) favours the emendation partly on the ground that the verse as it stands 'points to a concept of eternal life not usually found in the Old Testament' (p. 329). But the verse as it stands is a neat parallelism ('calamity . . . death; wicked . . . righteous; downfall . . . refuge') with the word order in the second line reflecting not that of the first line but the stress desired by the writer – typical of the glorious freedom of the Heb. poetic ethos to allow sense to dominate any rigidity of form.

40. Motyer, 'Psalms', in *NBC*, p. 495.

41. *hāsîd* is used of Yahweh's character (*e.g.* Ps. 145:17); as a general designation of the Lord's people, usually indeterminate in significance

(*e.g.* 2 Ch. 6:41; Ps. 132:9) but sometimes suggesting people divinely favoured (*e.g.* Pss. 79:2; 148:14) and sometimes, those marked by distinctive life (*e.g.* Ps. 85:8<9>). It describes those on whom divine favour rests (*e.g.* Pss. 4:4<3>; 16:10; 30:4<5>; 32:6; 116:5); and also people of a particular character (*e.g.* Pss. 12:1<2>; 18:25<26>; 37:28; 43:1). Ps. 50:5 holds together those who have been graced with the covenant and who show it in their lives.

42. For example, in the following verses of the Psalms, both *hāsîd* and *hosios* are used as general descriptions of those in good standing with the Lord (the references in brackets are to LXX): 30:5 (29:4); 37:28 (36:28); 50:5 (49:5); 79:2 (78:2); 85:9 (88:8); *etc.*

43. See J. R. W. Stott, *The Message of Acts*, BST (IVP, 1990), p. 76; D. W. Gooding, *True to the Faith* (Hodder & Stoughton, 1990), pp. 62–63.

44. See, however, NEB 'thy faithful servant' (Ps. 16:10), and *cf.* A. R. Johnson, *Sacral Kingship in Ancient Israel* (University of Wales Press, 1955), p. 22; JB has 'the one you love', *cf.* A. F. Kirkpatrick, *The Psalms* (CUP, 1910), pp. 18, 835–836.

45. *Cf.* M. D. Goulder, *The Prayers of David: Psalms 51–72* (JSOT Press, 1960).

46. P. C. Craigie, *Psalms 1–50* (Word, 1983), p. 158. See also Eaton, *op. cit.*, who writes: 'God will not abandon his . . . servant . . . to the power of death. Brought into close bond with God, he possesses life . . .' (p. 59). But in an additional note, Eaton takes the same view as Craigie. A. A. Anderson, *Psalms*, vol. 1 (Oliphants, 1972) says: '. . . God will deliver his servant from an untimely death . . . the danger of death during his allotted span of life. Yet it is just possible that the Psalmist may have hoped that . . . his fellowship with God would not come to an end . . . such a view would have been a novelty . . .' (p. 145). How odd, though, that the Egyptians could foresee their kings enjoying life in the world of the dead but for king David, knowing the living God as he did, it would be a novelty! The interpretation of Ps. 16 as *requiring* a setting in some mortal danger is itself derivative from the assumption that 16:9–11 *can only* refer to the banishing of some immediate threat of dying.

47. H. H. Rowley, *The Faith of Israel* (SCM, 1956), p. 174.

48. W. Zimmerli, *Man and his Hope in the Old Testament* (SCM, 1971), p. 41. Yet to say 'I believe . . . the resurrection of the body' in the Apostles' Creed is equally 'not substantiated further', but we are going far beyond 'venturing' it on a Sunday morning! Richard Baxter helped us to sing 'The heavenly hosts, world without end, Shall be my

company above; And Thou, my best and surest Friend, Who shall divide me from Thy love?' (from 'He wants not friends that hath Thy love'). But, in thus singing, we do not feel that we are identifying with a lone thinker 'venturing' an opinion. When truth gets into a creed or a hymn-book, it becomes the confident possession of the whole church.

49. See note 42 above. In addition, see Pss. 144:10; 148:14; 149:1, 5, 9.

50. R. C. Trench, *Synonyms of the New Testament* (Kegan, Paul, Trench, Trubner, 1894), pp. 328–334.

51. *Ibid.*, p. 334.

52. It is frequently urged that the Hebrew text should be emended to make these two verses identical. RSV and JB show two ways of doing this. But there is no plain ground for emendation and it destroys the balanced movement of the psalm. See Motyer, 'Psalms', in *NBC*, p. 517.

53. See pp. 55–56 above, and note 41 on p. 199.

54. Lit., 'when morning (re)turns' (Ps. 46:5).

55. C. S. Lewis, *The Last Battle* (Bodley Head, 1956).

56. *yāšār* is used of conduct right with God (Ex. 15:26); it is a 'title' for the Lord's people (Nu. 23:10; Ps. 111:1); it describes the Lord's character (Dt. 32:4; Pss. 25:8; 92:15<16>); it is 'the correct way' to do a thing (1 Sa. 29:6; Ezr. 8:21); God's law is *yāšār* (Ne. 9:13; Pss. 19:8<9>; 119:137), so is his word (Ps. 33:4) and his ways (Ho. 14:9<10>). It is a condition of heart (Ps. 7:10<11>) and describes those 'right with God' (Pss. 11:7; 32:11; 36:10<11>; 112:4); *etc.*

57. There are a number of other passages relevant to this great theme. In particular Pss. 17:14–15; 23:6 (see F. D. Kidner, *Psalms*, TOTC, vol. 1, IVP, 1973, but also A. R. Johnson, 'Psalm 23 and the Household of Faith', in J. I. Durham and J. R. Porter (eds.), *Proclamation and Presence*, SCM, 1970, pp. 255–271); Ps. 48:14 ('unto death', not as altered by NIV); Is. 26:19 (see J. A. Motyer, *The Prophecy of Isaiah*, IVP, 1993, pp. 218–220, but also R. E. Clements, *Isaiah 1–39*, Eerdmans/ Marshall, 1980, pp. 216–217); Jb. 19:25 (E. Dhorme, *A Commentary on the Book of Job*, Nelson, 1967, pp. 282–285; H. H. Rowley, *Job*, Oliphants and Nelson, 1970, pp. 172–174; *idem*, 'The Book of Job and its Meaning', in *From Moses to Qumran*, Lutterworth, 1963, pp. 179– 182; A. B. Davidson, *Job*, CUP, 1903, pp. 142–145, 291–296; see the masterly discussion in D. J. A. Clines, *Job 1–20*, Word, 1989, pp. 455– 466); Dn. 12:2 (J. G. Baldwin, *Daniel*, TOTC, IVP, 1978, pp. 204–205; A. Lacocque, *The Book of Daniel*, SPCK, 1979, pp. 234–246; N. Porteous, *Daniel*, SCM, 1956, pp. 170–171).

58. NIV has happily recovered this important use of 'take' in Ps. 73:24, obscured in AV, RV, RSV, NEB and JB as 'receive'. The use of the verb in the Enoch and Elijah narratives raises it to the status at least of a semi-technical term.

59. MT reads *'ên ḥarṣubbôt lemôtām*. The noun *ḥarṣōb* occurs elsewhere only in Is. 58:6, of the 'bondages' imposed by the wicked on the helpless. In Ps. 73, the text is more often than not emended by re-dividing the consonants of *lemôtām* ('at their death') to *lāmô ṭām* with the first word ('to them' = 'they have') allocated to the first half of the line and the second word (*ṭām* = 'sound, perfect') to the second: 'They have no bondages; whole and fat-fleshed is their body.' LXX (72:4) reads *en tō thanatō autou* ('in his death'). If 'bondages' can be used of the trials of life (as the emended text supposes), it can equally be used of trials at the time of death. It is only the supposed incongruity of a reference to death thus early in the psalm (see Kidner, *op. cit.*, who adopts the emendation) that would give weight to the altered text. If the reference to a painless death proves exegetically appropriate in the psalm as a whole, the MT must be retained.

60. *maššu'ôt* only occurs elsewhere in Ps. 74:3, 'ruins'. See note in M. Tate, *Psalms 51–100* (Word, 1990), with possible links with verbal roots 'emptiness' and 'deception'.

61. 'Terrors', a plural of amplification/majesty?

62. √*'ûr*, of God 'rousing himself' to action, Pss. 44:23<24>; 59:4<5>; Is. 51:9; Zc. 2:13<17>.

63. *Cf.* Ps. 39:6<7>. Tate, *op. cit.*, 'mere image . . . phantom-like . . .'; a bad dream whose influence the awakening sleeper shakes off.

64. *ba'ar*, cf. Pss. 49:10<11>; 92:6<7>; Pr. 12:1; 30:2.

65. *ḥēleq*, cf. Jos. 13:33; 18:17; Pss. 16:5; 142:5<6>; *etc.*

66. See J. R. W. Stott, *Christ the Controversialist* (Tyndale, 1970; reissued IVP, 1996), pp. 32–64; G. E. Ladd, *op. cit.*: 'There are a few intimations in the Old Testament that death will not . . . destroy the fellowship that God's people have enjoyed with him. Since God is the living God . . . he will not abandon his people to Sheol . . . The psalmists cannot conceive that communion with God can ever be broken, even by death' (p. 194).

8. CHRIST OUR HOPE

1. See pp. 33–35 above.
2. G. von Rad, *Genesis* (SCM, 1961), p. 90.

3. *Ibid.*, pp. 148–149.

4. In the key verses, √*barak* ('bless') is in the niphal in Gn. 12:3; 18:18; 28:14, and in the hithpael in Gn. 22:18; 26:4; *cf.* Ps. 72:17; Is. 65:16. No distinction can be drawn between these usages inasmuch as the niphal is fundamentally a reflexive mode of the verb, GKC 51c. But rather than the unacceptable 'bless themselves' or the uninformative 'congratulate themselves' (*cf.* Dt. 29:19<18>), something like 'enter into their blessedness' conveys the right sense. At its inception in Gn. 12:3, the contextual background is all the lost blessedness of Gn. 3 – 11.

5. For the 'triptych' view of Is. 13 – 27, see J. A. Motyer, *The Prophecy of Isaiah* (IVP, 1993), pp. 131–226.

6. C. Kaiser's *Creation and the History of Science* is a gloriously mind-enlarging experience (vol. 3 of P. Avis (ed.), *The History of Christian Theology*, Marshall Pickering, 1991).

7. √*bara'* occurs in an unelaborated sense, like Gn. 1:1 in, *e.g.*, Dt. 4:32 and Ps. 89:13. It includes within its ambience even the frustrations of life (Ps. 89:47<48>; Is. 45:7), and reaches forward to the eschaton (Is. 4:5; 65:17–18; Je. 31:22). The Creator is in control of his creation (Is. 40:26; 41:20; 45:8; 48:7; 54:16). In particular, he creates by his word (Ps. 148:5); his people are his particular care (Is. 43:1) and creation (Is. 43:7). Both birth (Ezk. 21:30<35>) and future generations (Ps. 102:18<19>) are his creation, and he is also the renewer of nature (Ps. 104:30), of spiritual life (Ps. 51:10<12>) and the giver of responsiveness (Is. 57:19), *etc.*

8. See pp. 67–68 above.

9. *ra'*, broadly translated 'evil', is used about 640 times in the Old Testament. Of these, moral evil – affronting God and his law or other humans – accounts for 356 instances, and physical calamity of any and every sort for 275 cases; it means 'unfavourable', 'displeasing' – even 'bad fruit' – about sixty-six times, and on fourteen occasions it means 'sad', 'downcast'. Regarding its root derivation, KB offers two roots: √*rā'a'* (I), to be bad, worthless (*e.g.* Gn. 21:11); and √*rā'a'* (II), to break, *e.g.* Mi. 5:5. BDB recognizes that *ra'* must derive from a √*rā'a'* but refuses to identify it, preferring to treat the verb *rā'a'* as a denominative. There seems to be no reason why the two roots identified by KB should not be recognized as one. This would suggest 'evil' as a true contrary to *šālôm* 'wholeness' (of life, within the personality, in society, and with God). 'Evil' is what breaks the true integrity of life.

10. The idea of control can so easily be degraded to fatalism, making

humans mere puppets, and it would be useful to look back to ch. 5 above for the subtle blending of the dominant and directive mind of God in inspiration, and the full action of the truly human mind of the prophet, as an example of the inner dynamic of the two forces active in the creation (see pp. 89–94).

11. 'Maker of heaven and earth' occurs with both unexpectedness and appropriateness in, *e.g.*, Pss. 121:2 and 124:8 – as if the psalmist, in the expectation or reality of trouble, suddenly grasped the significance of the fact that all trouble comes *in God's world* and therefore under his supreme and total management.

12. Motyer, *op. cit.*, p. 530.

13. *Cf.* C. R. North, *The Old Testament Interpretation of History* (Epworth, 1946), pp. 66–72; J. L. Crenshaw (ed.), *Theodicy in the Old Testament* (SPCK, 1983).

14. N. C. Habel, *The Book of Job* (SCM, 1985), notes that 'Job 28 is a brilliant but embarrassing poem for many commentators' (p. 391). Habel provides a useful summary of current views. His own view stems from his correct observation that 'the full significance of this chapter . . . is only evident when due consideration is given to the closing verse (v. 28)'. How true! For the chapter and its place in the book cannot be understood as long as it is classed simply as a 'poem on wisdom'. Its real point is that it is a poem on 'revealed wisdom'. Wisdom itself is indeed hidden in God, inaccessible to humankind, but God has spoken: 'He said to man, "The fear of the Lord – that is wisdom, and to shun evil is understanding."' But this is exactly what poor Job spent his life doing – and look where it got him! Within the sequence of the chapters, chapter 28 thus has its rightful place. Bildad (Jb. 25) has only succeeded in re-inventing the wheel, for our real problem is not to know about this or that divine attribute but to know God himself (26:14). Yet Job's basic commitment remains: to preserve a full integrity of life (27:2–6), urged thereto by the hopelessness (27:7–10) and fate (27:11–23) of the ungodly. The theological basis for this commitment to righteousness is explored in ch. 28: it is what God has revealed as pleasing to him. There was a time when such a life fulfilled its promise (29:1–20), but then everything went sour (29:21 – 30:31). And yet, as Job looks back, there was a perfect concord between his life and God's revealed wisdom (31:1–40). Seen in this light, the six chapters of Job's final speech are not only coherent but justify the concluding comment (31:40) that there is nothing more for Job to say! Rowley (*Job*, Oliphants and Nelson,

1970) makes a substantial point when he disallows chapter 28 to Job on the ground that it anticipates the truth affirmed in the Yahweh-speeches – and which then brought Job to comfort. If he knew it already, why was he not comforted before? But this is broadly the point Job made to Bildad in chapters 26 and 27. It is one thing to know about God and another thing to know God – and the knowledge of God can only be true knowledge when there is face-to-face communion. Only then does the hearing of the ear become the seeing of the eye (42:5).

15. See J. A. Motyer, *A Scenic Route through the Old Testament* (IVP, 1994), pp. 111–112. The theological rigour of the book of Job is that it makes us face up to a God who is always – at every time and in every place – perfect in wisdom, righteousness and power. This leaves us with no logical escape hatch to 'explain' the world as we meet it; we are shut up to faith.

16. See pp. 89–94 above.

17. See J. R. W. Stott, *Christ the Controversialist* (Tyndale, 1970; reissued IVP, 1996), pp. 44–64. For an essentially Sadducean approach to Christian truth, *cf.* W. R. Matthews, *The Thirty-nine Articles: A Plea for a New Statement* (Hodder & Stoughton, 1961).

18. J. Morris, *The Pax Brittanica Trilogy*, vol. 1 *Heaven's Command: An Imperial Progress* (The Folio Society, 1992), p. 153.

19. √*śāṭan* 'to bear a grudge (against), to oppose churlishly', *e.g.* Pss. 38:20<21>; 71:13; 109:4, 20, 29; *etc.* In Jb. 1 – 2 and Zc. 3:2, 'Satan' is used with the definite article, 'the Satan/the Adversary'. It is usually supposed that 1 Ch. 21:1, having no definite article, marks an evolution from a title to a proper name, 'Satan', and thereby offers an ameliorating gloss on the blunt statement of 2 Sa. 24:1 that the Lord incited David. But within the thought-world of Old Testament Theology, the attribution of this direct action to the Lord needs no 'gloss' or 'developmental adjustment'. Furthermore, there is no reason why 1 Ch. 21:1 should be understood as a reference to 'Satan'. In 1 Ki. 11:14, the same word (without a definite article) is used of a human opponent of Solomon, and 1 Chronicles could equally well point to some malignant adviser who caught David's ear. For a brief statement of the supposed evolution from 'The Satan' to 'Satan', see BDB p. 966, KB pp. 918–919. At greater length, see R. Braun, *1 Chronicles* (Word, 1986), pp. 216–217; and the more important comment in J. G. McConville, *Chronicles* (St Andrew Press, 1984), pp. 69–71.

20. This is just as true in the NT. Rev. 20 is an arena of much controversy

but this at least is unquestionable, that Satan is bound and loosed according to the will of God and, when loosed, it is to achieve the divine purpose of gathering the nations to the last battle. Satan's overthrow is a matter of consummate divine ease.

21. On the expression *kāʿēt ḥayyâh*, see Wenham, *Genesis*, vol. 2 (Word, 1994). F. Delitzsch, *New Commentary on Genesis*, vol. 2 (T. & T. Clark, 1889), offers 'about the time when it revives', 'about this time next year'.

22. From 'It came upon the midnight clear', E. H. Sears, 1849.

23. S. J. DeVries, *Yesterday, Today and Tomorrow* (SPCK, 1975); T. Boman, *Hebrew Thought Compared with Greek* (SCM, 1960), pp. 123–153; J. Barr, *Biblical Words for Time* (SCM, 1962). An old and forgotten book worth consulting is Nathan Wood, *The Secret of the Universe* (The Bookroom, Westminster Congregational Church, London, no date [probably 1930s]).

24. DeVries, *op. cit.*, pp. 36–37.

25. See Ex. 12:41, 51; 13:3–4; *cf.* 14:13, 30; Nu. 3:13; Dt. 9:7; 16:13; Jdg. 19:30; 1 Sa. 8:8; 2 Sa. 7:6; 1 Ki. 8:16; 1 Ch. 17:5; 2 Ch. 6:56; Is. 11:16; *cf.* 19:23–25; 25:9 and 26:1 with Ex. 15:1; Is. 51:9; Je. 7:22, 25; 11:4, 7; 31:32; 34:13; Ezk. 20:5–6; 30:9; Ho. 2:15; Zp. 1:15.

26. This would include such significant references as Ps. 118:24, 'This is the day'. See on Psalm 118, J. A. Motyer, 'Psalms', in *NBC*.

27. Am. 5:18–20 should be read as one continuous story of inescapable doom.

28. S. Mowinckel, *He That Cometh* (Blackwell, 1959), p. 145. For useful summaries and lists of references, see pp. 147 and 269.

29. This is the theological and conceptual error involved in denying Am. 9:11–15 to Amos: it makes him the advocate of a truncated theology and less than a Yahwistic prophet. Commentators, however, may be less inclined now than previously to deny a doctrine of hope to Amos. See D. Stuart, *Hosea–Jonah* (Word, 1987), pp. 396–397. Stuart takes Am. 9:11 (MT, *sukkat*, 'booth of') as the place name 'Succoth'. But even if we retain MT, there is no need to hold, with Mowinckel (*op. cit.*, pp. 18–19) *et al.*, that the 'fallen booth' of David must mean that the monarchy has come to an absolute end. 'David's booth' was very effectively dismantled by the egregious Rehoboam (1 Ki. 12). The book of Amos exercises the same 'prophetic logic' as pervades all 'Day of the Lord' thinking. Ordinary logic foresees no hope: the whole world (Am. 1 – 2) is guilty before God; total judgment is waiting in the wings for Israel (3:9 – 6:14); when it comes (chs. 7–9), Israel will be judged – and

saved! See J. A. Motyer, 'Amos', in *NBC*, pp. 795, 803, 807–808, especially the integrative analysis of Am. 7:1 – 9:15.

30. The same 'prophetic logic' operates in Zephaniah as in Amos. See the analysis in J. A. Motyer, 'Three in One or One in Three: A Dipstick into the Isaianic *Literature*', *Churchman* 108.1, 1994, pp. 26–27. Also, *idem*, 'Zephaniah', in T. McComiskey (ed.), *The Minor Prophets*, vol. 3 (Baker, 1996).

31. See Is. 2:10–20, 24:10, 14–16a with 25:1–10a; 30:25–26; 36–37; 63:4; 66:20–24.

32. See Je. 30:4–7 with 8–9, 12–15 with 16–22.

33. Ezk. 37:27–28 and 40:1 – 48:35 act as brackets around 38:1 – 39:29.

34. See pp. 54–55 above.

35. See p. 52 above. A further centrally significant line of 'truth going somewhere' is 'the Kingdom not of this world', see pp. 37–38 above.

36. It is the Psalms in the OT, not the Pharisees in the NT, through which we see OT religion. We need to recall the word of the Lord Jesus when he dismissed pharisaic Judaism as a plant his heavenly Father had not planted (Mt. 15:13).

37. See pp. 55–56 above.

38. See notes 71 and 72 on p. 216.

39. See also the comment by J. R. W. Stott, *The Message of Romans*, BST (IVP, 1994), pp. 116–117.

40. See, *e.g.* C. F. Whitley, *The Prophetic Achievement* (SPCK, 1963); E. W. Heaton, *The Old Testament Prophets* (Penguin, 1961). To the contrary, see H. H. Rowley, *The Unity of the Bible* (Carey Kingsgate, 1953); J. A. Motyer, 'Prophecy', in *IBD*, vol. 3.

41. See pp. 56–57 above.

42. See Motyer, 'Psalms', in *NBC*.

43. Note that in this section, the verse numbers for Psalm 51 are those of the English Bible. For the Hebrew enumeration, add on two.

44. Hyssop is mentioned also in Lv. 14:4, 6, 49, 51–52; Nu. 19:6, 18. The symbolism of 'efficacy applied' is constant throughout even when a branch of hyssop is not actually used as an instrument of sprinkling. As an ingredient, for example, in Lv. 14:4 it indicates that the spiritual realities represented by the other ingredients are intended to apply to the candidate.

45. See pp. 54–55 above.

46. This translation understands the verbs in Is. 53:7 as 'tolerative niphals'. See GKC 51c.

47. See S. Motyer, *Israel in the Plan of God* (IVP, 1989), p. 41.

48. In his parting 'blessing', Jacob faithfully gives Reuben his place as chronologically the firstborn, but between Gn. 37:21, when Reuben failed to exert leadership over his brothers in the matter of Joseph, and 43:8, where Judah is seen in leadership, things have changed. Judah shoulders full responsibility in 44:18ff. and is his father's emissary in 46:28.

49. This was Luther's great maxim concerning justification by faith, see, *e.g.*, T. P. Boultbee, *An Introduction to the Theology of the Church of England in an Exposition of the Thirty-nine Articles* (Longmans Green, 1973), p. 97.

50. Can any English rendering catch the telling assonance of *'im lō' ta"mînû kî lō' tē'āmēnû* (Is. 7:9) or, indeed, has anyone ever matched such succinctness in expressing the crucial necessity of faith? 'Live by faith or meet your fate' is reasonably assonantal, but is by no stretch of the imagination a translation of the Hebrew!

51. This outline is drawn from Motyer, *Isaiah*, pp. 92–98. See also G. J. Wenham, *Faith in the Old Testament* (TSF/IVP, 1976), pp. 10–17. Isaiah, of course, did not invent the idea of the remnant. As we have seen, the principle of selection within the favoured people was attested from the start in Genesis but it is equally plain in Amos' vision of the plumbline (Am. 7:7–9). 'Behold the Sovereign had taken his stand beside a plumbline-wall and in his hand was a plumbline.' A 'plumbline-wall' would be a wall built with a plumbline; the plumbline in his hand would mean that the wall would be tested at the end by a standard available from the beginning. It is a mistake, therefore, to identity the plumbline with the moral law of the Lord, for that was only one half of the Mosaic foundation: there was also the provision, through the sacrificial system, of atonement for sins and for offering an adequate obedience by the burnt-offering. Within the structure of Amos 7 – 9, the parallel to the plumbline is 9:7–10. Those who rest complacently on the mere calendar date of the Exodus (9:7) are in no better case than a Philistine or an Aramean! The Lord purposes a sieving, discriminating judgment (9:9), searching out the complacent whose opinion is that their past sin will never catch them nor lie in wait for them (9:10). Putting all this positively: there is a community within the community. It is marked by a life lived between the twin poles of grace and law, *i.e.* a truly Exodus-community, living by Exodus, Mosaic values; it has a solemn awareness of the seriousness of sin; it will enter the glory of the

Davidic future (9:11ff.). See Motyer, *Scenic Route*, pp. 100–101.

52. See likewise Is. 19:23–25; 27:12–13; Ezk. 25 – 32, with its recurring theme 'they shall know that I am the Lord' (missing only in the case of Edom). *Cf.* the 'west-east-south-north' coverage of Zp. 2:4–15.

53. C. S. Lewis, *The Last Battle* (Bodley Head, 1956).

54. *Cf.* the 'covenant of peace' of Is. 54:10; Ezk. 34:25; 37:26.

55. See Is. 1:26; 11:1; Ezk. 34:24; Am. 9:11; Hg. 2:23. Even the 'shape' of Haggai's book is Davidic, matching the shape of 2 Sa. 7. Each begins with the enterprise of building the Lord a house and ends with the promise that the Lord will build David's house. See J. A. Motyer, 'Haggai', in T. McComiskey (ed.) *The Minor Prophets*, vol. 3 (Baker, 1996).

56. See Is. 24:23; 33:17, 22; Joel 3<4>:16–17; Ob. 21; Mi. 4:7; Zc. 14:9.

57. On 'the branch', see Motyer, *Isaiah*, p. 65, on 4:2; *cf.* Zc. 3:8; 6:12–13. See J. G. Baldwin, 'Tsemach as a Technical Term in the Prophets', *VT* XIV.21, 1964.

58. J. Ellul, *The Meaning of the City* (Eerdmans, 1973).

59. *qiryat tōhû*, Is. 24:10: *i.e.* life reduced to Genesis 1:2, deprived of the ordering, illuminating, life-imparting hand of God (Je. 4:23–26).

60. *Cf.*, the truly 'world-Zion' of Is. 25:6–10a.

61. J. Bunyan, *The Pilgrim's Progress* (J. M. Dent, 1937), p. 193.

Bibliography

Achtemeier, P. and E., *The Old Testament Roots of our Faith* (SPCK, 1964).

Albright, W. F., *From Stone Age to Christianity* (Doubleday, 1957).

Alter, R., *The Art of Biblical Narrative* (NY Basic Books, 1981).

Anderson, A. A., *Psalms*, 2 vols. (Oliphants, 1972).

Atkinson, D., *The Message of Genesis 1–11*, BST (IVP, 1990).

Avis, P. (ed.), *The History of Christian Theology* (Marshall Pickering, 1991).

Baker, D. L., *Two Testaments, One Bible* (Apollos, 1990).

Baldwin, J. G., 'Tsemach as a Technical Term in the Prophets', *VT* XIV. 21, 1964.

—*Haggai, Zechariah, Malachi*, TOTC (IVP, 1972).

—*Daniel*, TOTC (IVP, 1978).

—*1 and 2 Samuel*, TOTC (IVP, 1988).

Barnes, W. E., *The Psalms*, 2 vols. (Methuen, 1931).

Barr, J., *Biblical Words for Time* (SCM, 1962).

—*Old and New in Interpretation* (SCM, 1966).

Bentzen, A., *King and Messiah* (Blackwell, 1970).

Berkouwer, G. C., *Man: The Image of God* (Eerdmans, 1962).

Bicknell, E. J., *A Theological Introduction to the Thirty-nine Articles of the Church of England* (Longmans, 1944).

Binns, L. E., *Jeremiah* (Methuen, 1919).

Blocher, H., *In the Beginning* (IVP, 1984).

—*Evil and the Cross* (Apollos, 1994).

Boman, T., *Hebrew Thought Compared with Greek* (SCM, 1960).

Boultbee, T. P., *An Introduction to the Theology of the Church of England in an Exposition of the Thirty-nine Articles* (Longmans Green, 1873).

Bradshaw, T., *The Olive Branch* (Paternoster, 1992).

Braun, R., *1 Chronicles* (Word, 1986).

Briggs, C. A., *Psalms*, 2 vols. (T. & T. Clark, 1909).

Bright, J., *The Kingdom of God* (Abingdon, 1953).

—*Early Israel in Recent History Writing* (SCM, 1956).

—*The Authority of the Old Testament* (SCM, 1967).

Brown, C. (ed.), *History, Criticism and Faith* (IVP, 1976).

Brown, R., *The Message of Deuteronomy*, BST (IVP, 1993).

Bruce, F. F., *This is That* (Paternoster, 1968).

Buchan, J., *Witchwood* (Nelson, 1948).

Bunyan, J., *The Pilgrim's Progress* (Dent, 1937).

Buswell, J. O., 'The Origin and Nature of Sin', in C. F. H. Henry (ed.), *Basic Christian Doctrines* (Holt, Rinehart & Winston, 1962).

Calvin, J., *Psalms* (Eerdmans, 1949).

—*Institutes of the Christian Religion*, 2 vols. (SCM, 1955).

Carey, G., *The Meeting of the Waters* (Hodder & Stoughton, 1985).

Carson, D. A., and J. D. Woodbridge (eds.), *Hermeneutics, Authority and Canon* (IVP, 1986).

Cassuto, U., *A Commentary on the Book of Genesis: Part One, From Adam to Noah* (Magnes, 1961).

Childs, B. S., *Exodus* (SCM, 1974).

—*An Introduction to the Old Testament as Scripture* (SCM, 1979).

Clements, R. E., *Isaiah 1–39* (Eerdmans/Marshall, 1980).

Clines, D. J. A., 'The Image of God', *TynB* 19, 1968.

—*Job 1–20* (Word, 1989).

—*What does Eve Do to Help?* (JSOT Press, 1990).

Clines, D. J. A., D. Gunn and A. J. Hauser, *Art and Meaning: Rhetoric in Biblical Literature* (JSOT Press, 1982).

Craigie, P. C., *The Book of Deuteronomy*, NICOT (Hodder & Stoughton, 1976).

—*Psalms 1–50* (Word, 1983).

Crenshaw, J. L. (ed.), *Theodicy in the Old Testament* (SPCK, 1983).

Dale, R. W., *The Atonement* (Congregational Union of England and Wales, 1905).

Davidson, A. B., *Job* (CUP, 1903).

Davies, P., *The Mind of God* (Simon & Schuster, 1992).

Davis, R. D., *Such a Great Salvation* (Baker, 1990).

Delitzsch, F., *Commentary on Psalms* (T. & T. Clark, 1880).

—*New Commentary on Genesis*, 2 vols. (T. & T. Clark, 1888, 1889).

Denney, J., *Studies in Theology* (Hodder & Stoughton, 1900).

De Vaux, R., 'Method in the Study of Early Hebrew History', in J. P.

Hyatt (ed.), *The Bible in Modern Scholarship* (Abingdon, 1965).

DeVries, S. J., *Yesterday, Today and Tomorrow* (SPCK, 1975).

—*1 Kings* (Word, 1985).

Dhorme, E., *A Commentary on the Book of Job* (Nelson, 1967).

Dodd, C. H., *The Authority of the Bible* (SPCK, 1960).

Driver, S. R., *A Treatise on the Use of the Tenses in Hebrew* (Oxford, 1892).

—'Propitiation', in J. Hastings (ed.), *Dictionary of the Bible* (T. & T. Clark, 1898–1904).

Dumbrell, W. J., *Covenant and Creation* (Paternoster, 1984).

Durham, J. I., and J. R. Porter (eds.), *Proclamation and Presence* (SCM, 1970).

Dyrness, W., *Themes in Old Testament Theology* (Paternoster, 1979).

Eaton, J. H., *Psalms* (SCM, 1967).

Eichrodt, W., *Man in the Old Testament* (SCM, 1951).

—*Theology of the Old Testament*, 2 vols. (SCM, 1961, 1967).

Ellison, H. L., *The Centrality of the Messianic Idea for the Old Testament* (Tyndale, 1953).

Ellul, J., *The Meaning of the City* (Eerdmans, 1973).

Feinberg, P., 'The Meaning of Inerrancy', in N. L. Geisler, *Inerrancy* (Zondervan, 1979).

Flew, A., *An Introduction to Western Philosophy* (Thames & Hudson, 1989).

Foh, S., 'What is Woman's Desire?', *WTJ* 37, 1974–75.

Ford, D. W. C., *A Key to Genesis* (SPCK, 1951).

Frankfurt, H., *Before Philosophy* (Penguin, 1949).

Geisler, N. L., *Christian Ethics: Option and Issues* (Apollos, 1989).

Goldingay, J. E., 'That you may know that Yahweh is God': A Study in the Relationship between Theology and Historical Truth in the Old Testament', *TynB* 23, 1972.

—*Songs from a Strange Land: Psalms 42–51* (IVP, 1973).

—*Approaches to Old Testament Interpretation* (IVP, 1981).

—*Theological Diversity and the Authority of the Old Testament* (Eerdmans, 1987).

Gooding, D. W., *True to the Faith* (Hodder & Stoughton, 1990).

Goulder, M. D., *The Prayers of David: Psalms 51–72* (JSOT Press, 1960).

Gow, M. D., *The Book of Ruth: Its Structure, Theme and Purpose* (Apollos, 1992).

Guest, J., *Jeremiah, Lamentations* (Word, 1986).

Guthrie, H. G., *God and History in the Old Testament* (SPCK, 1961).

Habel, N. C., *The Book of Job* (SCM, 1985).

Hammond, T. C., *Perfect Freedom* (IVF, 1946).

Hanson, P. D., *The Dawn of Apocalyptic* (Knox, 1975).

Hasel, G., *Old Testament Theology: Basic Issues in the Current Debate* (Eerdmans, 1975).

Hayes, J. H., and E. F. C. Prussner, *Old Testament Theology: Its History and Development* (SCM, 1985).

Healey, D., *The Time of My Life* (Penguin, 1990).

Heaton, E. W., *The Old Testament Prophets* (Penguin, 1961).

Hebert, A. G., *The Authority of the Old Testament* (Faber, 1947).

Henry, C. F. H. (ed.), *Basic Christian Doctrines* (Holt, Rinehart & Winston, 1962).

—*Christian Personal Ethics* (Eerdmans, 1971).

Herrmann, S., *Israel in Egypt* (SCM, 1970).

Higgins, A. J. B., *The Christian Significance of the Old Testament* (Independent Press, 1949).

Hillers, D. R., *Covenant: The History of a Biblical Idea* (Johns Hopkins, 1969).

Hodge, C., *Systematic Theology*, 3 vols. (Nelson, 1874).

House, P. R., *Zephaniah: A Prophetic Drama* (JSOT Press, 1988).

—*The Unity of the Twelve* (JSOT Press, 1990).

Hubbard, D. A., *Hosea*, TOTC (IVP, 1989).

—*Proverbs* (Word, 1989).

Hubbard, R. L., *The Book of Ruth*, NICOT (Eerdmans, 1988).

Hyatt, J. P., 'Circumcision', in *IDB*, vol. 1 (IVP, 1980).

Jackman, D., *Judges, Ruth* (Word, 1991).

Jacob, E., *Theology of the Old Testament* (Hodder & Stoughton, 1958).

Jeeves, M. A., *The Scientific Enterprise and Christian Faith* (Tyndale, 1969).

Joad, C. E. M., *Guide to the Philosophy of Morals and Politics* (Gollanz, 1944).

Job, J. (ed.), *Studying God's Word* (IVP, 1972).

Johnson, A. R., *The Vitality of the Individual in the Thought of Ancient Israel* (University of Wales Press, 1949).

—*The One and the Many in the Israelite Conception of God* (University of Wales Press, 1951).

—*Sacral Kingship in Ancient Israel* (University of Wales Press, 1955).

Jones, D. R., *Haggai, Zechariah and Malachi* (SCM, 1962).

Kaiser, C., *Creation and the History of Science*, vol. 3 of P. Avis (ed.), *The History of Christian Theology* (Marshall Pickering, 1991).

Kaiser, W. C., *Towards an Old Testament Theology* (Zondervan, 1991).

—*Towards Rediscovering the Old Testament* (Zondervan, 1991).

Kaufman, Y., *The Religion of Israel* (George Allen & Unwin, 1961).

Kidner, F. D., *Proverbs*, TOTC (IVP, 1964).

—*Genesis*, TOTC (IVP, 1967).

—*Psalms*, TOTC, 2 vols. (IVP, 1973).

—*The Message of Hosea*, BST (IVP, 1981).

—*The Message of Jeremiah*, BST (IVP, 1987).

Kirkpatrick, A. F., *The Psalms* (CUP, 1910).

Klein, L. R., *The Triumph of Irony in the Book of Judges* (Almond, 1988).

Kline, M. G., 'Divine Kingship and Genesis 6:1–4', *WTJ* 24, 1961–62.

Knight, G. A. F., *A Biblical Approach to the Doctrine of the Trinity*, Scottish Journal of Theology, Occasional Paper 1 (Oliver & Boyd, 1953).

—*A Christian Theology of the Old Testament* (SCM, 1959).

—*Law and Grace* (SCM, 1962).

Koehler, L., *Old Testament Theology* (Lutterworth, 1953).

—*Hebrew Man* (SCM, 1956).

Kraeling, E. G., *The Old Testament since the Reformation* (Lutterworth, 1955).

Lacocque, A., *The Book of Daniel* (SPCK, 1979).

Ladd, G. E., *A Theology of the New Testament* (Lutterworth, 1974).

LaSor, W. S., D. A. Hubbard and F. W. Bush, *Old Testament Survey* (Eerdmans, 1982).

Leggett, D. A., *The Levirate and Goel Institutions in the Old Testament with Special Attention to the Book of Ruth* (Mack Publishing Company, 1974).

Lewis, C. S., *Broadcast Talks* (Bles, 1943).

—*The Last Battle* (Bodley Head, 1956).

Lightfoot, J. B., *Galatians* (Macmillan, 1880).

Lilley, J. P. U., 'A Literary Appreciation of the Book of Judges', *TynB* 18, 1967.

Lindblom, J., *Prophecy in Ancient Israel* (Blackwell, 1963).

Litton, E. A., *Introduction to Dogmatic Theology* (James Clarke, 1960).

Long, J. P., *The Art of Biblical History* (Apollos, 1994).

McCarthy, D. J., *Old Testament Covenant* (Blackwell, 1972).

McComiskey, T., *The Covenants of Promise* (IVP, 1985).

—(ed.), *The Minor Prophets*, 3 vols. (Baker, 1992–1995).

McConville, J. G., *Chronicles* (St Andrew Press, 1984).

—*Law and Theology* (JSOT Press, 1984).

—*Grace in the End: A Study in Deuteronomic Theology* (Paternoster, 1993).

—*Judgment and Promise: An Interpretation of the Book of Jeremiah* (Apollos, 1993).

MacDonald, H. D., *Theories of Revelation* (George Allen & Unwin, 1963).

McKane, W., *Samuel* (SCM, 1963).

—*Proverbs* (SCM, 1970).

MacKay, D. M. (ed.), *Christianity in a Mechanistic Universe* (IVP, 1965).

—*Human Science and Human Dignity* (Hodder & Stoughton, 1979).

Martin-Achard, R., *From Death to Life* (Oliver & Boyd, 1960).

Matthews, W. R., *The Thirty-nine Articles: A Plea for a New Statement* (Hodder & Stoughton, 1961).

Mauchline, J., *1 and 2 Samuel*, NCB (Oliphants, 1972).

Mayes, A. D. H., *Deuteronomy*, NCB (Oliphants, 1979).

Mays, J. L., *Amos* (SCM, 1969).

—*Micah* (SCM, 1976).

Milne, B., 'Sin', in *IBD*, vol. 3 (IVP, 1980).

Montgomery, J. W. (ed.), *God's Inerrant Word* (Bethany, 1974).

Moo, D. J., 'The Problem of *Sensus Plenior*', in D. A. Carson and J. D. Woodbridge (eds.), *Hermeneutics, Authority and Canon* (IVP, 1986).

Morris, J., *The Pax Brittanica Trilogy*, vol. 1 *Heaven's Command* (The Folio Society, 1992).

Morris, L., *The Wages of Sin* (Tyndale, 1955).

—*The Apostolic Preaching of the Cross* (Tyndale, [3]1965).

—*Ruth*, TOTC (IVP, 1968).

Motyer, J. A., *The Revelation of the Divine Name* (Tyndale, 1959).

—*After Death* (Hodder & Stoughton, 1965; reissued Christian Focus Publications, 1996).

—'Bible Study and the Unity of the Bible', in J. Job, *Studying God's Word* (IVP, 1972).

—*Baptism in the Book of Common Prayer* (Fellowship of Evangelical Churchmen, 1974).

—*The Message of Amos: The Day of the Lion*, BST (IVP, 1974).

—*The Image of God: Law and Liberty in Biblical Ethics* (London Bible College [Laing Lecture], 1976).

—*Law and Life: The Meaning of Law in the Old Testament* (Lawyers' Christian Fellowship, 1978).

—'Circumcision' in *IBD*, vol. 1 (IVP, 1980).

—'Curse' in *IBD*, vol. 1 (IVP, 1980).

—'Messiah: in the Old Testament', in *IBD*, vol. 2 (IVP, 1980).

—*The Prophecy of Isaiah* (IVP, 1993).

—'Amos', in *NBC* (IVP, 1994).

—'Psalms', in *NBC* (IVP, 1994).

—'Three in One or One in Three: A Dipstick into the Isaianic Literature', *Churchman* 108.1, 1994.

—*A Scenic Route through the Old Testament* (IVP, 1994).

—'Haggai', in T. McComiskey, *The Minor Prophets*, vol. 3 (Baker, 1996).

—'Zephaniah', in T. McComiskey (ed.), *The Minor Prophets*, vol. 3 (Baker, 1996).

Motyer, S., *Israel in the Plan of God* (IVP, 1989).

—*Ephesians: Free to be One*, CBG (Crossway, 1994).

—*Remember Jesus* (Christian Focus Publications, 1995).

Mowinckel, S., *He that Cometh* (Blackwell, 1959).

Muilenberg, J., 'Form Criticism and Beyond', *JBL* 88.1, 1969.

Murray, J., *Principles of Conduct* (Tyndale, 1957).

—*The Imputation of Adam's Sin* (Eerdmans, 1959).

Nicholson, E. W., *Preaching to the Exiles* (Blackwell, 1970).

Noll, M., *Between Faith and Criticism* (Apollos, 1991).

North, C. R., *The Old Testament Interpretation of History* (Epworth, 1946).

Noth, M., *Leviticus* (SCM, 1965).

O'Donovan, O., *The Christian and the Unborn Child* (Grove, 1973).

Oesterley, W. O. E., *The Book of Proverbs* (Methuen, 1929).

—*Psalms* (SPCK, 1955).

Orr, J., *The Christian View of God and the World* (Andrew Elliott, 1907).

—*God's Image in Man* (Hodder & Stoughton, 1907).

Packer, J. I., *Contemporary Views of Revelation*, in C. F. H. Henry (ed.), *Revelation and the Bible* (Tyndale, 1959).

—*God has Spoken* (Hodder & Stoughton, 1979).

Pannenberg, W., 'Redemption Event and History', in C. Westermann (ed.), *Essays on Old Testament Interpretation* (SCM, 1963).

Payne, D.F., *Genesis One Reconsidered* (Tyndale, 1964).

Payne, J. B., *The Theology of the Older Testament* (Zondervan, 1962).

Pedersen, J., *Israel, its Life and Culture*, vol. 1 *Israel I and II*, vol. 2 *Israel*

III and IV (Oxford, 1926, 1940).

Peterson, D. L., *Haggai, Zechariah 1–8* (SCM, 1985).

Pfeiffer, R. H., *Introduction to the Old Testament* (A. & C. Black, 1953).

Pidoux, G., 'Sin', in J. J. Von Allmen, *Vocabulary of the Bible* (Lutterworth, 1958).

Pinnock, C. H., 'The Inspiration of Scripture and the Authority of Jesus', in J. W. Montgomery (ed.), *God's Inerrant Word* (Bethany, 1974).

Porteous, N., *Daniel* (SCM, 1956).

—'Image of God', in *IDB*, vol. 2 (Abingdon, 1962).

Pusey, E. B., *What is of Faith as to Everlasting Punishment?* (London, 1880).

Quick, O. C., *Doctrines of the Creed* (Nisbet, 1951).

Ramsey, G. W., *The Quest of the Historical Israel* (Knox, 1981).

Ringgren, H., *The Messiah in the Old Testament* (SCM, 1956).

—*Israelite Religion* (SPCK, 1966).

Rogers, R. A. P., *Short History of Ethics* (Macmillan, 1937).

Rowley, H. H., *The Unity of the Bible* (Carey Kingsgate, 1953).

—*The Faith of Israel* (SCM, 1956).

—'The Book of Job and its Meaning', in *From Moses to Qumran* (Lutterworth, 1963).

—*Job* (Oliphants and Nelson, 1970).

Sailhamer, J. H., 'Genesis', in F. E. Gaebelein (ed.), *EBC*, vol. 2 (Zondervan, 1990).

—*An Introduction to Old Testament Theology* (Zondervan, 1995).

Schmidt, W. H., *Introduction to the Old Testament* (SCM, 1984).

Scott, R. B. Y., 'The Literary Structure of Isaiah's Oracles', in *Studies in Old Testament Prophecy* (Edinburgh, 1950).

Sebass, H., 'Holiness' in C. Brown (ed.), *NIDNTT*, vol. 2 (Paternoster, 1976).

Selman, M., *1 Chronicles* and *2 Chronicles*, TOTC (IVP, 1994).

Simon, U. E., *A Theology of Salvation* (SPCK, 1953).

Simpson, C. A., *The Composition of the Book of Judges* (Oxford, 1957).

Smedes, L., *Mere Morality* (Lion, 1983).

Smith, G. A., *The Book of Isaiah I–XXXIX*, Expositor's Bible (Hodder & Stoughton, 1904).

Smith, H. P., *Samuel*, ICC (T. & T. Clark, 1912).

Smith, R. L., *Micah–Malachi* (Word, 1984).

Snaith, N., *The Distinctive Ideas of the Old Testament* (Epworth, 1944).

Soggin, J. A., *Joshua* (SCM, 1972).

Sproul, R. C., 'The Case for Inerrancy', in J. W. Montgomery (ed.), *God's Inerrant Word* (Bethany, 1974).

Stacey, D., *Isaiah 1–39* (Epworth, 1993).

Stibbs, A. M., *The Meaning of the Word 'Blood' in Scripture* (Tyndale, 1947).

Stott, J. R. W., *Christ the Controversialist* (Tyndale, 1970; reissued IVP, 1996).

—*Issues Facing Christians Today* (Marshalls, 1984).

—*The Message of Acts*, BST (IVP, 1990).

—*The Message of Romans*, BST (IVP, 1994).

Strom, M., *The Days are Coming: Exploring Biblical Patterns* (Hodder & Stoughton, 1989).

Stuart, D., *Hosea–Jonah* (Word, 1987).

Tate, M., *Psalms 51–100* (Word, 1990).

Temple, W., *Nature, Man and God* (Macmillan, 1940).

Thomas, W. H. G., *The Principles of Theology* (Church Book Room Press, 1945).

Thompson, J. A., *Deuteronomy*, TOTC (IVP, 1974).

—*Jeremiah*, NICOT (Eerdmans, 1980).

Trench, R. C., *Synonyms of the New Testament* (Kegan, Paul, Trench & Trubner, 1894).

Van Gemeren, W., 'Psalms', in F. E. Gaebelein (ed.), *EBC*, vol. 5 (Zondervan, 1990).

Vanhoozer, K. J., 'The Semantics of Biblical Literature', in D. A. Carson and J. D. Woodbridge (eds.), *Hermeneutics, Authority and Canon* (IVP, 1986).

Van Til, C., 'Original Sin', in C. F. H. Henry, *Basic Christian Doctrines* (Holt, Rinehart & Winston, 1962).

Verhoef, P. A., *The Books of Haggai and Malachi*, NICOT (Eerdmans, 1987).

Vischer, W., *The Witness of the Old Testament to Christ* (Lutterworth, 1949).

Von Allmen, J. J., 'Marriage', in *idem* (ed.), *Vocabulary of the Bible* (Lutterworth, 1958).

Von Rad, G., *Genesis* (SCM, 1961).

—*Old Testament Theology*, 2 vols. (Oliver & Boyd, 1962, 1965).

Vos, G., *Biblical Theology: Old and New Testaments* (Eerdmans, 1963).

Vriezen, T. C., *An Outline of Old Testament Theology* (Blackwell, 1960).

Walpole, H., *Vanessa* (Macmillan, 1932).

Watts, J. D. W., *Isaiah 1–33* (Word, 1985).

Webb, B. G., *The Book of Judges: An Integrated Reading* (JSOT Press, 1987).

Weinfeld, M., in *TDOT*, vol. 2 (Eerdmans, 1975).

Weiser, A., *The Psalms* (SCM, 1962).

Wenham, G. J., *Faith in the Old Testament* (TSF/IVP, 1976).

—'History and the Old Testament', in C. Brown (ed.), *History, Criticism and Faith* (IVP, 1976).

—*Leviticus* (Eerdmans, 1979).

—*Genesis*, 2 vols. (Word, 1987, 1994).

Wenham, J. W., *Christ and the Bible* (IVP, 1972).

Westermann, C. (ed.), *Essays on Old Testament Interpretation* (SCM, 1963).

—*Basic Forms of Prophetic Speech* (Lutterworth, 1967).

—*Isaiah 40–66* (SCM, 1969).

—*Biblischer Kommentar I* (Neukirchener Verlag, 1974, 1982).

—*Genesis* (T. & T. Clark, 1988).

Whitley, C. F., *The Prophetic Achievement* (SPCK, 1963).

Wilcock, M. J., *The Message of Chronicles*, BST (IVP, 1987).

—*The Message of Judges*, BST (IVP, 1992).

Williams, N. P., *Ideas of the Fall and Original Sin* (1927).

Wolff, H. W., *Anthropology of the Old Testament* (SCM, 1974).

Wood, N., *The Secret of the Universe* (The Bookroom, Westminster Congregational Church, London, no date [?1930s]).

Wright, C. J. H., *Knowing Jesus through the Old Testament* (Marshall Pickering, 1992).

—*Walking in the Ways of the Lord* (Apollos, 1995).

Wright, G. E., *God Who Acts* (SCM, 1952).

—'Reflections concerning Old Testament Theology', in *Studia Biblica et Semitica* (Wageningren, 1966).

Young, E. J., *The Study of Old Testament Theology Today* (James Clarke, 1958).

—*Studies in Genesis 1* (Baker, 1964).

Zimmerli, W., *Man and his Hope in the Old Testament* (SCM, 1971).

Index of authors

Index of Scripture references

Index of selected topics